WINNING THE
TAX GAME
2003

Tim Cestnick

WINNING THE TAX GAME 2003

A Year-Round Tax

and Investment

Guide for Canadians

VIKING
CANADA

VIKING CANADA

Published by the Penguin Group
Penguin Books, a division of Pearson Canada, 10 Alcorn Avenue, Toronto, Ontario,
    Canada M4V 3B2
Penguin Books Ltd, 80 Strand, London WC2R 0RL, England
Penguin Putnam Inc., 375 Hudson Street, New York, New York 10014, U.S.A.
Penguin Books Australia Ltd, 250 Camberwell Road, Camberwell, Victoria 3124, Australia
Penguin Books India (P) Ltd, 11, Community Centre, Panchsheel Park, New Delhi –
    110 017, India
Penguin Books (NZ) Ltd, cnr Rosedale and Airborne Roads, Albany, Auckland 1310,
    New Zealand
Penguin Books (South Africa) (Pty) Ltd, 24 Sturdee Avenue, Rosebank 2196, South Africa

Penguin Books Ltd, Registered Offices: 80 Strand, London WC2R 0RL, England

First published 2002

10 9 8 7 6 5 4 3 2 1

Copyright © Tim Cestnick, 2002

This publication contains the opinions and ideas of its author and is designed to provide useful information in regard to the subject matter covered. The author and publisher are not engaged in rendering legal, accounting, or other professional services in this publication. This publication is not intended to provide a basis for action in particular circumstances without consideration by a competent professional. The author and publisher expressly disclaim any responsibility for any liability, loss, or risk, personal or otherwise, which is incurred as a consequence, directly or indirectly, of the use and application of any of the contents of this book.

ATTENTION: CORPORATIONS
Books are available at quantity discounts with bulk purchases for educational, business, or sales promotional use. For information, please email or write to Special Markets, Penguin Canada, 10 Alcorn Avenue, Suite 304, Toronto, ON M4V 3B2. Email lorraine.kelly@penguin.ca. Please supply title of book, ISBN, quantity, how the book will be used, and date needed.

Printed and bound in Canada.

NATIONAL LIBRARY OF CANADA CATALOGUING IN PUBLICATION

Cestnick, Timothy J., 1966–
        Winning the tax game : a year-round tax and investment guide for
Canadians / Tim Cestnick.

Annual.
[1998]–
Imprint varies.
ISSN 1490-8468
ISBN 0-670-04333-8 (2003 edition)

        1. Tax planning—Canada—Popular works. 2. Income tax—Law and
legislation—Canada—Popular works. I. Title.

KE5682.C47   343.7105'2'05   C99-901060-3
KF6297.ZA2C48

For tax updates, visit **www.timcestnick.com**

Visit Penguin Canada's website at **www.penguin.ca**

Contents

Acknowledgments vii

Tax Planning Tip Sheet viii

Foreword: Stepping Up to the Plate xv

Changes Making the Headlines. xix

Chapter 1 Pre-Game Warm-Up: The Basics of Tax Planning 1

Playing by the Rules. 2

Knowing the Numbers Game 3

Timing Your Taxes. 7

Fighting When You're Right 12

Chapter 2 Home Team Advantage: Tax Planning for the Family 17

Splitting Family Income 18

Educating the Family 39

Heading for Home. 48

Claiming Family Care Costs. 53

Surviving Separation and Divorce. 58

Chapter 3 Signing with the Team: Strategies for Employees 66

Optimizing Employment Benefits 67

Claiming Employment Deductions 86

Driving Automobiles on the Job 91

Deferring Compensation 98

Calling It Quits 103

Chapter 4 Becoming a Free Agent: Strategies for Self-Employment 105

Jumping on the Bandwagon 106

Choosing Your Business Structure. 108

Claiming Business Deductions 115

Adding Up the Tax Hits. 127

Chapter 5 Bulls, Bears, and Baseball: Strategies for Investors 130

Investing in a Tax-Smart Manner 131

Understanding Tax-Smart Strategies 142

Sheltering Income with Life Insurance. 161
Borrowing to Invest: Upvesting. 167

Chapter 6 Earning the Gold Glove: Strategies for Retirement **176**
Understanding RRSP Basics 177
Contributing to Your RRSP 187
Withdrawing from Your RRSP 205
Benefiting from RRIFs and Annuities 216
Understanding Registered Pension Plans 220

Chapter 7 American League Rules: United States' Connections **226**
Reporting Your U.S. Income. 227
Profiting from U.S. Real Estate 229
Cutting Your Gambling Losses. 234
Staying Canadian. 236
Considering U.S. Estate Taxes. 238

Chapter 8 A League of Their Own: Provincial Tax Issues **240**
Walking to a Different Drummer 241
Understanding the Quebec Difference. 252

Chapter 9 Bottom of the Ninth: Planning for Your Estate **261**
Knowing What to Expect. 262
Giving It Away Today 263
Giving It Away at Death. 266
Providing Tax-Free Death Benefits 278
Planning for U.S. Estate Taxes 280

Glossary of Abbreviations. **285**

Marginal Tax Rates for 2002 286
Federal Personal Tax Rates for 2002. 291
Provincial Personal Tax Rates for 2002. 292
Personal Tax Credits for 2002 292
Minimum Annual RRIF Withdrawals 295

Index **297**

Dedication

I dedicate this book to my wife, Carolyn, my son, Winston (my Little Guy—who isn't so little anymore), my daughter, Sarah (my Sweet Pea), and our third child on the way. Thank you for understanding when I sit at the computer for hours at a time.

Acknowledgments

It's hard to believe that this book is now in its fifth year. A lot has changed in five years, and our tax laws are no exception. This version of the book continues the tradition of excellence in sharing the important changes in the world of tax here in Canada over the last year and providing valuable insight into how you can live a life less taxed. I must thank those who continue to make this a better book and me a better tax professional each year. Specifically, I want to thank Suzanne Schultz, CA, CFP, Leigh Vyn, CA, CFP, Frank DiPietro, and Kathy Stradwick. These folks work with me each day at AIC Limited and make my life much easier with the work they do. I also want to thank my good friends at Penguin Canada, particularly Andrea Crozier and Nicole deMontbrun, who go out of their way to accommodate this high-maintenance author. Finally, thanks again to my wife, Carolyn, for the sacrifices she has made in allowing me to work on this project.

Tax Planning Tip Sheet

This Tax Planning Tip Sheet has been designed to make you a winner in the tax game. It lists all the tax-saving tips that I discuss throughout the book. Start by reading a chapter, then come back here to review the tips for that chapter. For each tip, simply answer the question: Can this apply to me? That is, even though a strategy may not currently apply to your situation, can you make changes to your life to permit you to apply the strategy? Check *Yes* next to those strategies that either apply or could apply if you were to make certain changes to your life—your Fact Situation. If you're not sure about a strategy, check *Not Sure*. Once you're done, take a closer look at the *Yes* and *Not Sure* answers. These strategies will form the foundation of your tax plan.

Don't worry about putting all the ideas into practice in a single year. It's not likely to happen. Choose up to four to implement this year. Keep the other ideas on file and think about setting them in motion next year or the year after. And by the way, I highly recommend that you visit a tax pro with your Tax Planning Tip Sheet just to make sure you're on the right track. A tax professional will help you to do things right. Now, go hit that grand slam!

Tim's Tips	Strategy	Can This Apply to Me?		
		Yes	No	Not Sure
Chapter 1.	**Pre-Game Warm-Up: The Basics of Tax Planning**			
1.	Avoid taxes like the plague, but don't evade them.	○	○	○
2.	Understand this thing called your marginal tax rate.	○	○	○
3.	Know the difference between a deduction and a credit.	○	○	○
4.	Always wait to trigger a tax hit.	○	○	○
5.	Pay your taxes on time, but not ahead of time.	○	○	○
6.	Think of taxes when big things happen in life.	○	○	○
7.	Dispute your assessment when you think you're right.	○	○	○
8.	Consider requesting relief under the fairness rules when circumstances were beyond your control.	○	○	○

Tim's Tips	Strategy	Can This Apply to Me?		
		Yes	No	Not Sure
Chapter 2.	**Home Team Advantage: Tax Planning for the Family**			
9.	Split income for hefty tax savings, with smart strategies from A to Z.	○	○	○
10.	Consider family trusts for income splitting.	○	○	○
11.	Use an RESP to save for your child's education.	○	○	○
12.	Set up in-trust accounts properly; otherwise stick to an RESP.	○	○	○
13.	Change the ownership of a second property to multiply tax savings.	○	○	○
14.	Plan the family's move carefully to maximize tax benefits.	○	○	○
15.	Maximize the base for your childcare expenses.	○	○	○
16.	Challenge the tax collector if a disability credit is disallowed.	○	○	○
17.	Choose carefully whether to claim attendant care as a deduction or a credit.	○	○	○
18.	Claim the equivalent-to-married tax credit, if applicable.	○	○	○
19.	Avoid a tax hit when splitting retirement plan assets.	○	○	○
20.	Maximize Child Tax Benefits by applying for one-income status.	○	○	○
21.	Consider splitting real estate when dividing up assets.	○	○	○
22.	Deduct legal costs incurred to collect support payments.	○	○	○
23.	Consider preserving pre–May 1997 support agreements.	○	○	○
Chapter 3.	**Signing with the Team: Strategies for Employees**			
24.	Take non-taxable benefits as part of your compensation, with smart strategies from A to Z.	○	○	○
25.	Calculate whether a taxable benefit works to your advantage.	○	○	○

Tim's Tips	Strategy	Can This Apply to Me?		
		Yes	No	Not Sure
26.	Negotiate a loan from your employer instead of from a bank.	○	○	○
27.	Opt for stock options or similar tax-efficient compensation.	○	○	○
28.	Claim all the employment deductions you're entitled to.	○	○	○
29.	Say "thanks, but no thanks" when offered a company car.	○	○	○
30.	Claim automobile expenses that exceed your allowance or reimbursements.	○	○	○
31.	Defer tax with a Registered Pension Plan (RPP), RRSP, or Deferred Profit Sharing Plan (DPSP).	○	○	○
32.	Push the tax on your bonuses to a future year.	○	○	○
33.	Consider a leave of absence or sabbatical plan to defer tax.	○	○	○
34.	Roll as much as possible of your retiring allowance to your RRSP or RPP.	○	○	○
Chapter 4.	**Becoming a Free Agent: Strategies for Self-Employment**			
35.	Structure your work so that you're self-employed, not an employee.	○	○	○
36.	Understand the three most common business structures.	○	○	○
37.	Consider incorporation once your business has grown, but not before.	○	○	○
38.	Choose the right year-end for your business.	○	○	○
39.	Maximize your deductions for home office expenses.	○	○	○
40.	Maximize deductions related to business use of your automobile.	○	○	○
41.	Categorize your meals and entertainment expenses to maximize tax savings.	○	○	○
42.	Maximize your eligibility to claim capital cost allowance.	○	○	○

Tim's Tips	Strategy	Can This Apply to Me?		
		Yes	No	Not Sure
43.	Pay salaries to family members for a number of tax benefits.	○	○	○
44.	Recognize the special tax treatment for certain expenses.	○	○	○
45.	Deal properly with losses from your business.	○	○	○
46.	Understand the various "taxes" affecting your business.	○	○	○
Chapter 5.	**Bulls, Bears, and Baseball: Strategies for Investors**			
47.	Consider the impact that taxes can have on a non-registered portfolio.	○	○	○
48.	Call your profits *capital gains* and your losses *business losses*.	○	○	○
49.	Claim a capital gains reserve to spread your tax bill over time.	○	○	○
50.	Think about reporting your spouse's dividends on your own tax return where possible.	○	○	○
51.	Look into corporate mutual funds as a way to defer tax.	○	○	○
52.	Invest in labour-sponsored funds for tax efficiency and good growth potential.	○	○	○
53.	Look at flow-through shares for a tax deduction and diversification.	○	○	○
54.	Understand the new breed of mutual funds designed for capital protection and tax-smart returns.	○	○	○
55.	Consider an investment in a private company in certain situations.	○	○	○
56.	Consider an exempt life insurance policy for tax-sheltered growth.	○	○	○
57.	Learn how to use cascading life insurance to shelter investment growth from tax for years.	○	○	○
58.	Establish a back-to-back prescribed annuity for tax-efficient cash flow.	○	○	○

Tim's Tips	Strategy	Can This Apply to Me?		
		Yes	No	Not Sure
59.	Consider "upvesting" to accelerate wealth creation and provide tax deductions.	○	○	○
60.	Deduct as much of your interest cost as possible.	○	○	○
Chapter 6.	**Earning the Gold Glove: Strategies for Retirement**			
61.	Contribute to an RRSP for tax deferral and tax-free growth.	○	○	○
62.	Recognize that it's possible to have too much in your RRSP.	○	○	○
63.	Open a self-directed RRSP once your plan assets reach $20,000.	○	○	○
64.	Pay your RRSP fees from outside your plan up to age 69.	○	○	○
65.	Know your RRSP contribution limit each year, then avoid an accumulation of contribution room.	○	○	○
66.	Make a contribution *in kind* to your RRSP if you're low on cash.	○	○	○
67.	Consider borrowing to make RRSP contributions if you haven't got the cash.	○	○	○
68.	Have your employer contribute directly to your RRSP.	○	○	○
69.	Avoid over-contributing to your RRSP and invest any excess outside the plan.	○	○	○
70.	Over-contribute to your RRSP just before winding up the plan at age 69, if you have earned income.	○	○	○
71.	Boost the value of your RRSP with tax-free rollovers.			
72.	Ensure that your child files a tax return to maximize RRSP contribution room.	○	○	○
73.	Claim your RRSP deduction in the right year.	○	○	○

Tim's Tips	Strategy	Can This Apply to Me?		
		Yes	No	Not Sure
74.	Contribute to your RRSP instead of paying down your mortgage.	○	○	○
75.	Contribute to a spousal RRSP to equalize incomes in retirement.	○	○	○
76.	Make RRSP withdrawals during periods of no or low income.	○	○	○
77.	Consider the impact of using RRSP assets to buy a home.	○	○	○
78.	Consider the impact of using RRSP money for full-time education for you or your spouse.	○	○	○
79.	Take three steps to minimize the tax hit on RRSP withdrawals if you're planning to leave the country.	○	○	○
80.	Roll your RRSP to a RRIF or annuity to defer tax well beyond age 69.	○	○	○
81.	Defer tax on your RRIF withdrawals as long as possible.	○	○	○
82.	Consider opting out of your company pension plan if you have the choice.	○	○	○
83.	Look into an Individual Pension Plan (IPP) to avoid a big tax hit when leaving your company pension plan.	○	○	○
Chapter 7.	**American League Rules: United States Connections**			
84.	Claim a foreign tax credit when you've paid withholding taxes to Uncle Sam.	○	○	○
85.	Use the *net rental income method* on your U.S. rental property in most cases.	○	○	○
86.	Take two steps to minimize the tax hit on the sale of your U.S. real estate.	○	○	○
87.	Register at a casino or hotel to track gambling losses for tax savings.	○	○	○
88.	Understand the implications of becoming a resident of the U.S.	○	○	○

Tim's Tips	Strategy	Can This Apply to Me?		
		Yes	No	Not Sure
89.	Determine whether you're a candidate for U.S. estate taxes.	○	○	○
Chapter 8.	A League of Their Own: Provincial Tax Issues			
90.	Understand the various tax rates and credits that apply specifically to your province.	○	○	○
91.	Understand the basics of the Quebec tax system.	○	○	○
92.	Understand the differences between federal and Quebec taxes, and plan accordingly.	○	○	○
Chapter 9.	Bottom of the Ninth: Planning for Your Estate			
93.	Understand the deemed disposition of your assets upon death.	○	○	○
94.	Give assets away during your lifetime for tax and probate savings upon your death.	○	○	○
95.	Consider an estate freeze to minimize your tax bill on death.	○	○	○
96.	Leave it to your spouse to defer the tax hit longer.	○	○	○
97.	Minimize the tax on your RRSP or RRIF assets upon death by naming the right beneficiaries.	○	○	○
98.	Instruct your executor to make a final contribution to your RRSP after your death.	○	○	○
99.	Save your heirs tax by setting up a testamentary trust in your will.	○	○	○
100.	Consider an alter ego trust for probate savings and other benefits.	○	○	○
101.	Give to charity and save a bundle. But do it properly!	○	○	○
102.	Use life insurance to soften the blow of a tax bill at the time of your death.	○	○	○
103.	Forecast your U.S. estate tax and apply eight strategies to minimize the tax bill.	○	○	○

FOREWORD: STEPPING UP TO THE PLATE

If you want to win the game, you've got to step up to the plate.

L et me tell you about Renee. She visited my office for the first time not long ago. And from the moment she sat in the chair across from me, even before she said a word, I assumed two things. First, I assumed that she was feeling the weight of a tax burden that only Canadians can truly understand. Second, I assumed that she was in my office to learn what she could do to fix the problem. I was only half right.

While it was true that Renee was discouraged about the level of taxes she had come to expect as a Canadian taxpayer, she wasn't in my office to learn how to lighten the load. The fact is, Renee and her husband Gerrald had already decided to leave Canada, and they were looking for me to explain the tax implications of making the move.

I couldn't resist asking the question: "Renee, before we talk about leaving the country, what is it that you and your husband have done in the last couple of years to save income taxes?" Her response didn't surprise me.

"Tim, there's really nothing we can do. We're claiming the $1,000 pension credit and a deduction for our safety deposit box fees. But big deal—these things save us next to nothing each year."

You see, this couple had come to the conclusion that their only hope for a prosperous retirement was to get up and leave Canada. Given their net worth, level of income, and our Canadian tax burden, Renee and Gerrald were convinced that they were bound to run out of retirement savings before running out of retirement.

Here was a woman who was truly discouraged. You could see it in her eyes. It was as though someone had left her 100 kilometres from shore in a canoe without a paddle. If you had checked the dictionary on that day under the word "discouragement," you might have found the family's name with a picture of Renee and Gerrald.

Discouraged? Why Be Discouraged?

It was the day after my meeting with Renee that I learned a lesson about discouragement—and from an unlikely source, I might add. I was driving down Lakeshore Road in Oakville, Ontario, where I grew up, and I saw some kids playing baseball at Bronte Park. I grew up playing baseball at that same park, and I was reminiscing a little, so I got out of my car and walked over to the baseball diamond.

The kids were having a great time. They were laughing and cheering. They were even shouting the same insults that we used to shout as kids. You know, things like: "Batter needs a beach ball" and "Pitcher has a rubber nose, wiggles every time he throws." The point is, you couldn't find a glum face at that park.

I leaned over and asked one of the kids what the score was. A little boy smiled up at me and said, "Fourteen–nothing!" Impressed, I replied, "Fourteen–nothing, that's great, you're killing them!" "Nope," the boy corrected me. "We're losing fourteen–nothing!" Surprised me for sure. From the way the kids were laughing, you'd never know they were down for the count. I had to ask the question: "If you're losing fourteen–nothing, how come you're so happy? Why aren't you discouraged?"

I'll never forget what that little boy said next: "Discouraged? Why should we be discouraged? We haven't even been up to bat yet."

Good point. There's no use being discouraged if you haven't been up to bat.

Renee and Gerrald are like many Canadians: They had not yet stepped up to the plate.

If you want to win the tax game, you've got to step up to the plate.

Get in the Game

It's frightening to think of how many Canadians have done little or nothing to reduce their income taxes. Here's what I mean: According to Stats Canada, just 38 percent of taxpayers between the ages 25 and 64 contributed to RRSPs in 1999 (the most recent year for which data is available). In addition, 1.1 million Canadians under age 65 withdrew money from their RRSPs in 1999—an average of $5,245 each. A full 53 percent of those cashing in their RRSPs were under age 45 and did so for non-retirement purposes. These stats don't faze you? Try this on for size: A full 59 percent of Canadian tax filers did not use any of their available RRSP contribution room at all in 1999! Yikes. Do you think that Canadians who are not even putting money into their RRSPs are likely to implement other, more intricate, tax planning strategies? Don't count on it.

You should realize that the odds are against you. Seventy percent of the people who read this book cover to cover will simply file the information in a drawer at the back of their mind labelled "interesting tax stuff." Thirty percent will actually use the information to create tax savings. If you've read this far, then you've shown up at the ball park. The question is, will you choose to be part of that 30 percent who actually get into the game?

Making It Easy

I've made it very easy to get into this game we call tax planning. Throughout this book, you're going to find tip after tip of good tax ideas. Unlike in previous versions of this book, I want to encourage you to make note of more than simply the strategies that apply to you today. While you'll certainly want to implement those strategies, I'd like you to also consider those strategies that could apply if you were to make certain changes to your life. For example, you may otherwise choose to ignore Chapter 4 since you're not currently self-employed. But rather than bypassing the tips in that chapter, I'd like you to consider making certain changes to your life—your Fact Situation—to allow you to implement some of those strategies. Perhaps part-time self-employment makes sense for you.

This change in approach is the result of my belief that you can save much more tax over the long run if you're willing to make certain changes to your life. This is really the theme of my new book *The Tax Freedom Zone*, which explains how to go beyond paying the least amount of tax you're currently required to pay and shows you how to pay even less. I call this moving into the Tax Freedom Zone.

At the front of this book, you'll find your own Tax Planning Tip Sheet, listing all the tax-saving tips from each chapter. As soon as you've read a chapter, flip to the front of the book and review the tips for that chapter. Ask yourself, "Can this tip apply to me?" Then check ○ *Yes,* ○ *No,* or ○ *Not Sure* for each tip. Follow me? When you've finished this book, all those *Yes* and *Not Sure* answers on your Tip Sheet will form a complete list of tax-saving measures, ready for your use or further research. A visit to a tax pro will often make sense once you've finalized your list.

There's one more thing to keep in mind: Tax rules are always changing. The advice I offer here is current as of July 31, 2002. A good tax pro will be able to bring you up to date on late-breaking developments from the Department of Finance or the Canada Customs and Revenue Agency (CCRA).

Calling All Hitters

Have you heard of Charlie Grimm? Charlie was a baseball manager—he used to manage the Chicago Cubs. There's a story about a scout who called up Charlie Grimm one day. The scout was so excited he could hardly utter the words. "Charlie! I've just discovered the greatest young pitcher I have ever seen! I watched him pitch a perfect game. He struck out every man who came to bat. Twenty-seven stepped up to the plate, and twenty-seven struck out! Nobody even hit a foul ball until the ninth inning. I've got the kid right here with me. Do you want me to sign him?"

"No," replied Charlie. "Find the kid who hit the foul ball in the ninth inning and sign *him*. I'm looking for hitters."

Charlie Grimm was looking for hitters. And so am I. With these pages, I'm going to get you off the bench and put a bat in your hands.

But remember: If you want to win the tax game, you've got to step up to the plate.

CHANGES MAKING THE HEADLINES

In the world of tax, change is the only constant.

I f you're looking for a quick summary of what's changed in Canadian tax rules in the past year, you've come to the right place. Here's a summary of key changes and proposed changes up to July 31, 2002. Some of these were introduced in the federal budget of December 10, 2001, but some changes relate to press releases, government pronouncements, or court cases. Keep in mind that proposed measures are generally enforced by the Canada Customs and Revenue Agency (CCRA) even before they're passed into law.

Topic	What's New
Tax Calculations	
Federal tax rates	Federal tax brackets were indexed for inflation and increased by 3 percent for 2002. The brackets for 2002 are: $31,677 ($30,754 in 2001), $63,354 ($61,509 in 2001), and $103,000 ($100,000 in 2001).
Basic personal credit	The basic personal amount was indexed and increased by 3 percent along with federal tax brackets. The amount for 2002 is $7,634 ($7,412 in 2001). The basic personal credit is 16 percent of this amount.

Family Care

Canada Child Tax Benefit

The amount of the Canada Child Tax Benefit (CTB), National Child Benefit (NCB) Supplement, and the income threshold at which these benefits are clawed back was increased by 3 percent effective July 1, 2002. The basic CTB base amount has been increased to $1,151 ($1,117 in 2001) for the first child, and the NCB Supplement has been increased to $1,293 ($1,255 in 2001) for the first child. See Tip 20 for more.

Other personal credits

The following personal credits were also indexed upward by 3 percent for 2002 and are based on the following amounts: Spouse and equivalent-to-spouse amounts–$6,482 ($6,293 for 2001), age amount–$3,728 ($3,619 for 2001), disability amount–$6,180 ($6,000 in 2001), supplement to disability amount–$3,605 ($3,500 in 2001), and caregiver and infirm dependents amounts–$3,605 ($3,500 in 2001). The actual credit in each case is 16 percent of the respective amount.

Equivalent-to-spouse credit and joint custody

According to a technical interpretation issued by the Canada Customs and Revenue Agency (CCRA) on January 7, 2002 (document 2001-0101105), it may be possible for both spouses to claim a full equivalent-to-spouse credit where custody of children is shared jointly when the parents are living apart. This will generally take appropriate wording in a separation agreement. A visit to a tax professional will be important. See Tip 18 for more.

GST tax credit

Lower-income Canadians are entitled to a GST credit which is based on family income and information provided on the last personal tax return of the individual. The 2001 federal budget changed things so that it is now possible to have your GST credit calculated based on information available as recently as the last quarter. So, if your personal circumstances change (births, deaths, marriages, etc.) and the amount of your GST credit changes as a result, you can now have the amount of your payments changed quarterly.

Employment Measures

Automobile limits

Unlike the last few years, the prescribed limits that determine taxable benefits to employees and deductions for employers related to automobiles have not changed in the last year. The rates for 2001 still apply for 2002. See Tips 29 and 30 for more.

Employee gifts and awards

The CCRA revised its policy on employee gifts and awards. An employee may now receive from his employer, on a tax free basis, up to two non-cash gifts annually, provided the aggregate cost of the gifts does not exceed $500 (including GST, PST, and HST). In addition, up to two non-cash awards may be given to an employee on a tax free basis, provided the aggregate cost is not in excess of $500. The CCRA confirmed that air miles given to an employee and similar gifts are akin to cash and may be taxable, even if under $500.

Employer-provided computers

The CCRA has stated that home computers, printers, and internet access provided or paid for by an employer may not be a taxable benefit to the employee. The determining factor will be whether or not the employee or the employer is the primary benefactor of the computer equipment or internet access.

Apprentice mechanics' tools

The federal budget on December 10, 2001, stated that starting in 2002, apprentice mechanics can deduct a portion of the cost of tools acquired. The deduction allowed is the total cost of the tools less the greater of $1,000 and 5 percent of the apprenticeship income for the year. A GST/HST credit can be claimed for the sales tax paid on the deductible portion of the tools. If the deduction will not benefit the apprentice due to a very low income, the unused portion of the deduction can be carried forward and deducted in future years.

Investment Measures

Foreign investment entities and non-resident rusts

The Department of Finance has delayed by one year the implementation of proposed rules that are intended to ensure that Canadian residents do not defer tax on investment income earned outside of Canada through foreign entities and trusts. The rules will now be effective for tax years beginning after 2002.

Tax shelter investments

New rules were introduced by the Department of Finance on September 18, 2001, that will limit the ability of a taxpayer to claim deductions related to certain tax shelters (most notably film tax shelters). The rules apply to expenditures made after September 17, 2001, where a taxpayer finances the business expenses of another person in exchange for a right to receive future income from that business.

Business Measures

Reasonableness of salaries or bonuses

The CCRA confirmed that where a shareholder/manager owns shares of a business, even indirectly through a holding company or trust, the department will not generally challenge the reasonableness of salaries or bonuses paid to the individual provided the individual is actively involved in the operations of the business. There was some concern recently that if the individual did not own shares directly in the business that the "reasonableness test" would be more strictly applied.

Woodlot farmers   A taxpayer is generally able to transfer certain farm properties to the next generation on a tax-free basis. In the case of wood-lots, many operations have not met the strict definition of a farming property, making this tax-free transfer impossible. The 2001 federal budget solved this problem by allowing the transfer of certain woodlot properties to the next generation on a tax-free basis after December 10, 2001.

Construction work camps   The 2001 federal budget changed the rules around meal costs for employees in semi-remote work sites. Employers can now deduct the full cost (formerly just one half) of meals incurred at a temporary work camp constructed for employees working at the semi-remote site. Similarly, the full amount of GST/HST paid by the employer can be claimed as an input tax credit.

Assistance for Students

Deduction for assistance   Some adults choose to take basic education courses (primary or secondary level) and receive tuition assistance through certain government programs under the Employment Insurance Act or through Human Resources Development Canada. That assistance has generally been taxable in the past, with no offsetting tuition or education credit allowed. The 2001 federal budget changed this by allowing a deduction for certain assistance received, effectively making this assistance non-taxable.

Charitable Giving

Donation of securities   The Department of Finance announced on October 12, 2001, that it is extending indefinitely the measure introduced in the 1997 federal budget that cuts in half the capital gains inclusion rate on publicly traded securities donated to charity. See Tip 101 for more.

Canadian Residency

Residence status   The CCRA has changed its long-held view that where an individual resides outside of Canada for two years or more, he is presumed to have given up Canadian residency for tax purposes. The CCRA no longer makes this presumption.

Court Decisions

Interest deductibility   On September 28, 2001, the Supreme Court of Canada (SCC) rendered a decision in the case of *Singleton v. The Queen*. The decision was in favour of the taxpayer. The case dealt with a "debt swap" strategy in which Mr. Singleton withdrew $300,000 from the capital account of his law firm (a tax-free withdrawal) and then used the money to buy a home. Singleton then borrowed $300,000 from the bank using the home as collateral and contributed that money to his law firm. He deducted the interest costs, arguing that the borrowed money was used for business purposes. The taxman argued that Mr. Singleton effectively borrowed to buy the home, and his interest costs should not be deductible. Mr. Singleton won the case. The court shot down the "economic reality" test applied by the CCRA. It's the direct use of the borrowed money which should determine whether interest costs are deductible.

In another case, *Ludco Enterprises Inc. v. The Queen*, Ludco borrowed money to invest in common shares that were not expected to generate much dividend income. Rather, Ludco expected to realize capital gains as the shares grew in value. The CCRA disallowed the interest deduction since our tax law requires borrowed money to be used to generate income from a business or property (which does not include capital gains) to permit an interest deduction. On

September 28, 2001, the SCC sided with Ludco, saying that earning "income" does not mean earning "net income" (after interest deductions). Further, earning income from property need only be one purpose for the borrowed money, but not the sole purpose. This case is good news for investors who invest borrowed money in growth shares or mutual funds.

Finally, in the case *Dansereau v. The Queen* (2001), the Federal Court of Appeal held that mortgage interest could be deducted even though the taxpayer had disposed of the properties that had been acquired with the borrowed money. This case may be relevant to you if you have disposed of rental properties and still have debt owing related to those properties.

Note: At the time of writing, the CCRA was reviewing the issue of interest deductibility and may make new pronouncements subsequent to this edition. Speak to a tax pro for more information.

Reasonable expectation of profit

Two decisions handed down by the Supreme Court of Canada on May 23, 2002, have a profound impact on losses claimed by individuals. These cases are *Brian J. Stewart v. The Queen* and *The Queen v. Jack Walls et al*. In these cases, the SCC ruled that where an activity lacks any personal element, it should generally be considered commercial in nature and a source of income. Where the endeavour is commercial in nature, the old "reasonable expectation of profit" test (which the CCRA has used to deny losses from rental and other activities) should not be applied.

Employee v. self-employed

In the case *Lawrence Wolf v. The Queen*, it was determined by the Federal Court of Appeal that Mr. Wolf was an independent contractor rather than an employee. You may be interested in this decision if you hope to argue that you, too, are self-employed. In this case, the FCA found it relevant that Mr. Wolf's skills and expertise exceeded that which was available within the business that hired him.

Tax free RRSP withdrawal

In the case *Field v. The Queen* (2001), Mr. Field's estranged wife withdrew funds from his RRSP, executing documentation without his authorization, and took control of the funds for herself. Mr. Field was taxed on the withdrawal. He took the CCRA to court over that issue. The court decided that Mr. Field should not be taxed on the withdrawal since he did not "receive" (using the plain meaning of the word) the amount from the RRSP. Our tax law requires amounts out of an RRSP to be "received" to be taxable. This case may not have a big impact on many individuals but is interesting nonetheless.

Moving expenses

In the case *Gary Adamson v. The Queen* (2001), Mr. Adamson had incurred moving expenses as an employee who was required to provide his own office in his home. He decided to move to a new home to provide greater needed office space. The CCRA disallowed his moving expenses (presumably because he did not start new employment after the move), but the court allowed the deduction. This case supports the notion that it may not be necessary to start new employment following a move to be entitled to claim moving costs.

In the case *Kenneth Cavalier v. The Queen*, Mr. Cavalier moved to a temporary residence. The CCRA disallowed his moving expense by claiming that he did not ordinarily reside at the location since he was there such a short time. The court ruled that there is no minimum time during which the taxpayer must reside in a place to be considered ordinarily resident there. This case may apply to you if you are a seasonal employee who must move to a temporary residence for work or school.

Childcare expenses	In the case *Burlton v. The Queen*, the Tax Court of Canada held that boarding school costs were considered tuition and not childcare expenses. On the heels of a similar case I noted last year in this book, *Stewart A. Bell v. The Queen*, this case reminds taxpayers that unless the purpose of an expense is to provide childcare, the deduction will be denied, even if the activity is undertaken while the parents are at work. Activities related to education, sports, and recreation will not generally qualify as childcare expenses.
Home office expenses	In the case *Thomas Vanka v. The Queen*, the taxpayer, who is a doctor, was permitted to claim a deduction for home office expenses even though he did not physically meet patients at his home office. This case is important because it supports the notion that the requirement to meet customers, clients, or patients at a home office could potentially be met when those meetings take place by phone. The facts of this case may differ from your situation, so speak to a tax pro before claiming the deductions.
Non-competition payments	In the case *Tod Manrell v. The Queen*, the Tax Court of Canada ruled that non-competition payments received following the sale of shares should be considered capital gains. The argument was that the disposition of the right to compete counts as a disposition of capital property. The court decision is under appeal, but don't hold your breath for a different outcome.

Limitation on collection of taxes

In the case *Markevich v. The Queen*, the CCRA attempted to collect a tax debt in 1998 that had been outstanding and inactive since 1986. The Federal Court of Appeal held that Markevich was not required to pay the taxes owing since the limitation period in the applicable provincial *Limitation Act* had run out. The court decided that the Income Tax Act is not a complete piece of legislation when it comes to limitations on the collectibility of tax debts and that the *Crown Liabilities and Proceedings Act* applies to provide limitation periods as set out in the various provincial statutes. The CCRA is seeking leave to appeal this case to the Supreme Court of Canada. You can expect the Department of Finance to change the tax law to clarify limitations on the collection of taxes owing.

PRE-GAME WARM-UP: THE BASICS OF TAX PLANNING

Only fools come to bat without first tying their shoes.

1

To this day, I can still remember my first season—in fact, my first game—in the Oakville Minor Baseball Association. I was six years old, a pretty good hitter for a rookie, and knew next to nothing about running the bases. My first time at bat, I belted a line drive into left field then proceeded to run as fast as I could directly to third base. I can still remember the umpire showing me which way to run after hitting the ball.

Eventually, I became a pretty good base stealer—but only after I learned the basics. Once I had the basics down, my playing improved to a whole new level. And so will yours.

In this chapter, we're going to look at the basics of the tax game.

Playing by the Rules

Tim's Tip 1: Avoid taxes like the plague, but don't evade them.

There's a big difference between avoiding taxes and evading them: One's okay; the other's a definite no-no.

Tax avoidance simply involves structuring your affairs legally so that you're paying less tax than you might otherwise pay. You do, after all, have the right to pay the least amount of tax the law will allow. Avoiding tax could involve using loopholes, which are inadvertent errors in the Income Tax Act, but more commonly will involve using provisions of the law to your advantage.

Tax evasion, on the other hand, is an attempt to reduce your taxes owing or increase refundable credits by illegal means, such as making false statements about your income or deductions, or destroying records. Trust me, if the Special Investigations Unit of the Canada Customs and Revenue Agency (CCRA) catches you in the act of evasion, you're in for a rough ride. Here's what happens: You'll not only have to make good on the taxes you've evaded, but you'll face penalties equal to 50 percent of those taxes. In addition, you'll face interest charges from the year of the crime until the day you pay those taxes and penalties owing. To top it off, you could face criminal charges filed by CCRA that may result in additional criminal penalties of 50 to 200 percent of the taxes evaded and up to five years in prison. Yikes!

If you've been evading taxes and haven't yet been caught in the act, there's some good news for you. The tax collector has said, in Information Circular 00-1, that if you come forward and correct deficiencies in your past tax affairs—through what's called a voluntary disclosure—you'll be given a break. No penalties will be levied, and no prosecution will be undertaken. Folks, this is not such a bad deal. And by the way, once CCRA has begun an audit or enforcement procedure, you can forget about making a voluntary disclosure—it's too late at that stage.

TO MAKE A LONG STORY SHORT:

- Tax avoidance involves legally structuring your affairs to take advantage of provisions or loopholes in our tax law.

- Tax evasion is a no-no. It can bring civil and criminal penalties, and can mean up to five years in prison.

- A voluntary disclosure may be your best option to come clean if you've been evading taxes.

Knowing the Numbers Game

Tim's Tip 2: **Understand this thing called your marginal tax rate.**

You're going to hear a lot about marginal tax rates as you browse the pages of this book—and for good reason. Your marginal tax rate is used to calculate all kinds of things. In particular, if you want to know how much tax a deduction is going to save you, or what the after-tax rate of return on your investments happens to be, you'll need to know your marginal tax rate.

> A voluntary disclosure (VD) will allow you to come clean if you haven't exactly been honest, but it may open a can of worms too. You see, a VD could lead CCRA to take a hard look at your financial affairs, including bank and brokerage account transactions. Sure, a VD may be your best bet if you're talking about significant tax dollars, but a simple adjustment request (using Form T1-ADJ) to your prior years' tax returns may be a better option if the dollars are minimal. Talk to a tax pro before deciding which way to go!
>
> **Caution!**

Quite simply, your marginal tax rate is the amount of tax that you'll pay on your last dollar of income. Suppose, for example, you're living in Ontario and you earned $65,000 in 2002. How much more tax do you suppose you'd pay if you earned one more dollar of income? The answer is 39.39 cents. You'd keep just 60.61 cents for yourself. In other words, your marginal tax rate is 39.39 percent. Similarly, if your marginal tax rate happens to be 26 percent, then 26 percent of the last dollar you earn will disappear in taxes. For a list of marginal tax rates by province, check out the tables starting on page 286.

You're going to discover that marginal tax rates really depend on three things: your province of residence, your level of income, and the type of income earned.

Basically, the higher your level of income, the higher the percentage of that income the tax collector is going to take. Further, dividends and capital gains are taxed at lower marginal rates than interest, salaries, and other types of income.

*J*udi and Ned are shareholders in a small business, Money Inc., located in Manitoba. In 2002, Judi received a salary of $75,000, while Ned earned $35,000. In addition, each received dividends of $5,000 from the company. Who do you think had the higher marginal tax rate on the salary? Good guess. Judi did. In fact, Judi's marginal tax rate on her salary in 2002 is 43.40 percent in Manitoba, while Ned's marginal rate is just 37.40 percent. As for the dividend income, Judi will face a marginal tax rate of 31.33 percent, and Ned will pay 23.83 percent (see the tables starting on page 286).

TO MAKE A LONG STORY SHORT:

• Your marginal tax rate is generally the most important tax figure for you to know.

• Simply put, it's the amount of tax you'll pay on your last dollar of income.

• Your marginal tax rate depends on three things: your province of residence, your level of income, and the type of income earned. To determine your marginal tax rate for 2002, see the tables starting on page 286.

Tim's Tip 3: **Know the difference between a deduction and a credit.**

No doubt about it, you've heard of them before. Deductions and credits are the friends of every taxpayer. The question is, do you know the difference between the two? Most Canadians don't. Let me explain.

A *deduction* is claimed to reduce your taxable income. Once you've calculated your taxable income, it's multiplied by current federal and provincial tax rates to arrive at your tax bill both federally and provincially. Make sense? But we're not done yet. Once your federal and provincial taxes are determined, those amounts are reduced dollar for dollar by any *credits* that you claim in each jurisdiction, to arrive at your basic federal and provincial tax bills. Finally, you'll have to add provincial surtaxes where they apply to arrive at your total tax bill.

DEDUCTIONS AND CREDITS: WHAT'S THE DIFFERENCE?

	Federal	Provincial	Total
	Net Income		
Subtract	**Deductions**		
	Taxable Income	Taxable Income	
Multiply	Federal Tax Rate	Provincial Tax Rate	
	Federal Tax	Provincial Tax	
Subtract	**Federal Credits**	**Provincial Credits**	
	Basic Federal Tax	Basic Provincial Tax	
Add		Provincial Surtaxes	
	Total Federal Tax	Total Provincial Tax	Total Combined Tax

Notes
- The provinces (except Quebec) and territories currently use the federal definition of "Taxable Income" when applying tax rates.
- No surtaxes are levied federally anymore.
- Surtaxes are levied in 2002 by Ontario, Nova Scotia, PEI, Newfoundland, and Yukon.
- The federal government still collects taxes for the provinces (except Quebec).

What's the bottom line? A deduction will reduce your total tax bill by an amount equal to your marginal tax rate. Consider Roshaan's story.

*R*oshaan had income of $48,000 in 2002, which puts her marginal tax rate *at about 35 percent. She claimed a deduction of $10,000 for childcare expenses in 2002, which brought her taxable income down to $38,000. How much tax do you think Roshaan saved in 2002 because of her $10,000 deduction? The answer is about $3,500 (35 percent of $10,000).*

Some tax credits can be claimed on the tax return of either spouse. Where this is the case, you'll generally be better off claiming the credits on the higher-income earner's tax return. The reason? The higher-income earner is likely to pay more in provincial surtaxes where those taxes apply. The medical expense credit is an exception to this rule. Generally, medical expenses should be claimed on the lower-income earner's return since the lower the income, the greater the credits for medical expenses.

Since a deduction saves you tax at your marginal tax rate, you can expect to save about 25 percent if your income is under $31,677, 35 percent on income between $31,677 and $63,354, 42 percent on income between $63,354 and $103,000, and 46 percent on income over $103,000. These figures are Canada-wide averages for 2002.

A tax credit, on the other hand, will save you federal or provincial tax, dollar for dollar. That is, a $100 tax credit will actually save you $100 in taxes. And there's more. Those credits may also save you provincial surtaxes (where your province still levies a surtax—see Chapter 8). By 2001, all provinces and territories had moved to a tax-on-income system (TONI), where they used to levy a tax simply as a percentage of your basic federal tax (see Chapter 8 for more).

Here's one last word on credits. There are two types: *non-refundable* credits can be used to bring your total tax bill down to zero, but don't offer any relief beyond that point, and *refundable* credits, as the name implies, can result in a cash refund once your total tax bill reaches zero.

TO MAKE A LONG STORY SHORT:

- A deduction reduces your taxable income and offers tax savings equal to your marginal tax rate.

- A credit reduces your basic federal or provincial tax bill, dollar for dollar, and results in savings on provincial surtaxes where they apply.

- There are two types of credits: non-refundable and refundable.

Timing Your Taxes

Tim's Tip 4: **Always wait to trigger a tax hit.**

You know, there are lots of events in life that can lead to a tax bill. And most of the time, there are things that you can do to delay the tax collector's knock at your door. Here's an example: Every time you switch from one mutual fund to the next outside a Registered Retirement Savings Plan (RRSP) or Registered Retirement Income Fund (RRIF), you could be triggering a taxable event and could have some tax to pay. If you're intent on switching those funds, why not wait until January of the next year to make that switch? This will push the tax bill one year into the future.

Want another very common example? Kathie has a story to tell.

*K*athie: *Last year, I wanted to help my daughter, Laurie, who has been struggling to save the down payment for a home. Since I had some stocks that I had inherited a few years ago, I decided to give them to Laurie.*
Tim: You were in for a nasty surprise, weren't you?
Kathie: That's for sure. I didn't realize that simply giving something to my daughter could lead to a tax bill.
Tim: Yup. Any time you give an asset away, you are deemed to have sold it at fair market value. So if the property has gone up in value since you acquired it, you could have a tax bill to pay. A common exception is when you give the property to your spouse.* In this case, your spouse acquires it at your original cost so there won't be a tax bill to face until your spouse disposes of the property.
Kathie: I wish I'd known that earlier.

After speaking with Kathie, it became obvious to me that, despite the tax bill, Kathie is still glad she gave the stocks to Laurie. It was the only way she could help her daughter. The question is this: Could Kathie have waited to trigger the tax hit? Sure, she could have waited to give Laurie those stocks until Laurie was ready to buy the home that she is still saving for today. This way, Kathie's tax hit could have been put off for a year or two.

* For brevity I will use the term "spouse" to refer to both spouses and common-law partners (same sex or not). Both are afforded the same tax treatment under our tax law.

For guaranteed tax savings, do all that you can to push a tax bill to a future year. The amount you save will depend on your rate of return on the money between now and the time you have to pay your tax bill. If you owe $100 in taxes but can push the tax bill off for five years and can earn 15 percent on your money between now and then, you'll cut the real cost of your tax bill in half! Consider the following numbers:

True Cost of $100 Tax Bill			
Rate of Return	True Cost of $100 Tax Bill Paid in the Future		
	1 Year	5 Years	10 Years
5 percent	$95	$78	$61
10 percent	91	62	39
15 percent	87	50	25
20 percent	83	40	16

I can understand that there might be good reasons for switching your mutual funds, giving assets away, or involving yourself in other taxable events, but my point here is simple: Be sure to understand what kind of events can lead to a tax hit, and then wait to trigger that tax bill if you can.

TO MAKE A LONG STORY SHORT:

- Educate yourself about what kinds of events can lead to a tax bill.

- There may be good reasons for involving yourself in some of these taxable events, but wait until a future year to trigger the tax hit if you can.

Tim's Tip 5: Pay your taxes on time, but not ahead of time.

Wouldn't it be nice if you could simply wait until April 30 each year to pay your entire tax bill for the previous year? Sure it would. But forget it—the tax collector has other ideas. You see, the government figures that if you're earning income in a particular year you should make your tax payments throughout that year. I'm referring, of course, to source withholdings and installments.

Source Withholdings

I can still remember the feeling of receiving my first real paycheque after graduating from university. I was broke, so any amount of money seemed like a windfall. But still, my reaction was mixed. I was thrilled to have some cash to waste away, and shocked that the tax collector would have the nerve to take such a hefty portion for the government to waste away. That year, I claimed a number of deductions that saved me $3,000 in taxes, which came back to me as a refund when I filed my tax return. I was not amused: The last thing I wanted was a refund!

You see, most Canadians are of the opinion that, next to being shot at and missed, there's nothing more satisfying than a big tax refund each year. The problem with a refund is that it means just one thing: You have effectively made an interest-free loan to the tax collector during the year. Rather than allowing this to happen, why not request permission from CCRA to reduce the taxes that are deducted at source? Use Form T1213 to make this request, and file it with your local CCRA tax services office. Your employer will gladly go along with the idea as long as CCRA has given the green light. All that's necessary is to provide CCRA with proof that you're expecting a refund due to any number of deductions, such as RRSP contributions, charitable donations, medical expenses, alimony and maintenance payments, and so on.

Your aim should actually be to pay a small balance each year when you file your tax return; then you know you haven't made your tax payments ahead of time.

Installments

If you happen to be self-employed or you receive a decent income from your investments each year, you're an obvious candidate for making quarterly installments, since folks in these situations are not often subject to source withholdings. This leaves installments as the only other option to ensure the tax collector gets paid throughout the year. Installments are due on the 15th of the month in March, June, September, and December.

In a nutshell, you'll be required to make installments if the difference between your total tax payable (federal and provincial) and any amounts withheld at source is more than $2,000 in the current year and either of the two preceding years. If you live in Quebec, the threshold is $1,200 of federal tax, since provincial tax is not collected by CCRA in Quebec.

You've got three options for calculating your installments:

Second Prior Year Method. For each of your March and June installments, calculate one-quarter of your total tax liability from two years ago. For each of your September and December installments, start with your tax liability from last year, then subtract your March and June installments and divide the balance by two. This means that in 2003, your March and June installments would each be one-quarter of your total 2001 tax. The September and December installments would each be equal to your 2002 tax bill, less your March and June installments, divided by two.

Prior Year Method. Calculate each quarterly installment as one-quarter of your total tax liability from last year (2002 for the 2003 tax year).

Current Year Method. Estimate your tax liability for the current year (2003) and pay one-quarter of that amount each quarter.

You may want to choose the option that provides the lowest quarterly payments. Keep in mind that as long as your payments are made on time and in accordance with the Second Prior Year Method, you'll escape interest and penalties. If, however, you choose the Current or Prior Year Method, deficient installments could lead to interest and penalties.

TO MAKE A LONG STORY SHORT:

- Don't hope for a refund when you file your return. Aim for a small balance owing instead.

- Request to have source withholdings reduced when you expect a refund due to certain deductions (file Form T1213 with CCRA).

- You may have to make quarterly installments when your income is not subject to source withholdings.

- Consider the installment method that results in the lowest quarterly payments.

Tim's Tip 6: Think of taxes when big things happen in life.

Matthew paid me a visit not long ago. He wasn't sure if there were any tax issues to worry about in his situation, so he thought he'd play it safe and visit me to find out. When I asked him to tell me what's been happening, he replied in a single breath:

> "Tim, my wife and I aren't getting along so well so we decided to separate earlier this year and my son is away at school for the first time and has been withdrawing funds from the Registered Education Savings Plan we set up for him 10 years ago and my California condominium was sold in the year because we haven't been using it very much and my wife and I are going to split the money from that sale then I became concerned about my personal liability in my business so I set up a corporation but only after I gave my brother some money to help him buy a farm. Is any of this going to affect my taxes?"

"Yes, Matthew, I would say so," I said.

Folks, any time a big event happens in life, ask yourself the question, "Will this affect my taxes?" While I couldn't possibly list every event to watch for, here are some of the most common that cross my desk:

- getting a separation or divorce
- negotiating salary or other compensation
- moving to another province or country
- setting up a business in another country
- investing offshore
- buying or selling a vacation or rental property
- starting or incorporating a business
- investing in someone else's small business
- inheriting assets
- creating or revising a will
- giving assets away during your lifetime

> **Did You Know?**
>
> Income taxes were first introduced in Canada in 1917. *The Income War Tax Act* levied a 4-percent tax on Canadians to help finance World War I. It is commonly believed, based on comments made by Sir Thomas White, the finance minister of the day, that income taxes were to be a temporary measure.

Whom should you visit when it's time to see a tax pro? Many people out there call themselves tax experts. Some are really just tax preparers. If in doubt, your best bet is to visit a tax professional who has completed the Canadian Institute of Chartered Accountants' In-depth Tax Course. This is a two-year comprehensive course that only those specializing in tax full time are permitted to take. Most students of the course are chartered accountants, but you'll also find a handful of lawyers and certified general or certified management accountants as well.

If these or other big events appear on your horizon, visit a tax professional—sooner rather than later. You'd hate to find out after the fact that the tax collector wants more than you bargained for.

TO MAKE A LONG STORY SHORT:

- Think of taxes any time big events happen in life.

- Visit a tax professional before the events take place, if possible.

Fighting When You're Right

Tim's Tip 7: Dispute your assessment when you think you're right.

If one thing can be said about Canadian taxpayers, it's that we're a passive bunch. By this I mean that many Canadians are content to accept any assessment issued by CCRA, under the assumption that CCRA must be right. I admit, when the government receives your tax return, takes a look at it, and then issues you an assessment notice making changes to the return you've filed, it's easy to assume that you—or your tax preparer—probably made a mistake when filling out the forms. Bad assumption. The folks at CCRA are prone to making mistakes as often as anyone else.

Notice of Objection

After filing your tax return, you can expect to receive a Notice of Assessment from CCRA within 8 to 12 weeks. If you disagree with CCRA's assessment of your tax return, don't let it go. Your first line of attack is to call your local CCRA taxation office to talk over your concerns. You might just resolve the whole issue at that time. If that call doesn't resolve the problem to your satisfaction, then you should consider filing a Notice of Objection.

A Notice of Objection can be filed on Form T400A, but doesn't have to be. You can also file an objection by detailing the facts and your reasons for objecting in a letter addressed to the Chief of Appeals at your local tax services office or taxation centre. Remember, you've got to file your objection on time—otherwise CCRA is not obligated to hear you out. For individuals and testamentary trusts, the deadline for any Notice of Objection is 90 days after the mailing date noted on your assessment, or one year after the due date of the tax return you're fighting, whichever is later. If, for example, your 2002 assessment notice is dated May 15, 2003, you'd have until April 30, 2004 (one year after the due date of your 2002 return) to file an objection. The same deadlines apply in Quebec.

> **Action Step**
>
> Try to resolve your beef with CCRA without filing a Notice of Objection. But keep an eye on the filing deadline, and be sure to file your objection on time to preserve your right to appeal if the discussions don't go your way. When a Notice of Objection is your best bet, visit a tax pro to have it prepared properly. Why wait to file? If you jump right to the Notice of Objection first, there's always a chance that your objection could be denied, leaving you with no alternative but to take the tax collector to court. Keep your options open.

Take 'em to Court

What happens if you file a Notice of Objection and the tax collector still refuses to assess your return as you think it should be assessed? Your next option is to take CCRA to court—to the Tax Court of Canada (or the Court of Quebec for Quebec tax issues).

At the Tax Court of Canada, you've got two options: the *informal* or the *general* procedure. With the informal procedure, you can represent yourself, or have anyone else (your accountant, lawyer, another advisor, or your brother's friend's cousin, for example) lend a hand in the appeal, and you can expect to have a judgment on your case in 6 to 12 months. To be eligible for the informal procedure, the amount of federal tax in dispute has to be less than $12,000 (about $19,000 including provincial taxes, excluding Quebec tax) for each year in question, or less than $24,000 in disputed losses where disallowed losses are the issue. If you don't qualify for the informal procedure, the Court's general procedure is your other option.

The general procedure is going to mean a visit to a lawyer who will represent you in court. Don't get me wrong: You can represent yourself in court under the general procedure as well, but I wouldn't recommend it. Formal rules of evidence and other legal procedures will apply, and unless you're completely familiar with these, you won't stand a chance on your own.

If the Tax Court of Canada judgment doesn't work out in your favour, you can usually appeal to the Federal Court of Appeal. The final step is to request an appeal to the Supreme Court of Canada, although very few cases (fewer than five or so) make it that far each year.

TO MAKE A LONG STORY SHORT:

- If you disagree with your Notice of Assessment, call CCRA to straighten things out.

- If a phone call doesn't help, consider filing a Notice of Objection within the required time limits.

- Your last line of attack is to take CCRA to court, starting with the Tax Court of Canada's informal or general procedure, and potentially ending at the Supreme Court of Canada.

Tim's Tip 8: Consider requesting relief when circumstances were beyond your control.

Have you ever been subject to interest, penalties, or other tax treatment that you thought was unfair? There may be relief today. You see, our tax law contains fairness rules that give CCRA the ability to waive interest and penalties and perform other acts to help you out in certain situations—particularly when circumstances were beyond your control. For example, a serious illness, an accident, or a natural or human-made disaster might cause you to file your tax return late, or to make payments late. Specifically, CCRA may be able to provide you with some relief under the fairness rules including:

- forgiving interest and penalties on overdue tax filings and payments
- issuing tax refunds after the late-filing deadline (typically three years after the original due date)
- accepting certain tax elections that are filed late

Keep in mind that the tax collector is not obligated to give you relief under the fairness rules—but there's nothing shameful in begging for it (I'll do anything for $5). You should be aware that CCRA will take a look at your history when assessing whether they'll grant you relief. So, if you've filed your tax return late every year for the last 10 years, you're not as likely to find relief when you really need it. CCRA will also look at the promptness with which you've made your request. And if you're asking for relief in a situation where you were simply negligent or didn't understand the rules—forget it, the tax collector isn't that merciful.

Finally, while the provinces and territories don't have similar fairness legislation, they often will offer the same type of relief that the feds offer. So don't forget to ask.

TO MAKE A LONG STORY SHORT:

- If you have faced circumstances beyond your control that led to interest, penalties, or other unfair tax treatment, don't be afraid to ask for relief under our tax law's fairness rules.

- CCRA is not obligated to provide relief, and they will look at your history when making a decision.

- Your province or territory may also offer similar relief if you ask.

Getting into the Game

Okay, you've taken the first step: You know the tax basics. It's time to turn to the Tax Planning Tip Sheet at the front of the book and review the strategies introduced in Chapter 1. Ask yourself, "Can this tip apply to me?" Each *Yes* or *Not Sure* could bring you one step closer to winning the game.

HOME TEAM ADVANTAGE: TAX PLANNING FOR THE FAMILY

The thing that a parent will never understand is why all bachelors aren't rich.

2

I t seems like only yesterday that Carolyn and I got married. In fact, we tied the knot on August 3, 1997. I have to admit, one of Carolyn's virtues—and she has many—is that she can cook like no one else I know. I can't even make my way around in the kitchen except to raid the fridge. In fact, some people accuse me of getting married solely for the culinary benefits. That's ridiculous. After all, there are countless income tax benefits as well.

Here's some advice for you: When you think of tax planning, think of it as a family affair. Just think of the fun it could be—you, your spouse, and your kids if you have any, sitting around the table sharing tax strategies. It's not something my family did when I was young. Too bad. I think my sisters would have enjoyed it. So, next time you're tempted to pull out the Monopoly board, think twice, and pull out this book instead.

You need to realize that any effective tax plan will involve your family members. And I realize that families come in all shapes and sizes. Some involve single parents, adoptive parents, or common-law partners,* including same-sex relationships. The strategies in this chapter apply, for the most part, to all families. I should mention that 2001 represented the first year that same-sex couples were given the same tax treatment as legally married couples—for better or worse!

Let's take a look at some of the best ideas available to make tax planning a family affair.

Splitting Family Income

Tim's Tip 9: Split income for hefty tax savings, with smart strategies from A to Z.

Maybe you've heard the term *income splitting* before. It's not a complicated tactic, but it's certainly one of the pillars of tax planning. Income splitting involves moving income from the hands of one family member, who is going to pay tax at a higher rate, into the hands of another, who will pay tax at a lower rate. The savings can be substantial. Check out Ron and Becky's situation.

*I*f Becky earned $60,000 in 2002 in Ontario and was the only spouse earning income, the family's tax bill would amount to $12,682. But things change dramatically if both Becky and Ron each bring home $30,000. With two income earners in this case, the family's total income remains at $60,000, but the family's tax bill drops to just $9,858, for savings of $2,824 each year. Why the tax savings? Simple. Think back to our talk about marginal tax rates in Chapter 1, Tip 2. With each spouse earning just $30,000, nearly every dollar earned by the family is taxed at the lowest marginal tax rate possible for

---

* For brevity I will use the term "spouse" to refer to both spouses and common-law partners (same sex or not). Both are afforded the same tax treatment under our tax law.

employment income—about 25 percent. When Becky earned all the money herself, every dollar over $31,677 was taxed at a higher marginal rate—about 35 percent—giving rise to a higher tax bill.

Not impressed so far? The truth is, your tax savings from splitting income can be as high as $12,960 (Canada-wide average) annually! The actual savings from splitting income depend on your province of residence and the difference between your marginal tax rate and that of your family member.

THE VALUE OF SPLITTING INCOME			
	Becky's Income	**Ron's Income**	**Total**
One Income Earner			
Employment income	$60,000	$ –	$60,000
Tax to pay	$12,682	$ –	$12,682
Two Income Earners			
Employment income	$30,000	$30,000	$60,000
Tax to pay	$ 4,929	$ 4,929	$ 9,858
Tax saved annually			**$ 2,824**

The Attribution Rules

The problem is this: The tax collector will not allow you simply to hand a portion of your income to your spouse or child to be taxed in their hands. If you try this, you'll be caught under the *attribution rules* found in our tax law. These rules say that, when you try to pass income to your spouse or common-law partner, children, in-laws, nieces or nephews by transferring income-producing property to them, *you* will be taxed on the income, and not the person whom you intended to pay the tax.

By the way, a common-law partner is someone, same sex or not, with whom you've been living in a conjugal relationship for 12 months or more, or one you're living with who is also a parent of a child of yours.

	THE ATTRIBUTION RULES IN A NUTSHELL		
	Type of Transfer		
Transfer To	**Gift**	**Loan With No Interest**	**Loan at Interest***
Spouse**	Attribute all investment income and capital gains back to transferor	Attribute all investment income and capital gains back to transferor	No attribution
Minor Child	Attribute all investment income, but not capital gains, to transferor	Attribute all investment income, but not capital gains, to transferor	No attribution
Adult Child	No attribution	Attribute all investment income and capital gains if loan made specifically to avoid tax	No attribution

* Interest charged must be CCRA's prescribed rate, or commercial rates if these are less.
** Transfers to a spouse or common-law partner are treated the same.

Never fear. There are ways to sidestep the attribution rules. What follows is the A to Z of income-splitting strategies.

a. Lend money and charge fair interest.

Set up a loan between you and the family member you'd like to split income with. As long as you charge interest on the loan at the rate prescribed by the Canada Customs and Revenue Agency (CCRA) or at current commercial rates (you should choose whichever rate is lower), then you'll avoid attribution back to you of any income earned on the money you've lent. The interest must be paid to you by January 30 following any year the loan is outstanding, and will be taxable to you. Your family member can deduct the interest paid on the loan. One last thing: You're required to set the rate on the loan permanently at the time the loan is set up—which can be great news if interest rates happen to be low at that time.

b. Lend money, then take repayment.

This idea works well if you'd rather not charge interest on money lent to family members. It works this way: Lend money to a family member for investment purposes—say $15,000—then take back those funds after five years. Those funds will earn, say, $1,200 each year, which, in most cases, will be taxed in your hands because of the attribution rules. Here's the kicker: That $1,200 can be reinvested each year, and any second-generation income—in other words, income on income—will not be attributed back to you. By lending money to a family member for five years or more, there will be enough time for the second-generation income to grow and take on a life of its own. Soon, your family member will have a sizeable portfolio growing and facing tax in his or her hands—not yours. You'd be wise to transfer the income earned each year to a separate account to keep the second-generation income segregated.

c. Transfer money for business purposes.

You'll manage to avoid the attribution rules if you lend or give money to family members for use in a business. If it's a loan, there's no need to charge interest to avoid the dreaded attribution rules, but there are right ways and wrong ways to invest in a small business. I'll talk more about this issue in Chapter 5, Tip 55.

Action Step

When you set up a loan between family members for the purpose of splitting income, be sure to properly document the loan. A promissory note signed by the borrower should do the trick. The promissory note should detail the date and amount of the loan; the interest rate charged (if any); the method for calculating interest (compounded daily, monthly, or annually); and the terms of repayment (perhaps simply due upon demand), including when interest will be paid. Remember: To avoid the attribution rules, pay the interest by January 30 each year.

d. Transfer money to cover interest on investment loans.

When a family member borrows money to invest, make sure that a higher-income family member does not guarantee the loan or give the borrower funds to repay the loan principal. The problem? Quite simply, the attribution rules. These rules will cause any income earned on the borrowed funds to be taxed in the hands of the person guaranteeing or effectively making payments on the loan.

The fact is, when you've transferred money to a lower-income family member, and those funds are used to pay for expenses and not to invest, the attribution rules won't apply. So, why not give cash to your family member in order to pay the interest on any investment loans? Giving that family member the cash to make those interest payments will make it much easier for that lower-income family member to borrow for investing. The result? Investment income is taxed at a lower marginal tax rate in the hands of your family member. Be careful that you do not provide collateral, guarantee the loan, or make principal repayments—otherwise you'll wind up with the tax bill, not your lower-income family member.

e. Swap assets with another family member.

We've been talking, so far, about splitting income by passing investment assets to other family members who are going to face a lower marginal tax rate than you are. Why not swap assets to make this happen? Here's how: "Sell" some of your investments to your spouse or child in exchange for another asset you take back in return. The asset you take back should be worth at least as much as the investments you're handing over, and should not produce an income of any kind. I'm talking about things like jewellery, artwork, a coin or other collection, or even your spouse's half of the family home—provided your spouse actually contributed to its purchase. If the house was purchased with your money alone, the attribution rules will catch up to you. Keep in mind that, for tax purposes, any swap is considered to be a sale at fair market value, so there could be tax to pay on any accrued gains when you make the swap.

f. Generate capital gains in the hands of your kids.

One of the most common ways to split income with the kids is to give or lend them cash to invest. Regardless of the age of your kids, there will not generally be attribution of capital gains on the invested money back to you. That is, your kids will pay the tax on any capital gains generated. The best part, of course, is that your kids can earn up to $15,268 in capital gains in 2002 without paying any tax if they have no other source of income. Besides cash, you could also transfer existing investments to your kids. But beware: When you give assets away, you are deemed to have sold those assets at fair market value. So, if those assets have appreciated in value, there could be some tax to pay on the gains. This tax cost, however, could pale in comparison to the taxes you'll save by splitting income with the kids.

g. Transfer any investment income to your adult child.

While you'll generally be able to move capital gains to the hands of your children and avoid attribution, it's a whole new ball game when we talk about interest, dividends, rents, royalties, and other *income from property*. If you transfer money to your minor children for investment, you're going to pay the tax on any income from property. But there's good news. Any income generated on assets given to an adult child (18 years or older at the end of the year) will avoid attribution, no matter what the type of income. The only catch is that your child now owns and controls the assets. To avoid having your child spend your hard-earned money on the finer things in life, consider setting up a formal trust to maintain control over the assets. One last point to note: If you transferred the money to your adult child as a loan rather than a gift, and the tax collector decides that your primary motive was to avoid tax, you're going to face the attribution rules.

h. Give funds to your adult child, then charge room and board.

When you give money to a child who has reached age 18 by December 31, you'll avoid attribution on any income earned. Of course, you may not want to give up the income you were enjoying on those investments, so here's a plan: Charge your child room and board for living at home. This will enable you to recover the income that you've given up by giving away your money. If you're not thrilled with the idea of handing over a sum of money to your semi-responsible 18-year-old, consider transferring the assets to a trust. This will allow you to accomplish the same thing, but will give you control over the money as long as you're a trustee and the trust is set up properly.

i. Make a corporate loan to a related student.

If you're a shareholder of a corporation, consider setting up a loan from the corporation to a student who is not dealing at arm's length with you and who will be 18 or older in the year. If the loan is not repaid within one year of your company's year-end, the loan is going to be taxed in the hands of the student. That's no big deal: The student will likely pay little or no tax on the amount if he or she has very little other income. But there's more. Once that student graduates and is earning a regular income, the loan can be repaid, and the student will be allowed a deduction for the amount of the repayment. Not a bad deal! Little or no tax to pay when the loan is included in income, but a healthy deduction when it's repaid later. This idea is great where the student doesn't work in the business and it would be tough to justify paying salary or wages. Keep in mind that the company won't be entitled to a deduction for the cash paid to the student. After all, it's a loan.

j. Pay an allowance to your working child.

I know, I know, you've been looking forward to the day when your children are out working, earning their own spending money, if only because it will teach them responsibility. What if I were to tell you that paying your children an allowance makes sense once they're earning their own money? Here's why: Giving your children an allowance will free up their earnings for investment. When they invest their own income, the attribution rules won't apply and you will have effectively split income. By the way, a child who has earned income will be entitled to RRSP contribution room, which will save tax down the road when the child starts contributing to that RRSP.

k. Pay an adult child to babysit the younger kids.

If you haven't got investments or cash simply to hand over to the kids to split income, try this idea on for size: Pay your adult child who was 18 or older in the year to babysit your younger kids who were 16 or under in the year. Babysitting fees, like other childcare expenses, may be deductible if they were paid out to allow you to earn income. Follow me now: You're entitled to a deduction for the payments to your adult child, and that child will report the payments as income. There's a very good chance, however, that your child will face little or no tax on those payments. In this case, you've managed to split income by moving income directly from your tax return to your kid's return. Oh, and there's another big benefit: This *earned income* will entitle your child to RRSP contribution room.

l. Pay an adult child to help in a move.

Where you're entitled to claim moving expenses, why not pay your adult child to help you with the move? Let's face it, someone's got to drive the truck or lift the furniture. It might as well be a family member. You'll not only keep the money in the family, but you'll be entitled to a deduction for the payment made—subject, of course, to the usual moving expense rules (see Tip 14). Your child will have to report the income, but may not pay much tax, if any, when his or her income is low. The payment will also entitle your child to RRSP contributions, since it's earned income. There's nothing quite like moving income directly from your tax return to your child's—and this is what you're accomplishing here.

m. Transfer assets before leaving the country.

Suppose that you and your spouse have decided to leave Canada. Did you realize that you could face an ugly tax hit when you leave? Here's why: When you leave, you are deemed to have "sold" everything you own at fair market value, with some exceptions, and so you could face tax on certain property that has appreciated in value. You could minimize this tax hit with a clever tactic used by Burt and Margaret.

After spending several winters in the sunny south, Burt and Margaret decided to retire in California in January 2003. At the time the couple decided to move, Burt owned stocks worth $20,000 that he had paid $5,000 for. Burt was due to face a tax bill on the $15,000 ($20,000 minus $5,000) accrued capital gain when leaving Canada, thanks to the rule that deems him to have sold these stocks. In December 2002, just before leaving, Burt gave the stocks to his wife Margaret (with no tax effect to himself since assets transferred to a spouse generally transfer at original cost). On January 5, 2003, Burt left for California and became a resident of the U.S. Margaret left one month later to join Burt and became a resident of the U.S. in February 2003.

When Margaret left, she owned the stocks with the $15,000 gain, and had to pay tax on that gain when leaving. Normally, the attribution rules would require the gain to be taxed in Burt's hands, but not in this case, since Burt is no longer a resident of Canada. Instead, Margaret paid the tax on the $15,000 gain at her lower marginal tax rate. The couple successfully split income.

By the way, normally the tax collector will consider two spouses to have given up residency on the same day. In Burt and Margaret's case, Margaret had business reasons to stay behind. I should also mention that there is a court case, *Min Shan Shih v. The Queen* (2000), which supports the notion that a spouse can, in some cases, be a non-resident of Canada at the same time that the other spouse is resident here. Make sure you visit a tax professional to talk over the residency issue before trying this idea.

n. Transfer capital losses to your spouse.

When I met Paul a couple of years ago, he had a common problem: unrealized capital losses. You see, Paul paid $20,000 for shares in XYZ Corp. that today are worth just $5,000, so Paul has an unrealized capital loss of $15,000. While Paul does not have any capital gains against which to deduct this loss, his wife Esther does. Esther has about $15,000 of realized capital gains this year. Wouldn't it be nice if we could transfer Paul's $15,000 unrealized capital loss to Esther? She could then shelter her capital gains from tax. The good news is, we can. There are three steps to take.

Caution!

If you're leaving Canada, be sure to visit a tax professional who can help you to determine, in advance, whether or not you are properly giving up residency for tax purposes. CCRA will make this determination for you if you complete Form NR73, but I rarely recommend sending a completed Form NR73 to the tax collector! You see, if there's any way to call you a resident of Canada—the tax collector will. In most cases, there's no need to send anything to the tax collector before giving up residency.

Step 1 Paul will sell his XYZ shares on the open market and trigger the $15,000 capital loss. As you'll see in a second, Paul won't actually be able to claim the loss. Not to worry—this is precisely what we want!

Step 2 Esther will then acquire the same number and type of XYZ shares on the open market immediately (or within 30 days) after Paul sells his. This step has two results: First, Paul's $15,000 capital loss is denied. You see, the *superficial loss rules* in our tax law will not allow you to claim a capital loss if you or a person affiliated with you (your spouse, for example) acquires identical property within a certain time frame (30 days prior to and 30 days after your sale of the property, a 61-day window). The second result is that Esther will pay just $5,000 for her XYZ shares, but the $15,000 loss denied to Paul will be added to her cost, providing her with an adjusted cost base (ACB) of $20,000. That's right, the taxman won't deny Paul's loss forever. It's handed to Esther in the form of a higher ACB so that when she ultimately sells the shares, she'll have a lower capital gain or greater capital loss at that time.

Step 3 Esther will wait until that 61-day superficial loss time window is over (this is necessary to ensure the loss is denied to Paul), and then will sell the XYZ shares on the open market. Don't forget, Esther's ACB is $20,000, but the shares are worth just $5,000—so she'll realize a $15,000 capital loss. Esther can then use this capital loss to offset the capital gains that she has already realized this year.

By the way, it's not critical that Esther have capital gains in the same year that Paul has capital losses. Why? Because capital losses can be carried back up to three years, or forward indefinitely, to offset gains in those other years. So, if Esther reported gains in a prior year, it may be possible for her to take that $15,000 capital loss and carry it back to recover taxes paid in a prior year. Form T1A is used to carry losses back, and must be filed with your tax return in the year the losses are realized.

Here's the bottom line: Don't try this stunt at home. Visit a tax professional for help. You'll want to do it right since the superficial loss rules can be complex.

o. Transfer personal tax credits.

There are a few non-refundable personal tax credits that can be transferred from one spouse to the other. The idea here is to transfer these credits to the higher-income spouse when possible. Overall, this could save the family taxes—largely due to the provincial surtax savings you'll enjoy where your province levies a surtax (see Chapter 8). Which credits can be passed by your spouse to you? Four in particular: the age credit (if your spouse was 65 years or older in the year); disability credit (where your spouse had a severe mental or physical impairment, supported by a signed Form T2201—see Tip 16); pension credit (where your spouse had pension income); and tuition and education credits (where your spouse attended a qualifying post-secondary school).

p. Pay household expenses through the higher-income spouse.

This is, perhaps, the simplest technique for splitting income. Let's suppose that you have a higher income and marginal tax rate than your spouse. If you pay for all or most of the household expenses, this will free up your spouse's income for investment. You can even pay your spouse's income taxes. There won't be any attribution of income in this case, since you are not giving money to your spouse to earn income. The result? This will free up some of your spouse's income to invest, and your spouse will face the tax on those investment earnings at his or her lower marginal tax rate.

q. Invest inheritances in the right name.

Make sure that any inheritance received by the lower-income spouse is kept separate and apart from any joint accounts you might have as a couple. As long as the inherited money is invested solely in the name of the lower-income spouse, the investment income will be taxed in the hands of that spouse alone, which will spell tax savings for the family. Likewise, where money has been left to both of you, be sure to invest the lower-income spouse's half separately rather than keeping the money in a joint account. The tax savings on an inheritance properly invested could be enough to pay for a family vacation each year!

r. Invest Child Tax Benefits in the child's name.

It was in January 1993 that the tax collector replaced the old Family Allowance system with the Child Tax Benefit system. You know what I'm talking about. Canada Child Tax Benefits are those payments that many Canadian families are entitled to receive on a monthly basis until the children reach age 18. Did you realize that benefit payments can be invested in your child's name without the attribution rules kicking in? You better believe it. And it makes good sense. Ensure that the payments are deposited directly into an investment account for the child, and not co-mingled with funds you might have given the child. Then consider investing those funds for the long term—perhaps to help with your child's education.

Action Step

When investing Canada Child Tax Benefits in the name of your child, your best bet is to open an investment account in the name of the child alone. Many financial institutions will do this for you. Obtain a Social Insurance Number (SIN) for your child and visit your financial institution armed with that SIN to open the account properly. This will avoid any confusion with the tax collector when it comes time to report the income on the child's tax return.

s. Contribute to a spousal RRSP.

Your goal for retirement should be for you and your spouse to have equal incomes. Why? Because this will accomplish a perfect splitting of incomes. To make it happen, you may need to help your spouse by contributing to a Registered Retirement Savings Plan (RRSP) for him or her. I'm talking about a spousal RRSP. It works this way: You'll contribute to an RRSP under which your spouse is the annuitant. This simply means that your spouse will be the one to make withdrawals from the plan, and your spouse will pay the tax on those withdrawals. The good news is that you'll be entitled to a deduction for the contribution you've made to the spousal RRSP. I'll take a closer look at spousal RRSPs in Chapter 6, Tip 75.

t. Consider an RESP for a child's education.

Registered Education Savings Plans (RESPs) are special plans registered with the government to help save for post-secondary education. Here's the deal: You won't be allowed to deduct your contribution to an RESP, but the funds will grow tax-deferred in the plan over the years. When the money is withdrawn from the RESP for education purposes, the income that had accumulated in the RESP will be taxed in the hands of the student. I like it—a perfect splitting of income. By the way, RESPs are also attractive because the government will pay grant money into the plan with your own dollars for eligible kids. I'll be talking more about RESPs in Tip 11.

u. Split the tax bill on your CPP benefits.

Here's an income splitting idea that the tax collector openly endorses. You're entitled to take up to one-half of your Canada Pension Plan (CPP) benefits and report the amount on your spouse's tax return provided you're both over age 60. The arrangement is actually reciprocal so that the same proportion of your spouse's CPP benefits will have to be reported on your tax return. As long as your benefits are higher than your spouse's, and you have a higher marginal tax rate, you're going to save some tax. Be sure to contact Human Resources Development Canada to arrange for this splitting of benefits.

The tax rules say that when you transfer dividends from one spouse to the next, you'll have to transfer all the dividends. You can't simply pick and choose which dividends to transfer. Watch out! Transferring all the dividends to the higher-income spouse's tax return might increase that spouse's income enough to cause a clawback of Old Age Security benefits. In this case, you might want to avoid this type of transfer.

Caution!

v. Report your spouse's dividends on your tax return.

What if I told you that reporting someone else's income on your tax return could actually save you tax? You'd probably have me committed. The truth is, the idea can work. You see, you can elect to report all of your spouse's Canadian dividends on your own tax return. It can make sense if your spouse's income is quite low. By putting your spouse's dividends on your return, you'll reduce your spouse's income, which may, in turn, increase the spousal tax credit you're entitled to claim. In fact, you'll only be allowed to make this election if it increases your spousal tax credit. Since you'll also be entitled to claim a dividend tax credit on the dividends reported, your family could save hundreds of dollars in tax by making this swap (see Tip 50 for more).

w. Pay family members a salary.

If you happen to run a business of any kind, you'll be able to pay your family members a salary or wage to work in that business. The only catch is that the amount you pay must be reasonable for the services provided. What's reasonable? Consider what you would pay an unrelated third party and this should give you a pretty good idea. Your business will claim a deduction, and your family member will report the income. More on this in Tip 43.

x. Become a partner with family members.

Did you know that a partnership does not pay taxes itself? Rather, the income or loss of the partnership is passed along to each of the partners, who are then responsible for reporting the income or loss to the tax collector. If you become a partner with your spouse or children, you'll split income by having some of your profits taxed in their hands, in accordance with your partnership agreement. By the way, a written partnership agreement is critical to avoid misunderstandings with family and to satisfy CCRA of the partnership allocations.

y. Own a corporation with family members.

If you're a co-shareholder with your spouse or kids, you can split income with them in a number of ways. As shareholders, your family members are entitled to dividends from the corporation. In addition, they may be entitled to directors' fees if they are directors of the company, or salary if they are actively employed by the company. It's also common to see family trusts set up where the trust owns shares in the corporation, and the kids are beneficiaries of the trust. Dividends can be paid to the trust and allocated out to the children to be taxed in their hands, although the 1999 federal budget made this tactic unattractive for minor children as of January 1, 2000. (I'll talk more about this in Tip 10.) Adult family members can receive up to $28,820 in dividends from a Canadian corporation in a year and pay little or no tax if they have no other income, thanks to the dividend tax credit.

z. Use two corporations to transfer money.

The ugly attribution rules we've been talking about apply to transfers of assets between two individuals or between an individual and a corporation—but not between two corporations. If, for example, you and your spouse own separate corporations, funds can be lent from your corporation to your spouse's without attribution. If those funds were used in a business or invested inside your spouse's corporation, your spouse could access the funds by taking dividends. Your spouse will be able to take up to $28,820 in dividends from his or her corporation and pay little or no tax (varies by province), thanks to the dividend tax credit, provided those dividends are your spouse's only source of income. Be sure to visit a tax pro before trying this idea. You'll have to set things up properly to satisfy the anti-avoidance provisions in the *Income Tax Act*.

TO MAKE A LONG STORY SHORT:

- Splitting income involves moving income from the hands of one family member, who will be taxed at a higher rate, to the hands of another, who will face tax at a lower rate.

- The attribution rules prevent many attempts at passing income to other family members.

- Splitting income most commonly entails investing money in lower-income hands, making deductible payments to lower-income family members, and claiming deductions and credits on the most appropriate tax return.

Tim's Tip 10: Consider family trusts for income splitting.

Trusts can offer a ton of flexibility in managing your affairs and controlling the use of your property. And a trust can be as simple to set up as a visit to your lawyer. Sure, it's going to take some legal fees up front and some accounting fees each year to file the appropriate T3 income tax and information return for your trust, but the costs could be well worth it.

How a Trust Works

A trust is not a legal entity itself. It's a *relationship* between three parties: the settlor, the trustee, and the beneficiary. The settlor creates the trust by transferring property to the trustee. The trustee holds legal title to the trust property for the benefit of the beneficiary, rather than for the trustee's own benefit. Of course, it's possible to have more than one beneficiary. In fact, it's possible to have more than one settlor and trustee, too.

William is elderly and has two sons, Scott and Jason. Jason is mentally impaired. William wants to ensure that Jason will always be provided for, so he gave $300,000 to Scott to hold in trust for Jason. A trust agreement was drawn up so that Scott is able to use the funds to provide for Jason's needs. Scott is responsible for investing the funds until they are paid out for Jason's benefit. Scott is legally bound to use the funds for Jason's benefit alone. In this case, the trust agreement provides that an annual fee is paid to Scott for his services. William is the settlor of the trust, Scott is the trustee, and Jason is the beneficiary.

How is a trust taxed? Just like any other individual. That's right, the trust will have to file a tax and information return each year (called a T3 return) and will have to report any income earned in the trust. There's a way for the trust to avoid tax on its income, and that is to pay out to the beneficiary, or make payable to the beneficiary, any income earned in the trust each year. This way, the beneficiary will pay tax on the income instead.

Here's an important point: A trust that is set up while the settlor is alive is called an *inter vivos* trust and will face tax at the highest marginal tax rates going! All this

> **Caution!**
>
> You should remember that whenever you transfer any property to another individual or to most trusts, you're deemed to have sold that property at its fair market value at the time of the transfer. What does this mean for you? It means that, if the property has appreciated in value, you could end up with some tax to pay on the capital gain. You won't have to worry about this with cash and near-cash investments, like Guaranteed Investment Certificates and Canada Savings Bonds, because these don't appreciate in value.

means is that you'll generally want to ensure that any income in an inter vivos trust is taxed in the beneficiaries' hands, and not in the trust. A *testamentary* trust, on the other hand, is created through the will of a deceased individual. This type of trust is taxed just as you and I are, at graduated tax rates.

A family trust can be set up for lots of reasons—including some not related to income tax, such as:

- protecting assets from creditors or ex-spouses
- protecting the privacy of asset owners
- providing for the needs of disabled children
- avoiding probate fees

Of course, trusts are also useful for splitting income to reduce income tax.

Trusts for Income Splitting

Let's talk about inter vivos trusts now. Testamentary trusts can also be an effective income splitting tool, but these relate more to estate planning, so I'll cover them in Tip 99.

Before we jump to it, let me just say that splitting income using inter vivos trusts has some advantages over other income-splitting strategies. For example:

- Parents or grandparents can retain control over the property even after transferring beneficial ownership to the kids to split income.
- The assets in a trust are generally protected from the creditors of the settlor, trustee, or beneficiaries.
- It's possible to transfer ownership to the beneficiaries of the trust without having to decide yet which specific child or children will ultimately end up owning the properties or assets held in the trust.

The two most common uses of inter vivos family trusts for income splitting are to hold portfolio investments and to hold shares in a private corporation.

Portfolio Investments

The name of the game here is splitting income from investments. Most commonly, parents or grandparents "settle" a trust by transferring assets (usually cash) to the trustee for the benefit of minor children, who are usually the beneficiaries.

While the trustee and the settlor can be the same person, this isn't ideal from a tax point of view. You see, where the settlor is also the sole trustee, Subsection 75(2) of our tax law will kick in and cause the settlor rather than the beneficiaries to pay all the tax on income that is earned in the trust. The bottom line? If you're the settlor, you'd be wise to name your spouse, other family members, or an advisor to be trustees (perhaps in addition to yourself).

You should visit a tax pro with experience in trusts to make sure the trust is settled properly and to give proper consideration to tax and other legislation before naming the trustees.

Once the trust has been created, the funds must be invested carefully. The reason? If you're not careful, the ugly attribution rules I spoke about in Tip 9 could cause the income to be taxed in the hands of the settlor rather than the minor beneficiaries. Simply inserting a trust into the tax plan doesn't allow you to escape the attribution rules. Those rules look right through a trust. As a result, it's common to see trust funds invested to generate capital gains rather than interest or dividends. After all, capital gains escape the attribution rules and will be taxed in the hands of the minor beneficiaries (refer to Tip 9*f*). Once the beneficiaries reach 18 years of age you've got no problem: The attribution rules are generally shut down at that point (refer to Tip 9*g*). To generate capital gains rather than current income, consider investing in equity mutual funds with a "buy and hold" value approach to investing. A financial advisor can help you to choose the right investments.

From a practical point of view, any income in the trust that is *paid* or made *payable* to the beneficiary is deducted from the income of the trust on its tax return. The beneficiary gets a T3 slip for the same amount, and must report the income on his or her own tax return. If there's more than one beneficiary, the deducted amount will be split between the beneficiaries in whatever manner the trust agreement specifies.

Private Corporation Shares

If you're a shareholder in a private company, you may be able to split income with family members through a family trust. In the past, the structure has looked something like this: a grandparent transfers a gold coin to the trustee; the trustee then borrows a few dollars on behalf of the trust to buy shares in the family corporation for a nominal amount. The trust now owns shares in the family company. The minor children or grandchildren are typically the beneficiaries.

There's a clear reason why Grandma or Grandpa settles the trust with a gold coin, rather than with enough cash to buy the shares in the family corporation. You see, the gold coin is not an income-producing asset, and so the income from the trust will not be attributed back to the settlor (the grandparent).

Once the trust owns shares in the family corporation, the corporation can pay dividends to the trust. Who do you suppose is going to pay the tax on these dividends? You got it— the beneficiaries. In the past, the dividend tax credit made it possible to pay up to about $24,000 in dividends to the trust for each beneficiary, with little or no tax to pay if the beneficiary had no other source of income.

Changes introduced in the 1999 federal budget have put a stop to this for minor beneficiaries through something tax pros call the "kiddie tax," as I discuss below. But the trust structure I've been talking about here will still work to pass along dividends of $28,820 annually to adult children or to a spouse or common-law partner. And adult beneficiaries with little or no other income will pay little or no tax on the dividends.

> ## Did You Know?
>
> Any income earned in a trust can be taxed in the hands of the beneficiaries rather than the trust if the income is paid out or made payable to the beneficiaries. "Paid out" does not just include direct payments to the beneficiaries alone. In fact, the tax collector has said that payments to third parties (for example, summer camps or private schools) or to parents to reimburse them for costs incurred on behalf of a child beneficiary also qualify. Be sure to keep all receipts to show that the payments were for the child's benefit.

The Kiddie Tax

There's no question that family trusts holding shares of family corporations have, in the past, meant big tax savings for some. Through a tactic known as "dividend sprinkling," it was possible for a private company to pay dividends to a trust for the benefit of minor children. The kids would typically pay no tax on those dividends with the result that money could be extracted from the private company on a very tax-efficient basis.

The tax collector wasn't thrilled with this set-up and took steps in 1999 to minimize dividend sprinkling. So the 1999 federal budget took a shot at dividends paid directly or indirectly to minors. Minor beneficiaries will now pay a tax at the highest rate—about 32 percent on dividends. This is called the "kiddie tax." Here's a closer look at the rules:

- A special tax, at the top marginal rate, will be imposed on certain income (called "split income") received by individuals under age 18 throughout the year. This special tax will apply to taxable dividends and other shareholder benefits from private companies (both Canadian and foreign), including dividends received indirectly through a trust.
- The tax will also apply to income from a partnership or trust that supplies goods or services to a business carried on by a relative of the child or in which the relative participates.
- Income subject to this tax will not be eligible for any deductions or credits, except the dividend tax credit and the foreign tax credit where they apply.
- The measures do not apply to payments to or for adults (those 18 or older in the year).
- The measures do not apply to dividends from publicly traded shares.
- The measures apply to transactions in 2000 and future years.

Trusts Still Make Sense

If you've already set up a family trust or are wondering whether or not it still makes sense to create a family trust to hold shares of your private company, you'll be glad to know that tax savings can still be had.

Here's what I mean: Any dividends that are paid from your private company to your family trust will face tax at the highest rate going due to the kiddie tax rules. The good news, however, is that the money remaining, after taxes, can then be invested in the trust with no concern whatsoever about the kiddie tax or attribution rules.

---

*P*eter *and Janice are married and have three minor kids: Tori, Lincoln, and Virginia. Peter is a shareholder in his own corporation specializing in landscaping and lawn care in B.C. A family trust was set up a few years ago to hold shares of the corporation, and the kids are beneficiaries. In 2002, the corporation will pay $20,000 in dividends to the trust for each child. Each* *child will face taxes of $6,317 on those dividends, but a total of $41,049 will remain in the trust, after taxes, and will be invested in publicly traded securities and mutual funds. It doesn't matter what type of investment portfolio income is earned in the trust; all the income earned will be taxed in the hands of the children at their graduated tax rates, with no more application of the kiddie tax or the attribution rules.*

Why is it that the kiddie tax and attribution rules won't apply anymore to the portfolio income in the story above? The kiddie tax won't apply since this investment income is not derived from a private company, and the attribution rules won't apply because this is all second-generation income. Further, it's quite likely that when the trust in the above example was set up, it was settled by a gold or silver coin provided by the grandparents of the beneficiaries, and a coin is not an income-producing asset. This alone allows avoidance of the attribution rules.

In closing, let me say that there is no shortage of tax laws dealing with trusts. I've only touched on the basics here. In addition, I have dealt with the issue of alter ego trusts (a type of inter vivos trust for seniors) in Tip 100. Alter ego trusts are really an estate-planning tool. If you're considering a family trust, be sure to visit a tax pro. You've heard it before: Don't try this by yourself at home.

TO MAKE A LONG STORY SHORT:

- Every trust has at least one settlor, one trustee, and one beneficiary, along with trust property.

- A trust is commonly used to split income by holding investment portfolios or private company shares.

- When setting up a trust, be sure to visit a tax pro to ensure that the trust is settled, the trustees are named, and the trust documentation is prepared properly.

- The "kiddie tax" is legislation introduced in the 1999 federal budget that will cause tax to be paid at the highest rate by minor beneficiaries who receive certain types of income from a private company—even through a trust.

- There are still opportunities to use these family trusts to split second-generation income.

- Alter ego trusts are an estate-planning tool that seniors may want to consider. I'll talk about these trusts in Tip 100 in Chapter 9.

Educating the Family

When it comes to saving for education, there are a number of tax-smart strategies you can consider. I want to focus here on the two most common: Registered Education Savings Plans and in-trust accounts. I also cover the subject of education briefly in other parts of the book. Refer back to Tip 9*i* if you're a shareholder in a closely held corporation, or check out Tip 78 in Chapter 6 if you're wondering about using RRSP savings for education. For a more detailed look at education planning, pick up a copy of my book, *Winning the Education Savings Game*, which is full of bright ideas (see www.timcestnick.com). Now let's talk about those two most common strategies I was referring to.

Tim's Tip 11: Use an RESP to save for your child's education.

Do you have any idea what it's going to cost to send that special child in your life to post-secondary school? Plenty. In my book, *Winning the Education Savings Game*, I spell out the expected costs of an education down the road. If your child or grandchild enrolls at a college or university away from home in, say, 15 years, you can expect the cost to be approximately $130,000 for a four-year program.

Even if your child lives at home, the four years will still cost about $97,000. And this is the cost for just *one* child. What if you have three or more kids at school? All of a sudden, your savings goals look like a huge challenge.

The bottom line is that saving for your child's education should not be left to the last minute. It's going to take some careful planning. In *Winning the Education Savings Game*, I walk through the five strategies to pay for your child's education: begging, borrowing, stealing, sweating, and saving. At this point, I want to talk about the fifth strategy: saving for education.

Choosing an RESP

There's no doubt in my mind that a Registered Education Savings Plan should form the cornerstone of any planned savings program. Here's why:

- The Canada Education Savings Grant (CESG), available from Ottawa, can boost your RESP savings.
- An RESP offers 100-percent-guaranteed tax-free compounding inside the plan.
- The plan is simple to administer once you set it up. No annual tax filings are required.
- RESPs can provide all the investment choices you'll ever really need to save effectively for an education.
- It's possible to claim a refund of your contributions to the plan if you want.
- RESPs are quite flexible, allowing some practical alternatives if your child doesn't enroll in a qualifying educational program.
- RESPs let you split income, since the income that accumulates in the plan will be taxed in the beneficiary's hands when it's paid out as educational assistance payments.
- There's a psychological advantage to an RESP: The deadline each December 31 provides a sense of urgency about contributing, and the plan's specific purpose discourages you from using the funds for other things.

RESP Rules

I couldn't possibly cover all the rules around RESPs in one tip, which is why I wrote *Winning the Education Savings Game*. But let me share with you the most important rules:

- The RESP subscriber can contribute up to $4,000 each year for each beneficiary, with a lifetime maximum of $42,000 per beneficiary.
- Contributions are not tax deductible, but the assets in the plan can compound tax-free over the years.
- The student beneficiary will be taxed on the accumulated income when educational assistance payments are made from the plan.
- At any time, the subscriber may withdraw any contributions made to the plan (although a particular RESP promoter may place restrictions on withdrawals even though our tax law does not).
- If a child does not enroll in a qualifying educational program, the subscriber can do one of six things: (1) name a new beneficiary under the plan; (2) allocate the accumulated income to other beneficiaries already on the plan (this is possible under "family plans" where each beneficiary is connected to the subscriber by blood or adoption); (3) transfer the assets to another RESP for other beneficiaries; (4) roll up to $50,000 of RESP assets into an RRSP, provided the subscriber has sufficient RRSP contribution room; (5) donate the accumulated income in the plan to a college or university; or (6) withdraw the contributions (called a "refund of payments") and accumulated income (called "accumulated income payments") from the plan for the subscriber's own use. The accumulated income payments in this last option are fully taxable to the subscriber, and a 20-percent penalty tax will also apply.

Canada Education Savings Grants

The 1998 federal budget improved RESPs with the Canada Education Savings Grant (CESG). The CESG works alongside any RESP. Any contributions made to an RESP after 1997 for a child who is 17 or under in the year will net you a grant from the federal government, paid directly to the RESP. The grant is equal to 20 percent of the contributions made to the RESP, but only to the extent the child has CESG contribution room.

You see, the CESG is a distant cousin to your RRSP. Each child 17 or under in the year is entitled to CESG contribution room of $2,000 per year. If no contributions are made to an RESP in a given year, that contribution room is carried forward to a future year. When you contribute to the RESP, you use up that amount of contribution room, and the RESP receives a grant equal to 20 percent of the contribution room used. Keep in mind, however, that you're restricted to maximum RESP contributions of $4,000 per beneficiary each year under the usual RESP rules, so the biggest CESG grant you'll receive in any given year will be 20 percent of $4,000—or $800. I should mention that any contributions over and above the CESG contribution room cannot be carried forward to attract a CESG payment in a future year. Confused? Consider Jake's story.

Jake is four years old and his CESG contribution room for 2002 is $2,000. In February 2002, Jake's father contributed $800 to Jake's RESP. A CESG payment of $160 (20 percent of $800) is paid directly to the RESP in the following month. A few days later, Jake's grandmother made a $2,500 contribution to another RESP on behalf of Jake. Since only $1,200 of Jake's CESG contribution room is available at the time of Grandma's contribution (his dad used up $800 of it), only $1,200 of her contribution qualifies for a CESG payment. The remaining $1,300 of her contribution will not qualify for a CESG payment in the following year. By the way, if no contributions other than Dad's had been made, the remaining $1,200 of Jake's CESG contribution room would have been carried forward for use in a future year.

Action Step

If you're going to make use of an RESP, be sure to contribute enough to take maximum advantage of the CESG payments the government is offering. This will mean contributing at least $2,000 each year or $4,000 every two years. The truth is, the more you can sock away the better, because post-secondary school is not going to be cheap.

To ensure that Canadians are making use of RESPs on a regular basis, there's another catch to be aware of. If you're hoping to put money into an RESP for a child who is 16 or 17 in the year, you're going to receive CESG payments only where one of two conditions are met:

- a minimum of $2,000 in RESP contributions must have been made on behalf of the child before the year he or she turns 16, *or*
- a minimum of $100 in annual RESP contributions must have been made on behalf of that child in any four years before the year the child turns 16.

A child who turned 16 or 17 in 1998 will be eligible for CESG room for 1998 if he or she was a beneficiary of an RESP during any four years before 1998.

Get the drift? Make an RESP a regular habit if you want the benefits of the CESG.

TO MAKE A LONG STORY SHORT:

- RESPs should form the cornerstone of any planned education savings.

- The Canada Education Savings Grant (CESG) means a direct contribution by the government to a child's RESP, making these plans hard to resist.

- Read my book, *Winning the Education Savings Game*, for some bright ideas on education planning, or go to **www.timcestnick.com**.

Tim's Tip 12: **Set up in-trust accounts properly; otherwise stick to an RESP.**

In-trust accounts are more common than ever and are often used by parents, grandparents, or others to save for a child's education. The account is used to invest funds for a minor and, typically, an adult looks after the investment decisions on behalf of the child. These accounts are *informal* or *bare* trusts.

Normally, in-trust accounts are set up with the intention that the child, and not the adult, should pay the tax on any capital gains on the investment (see Tip 9*f*).

After all, the child's income is usually so low that reporting the gains in the child's hands won't trigger a tax hit at all. Of course, any interest or dividends earned by the investment will be taxed in the hands of the adult under the attribution rules, so it's typical to invest in mutual funds or securities that will generate primarily capital gains.

Doing it Properly

Here's the problem: If the in-trust account is not set up properly, you could be in for a nasty tax surprise. In a nutshell, our tax law says that there must be a real and irrevocable transfer of property to the child. That's right; if you've set up the in-trust account with the belief that you can simply access that money down the road for your own benefit—maybe to buy a new car or a set of golf clubs—you're mistaken. In the words of CCRA, you have to "divest, deprive, or dispossess" yourself of title over the money you've transferred to the account.

If you fail to make this type of transfer, then you're still considered to effectively own the assets. And if you're still the owner, guess who pays tax on every cent of income from the investment, including capital gains? Right. You do. That will defeat the purpose of setting up the account in the first place!

*R*andy *wanted to ensure that he wasn't offside with the tax collector, so he took two steps to make sure the in-trust account for his daughter, Chloe, passed the smell test.*

 Step 1
When Randy set up the in-trust account for Chloe, he ensured that the contributor (known as the settlor) of the account was not also the trustee. Since Randy contributed the money to Chloe's account, he ensured that someone else—his wife Skye—was named trustee. Naming the account "Skye Doe, in trust for Chloe Doe" provides some assurance to the tax collector that Randy has made a true transfer of assets when he set up the account.

Step 2
Randy signed an agreement providing that: (1) the property cannot revert back to Randy; (2) Randy will not require that the property be passed to persons to be named by him after setting up the account; and (3) Randy will not require that his consent or direction be obtained before the assets in the

account are disposed of. Signing this agreement is not absolutely necessary to satisfy the tax collector, but it's going to help. The agreement should simply be kept by the trustee in a safe place.

By the way, what you actually do with money in an in-trust account will speak volumes to CCRA about whether there was a true transfer of property. Be sure that the funds in the account are reserved only for the beneficiary child. Let's take it a step further. You should realize that the in-trust account arrangement is really a bare trust: The trustee's authority is limited to holding those funds until the child reaches the age of majority, then passing those funds to the child at that time.

Hmm. Food for thought.

In-Trust Accounts versus RESPs

There's only one question more perplexing than "Which came first, the chicken or the egg?" and that would be "Which is better for a child's education savings, an in-trust account or an RESP?" Both are good questions. Neither has an easy answer. In my opinion, both can have a place in any education savings program. The RESP is extremely valuable because of the free money available through the CESGs, and in-trust accounts can be useful when the RESP contribution limits make it difficult to save enough for your child's education through an RESP alone. See the table on pages 46–47 to compare the two.

TO MAKE A LONG STORY SHORT:

- In-trust accounts are a popular method of saving for a child's education but are often set up improperly. There are two steps involved in setting up an in-trust account properly.

- Once the money is in the in-trust account, forget about getting it back—it belongs to the child and he or she has a right to it at age of majority for education or otherwise.

- Both RESPs and in-trust accounts can play a significant role in paying for a child's education.

REGISTERED EDUCATION SAVINGS PLANS AND IN-TRUST ACCOUNTS

	Registered Education Savings Plans	In-Trust Accounts
Contribution limits	$4,000 per beneficiary per year. Lifetime maximum of $42,000 per beneficiary.	No limit.
Investment options	All investments eligible for RRSPs also qualify for RESPs. There are, however, no foreign content restrictions with RESPs.	Generally no restrictions, although some have expressed concern due to provincial trustee legislation. These concerns will likely be put to rest over time.
Government assistance	Canada Education Savings Grant. The grant is 20 percent of contributions made within the child's grant room—a maximum of $400 for each year.	None.
Control over assets	The subscriber controls the investments and decides when to pay the assets to the beneficiary.	The trustee of the account controls where the money is invested. The assets, however, must be held for the child until age of majority when the assets revert to the child.

continued

continued

	Registered Education Savings Plans	In-Trust Accounts
Use of assets	A beneficiary must use the plan assets for post-secondary education; otherwise, assets revert to the subscriber. If assets revert to subscriber, income tax plus a 20-percent penalty will be due on the accumulated income in the plan, unless the assets are transferred to the subscriber's RRSP.	Child may use the assets for any purpose once reaching age of majority. Contributor may not use the assets in any way, since the assets belong to the child.
Recovery of capital	Subscribers may receive a tax-free return of original capital at any time. Certain trustee or administration fees may apply.	Contributor has no right to recover the assets in the account since the assets belong to the child.
Taxation of assets	Assets grow tax-deferred over the years. When the student withdraws this money to attend a qualifying educational program, the student will pay tax on accumulated income in the plan.	Interest and dividends are taxed in the hands of the contributor annually. Realized capital gains and second-generation income are taxed in the hands of the child annually.
Tax filings	No annual filings are required until the student makes withdrawals from the RESP. Then the student must file returns to report the taxable income.	Technically, you must file a tax return for the child to report capital gains. A trust tax return should also be filed annually, but CCRA has not, to date, enforced these filings for in-trust accounts.

Heading for Home

When Dorothy returned from Oz, she declared, "There's no place like home." I'd have to agree and not simply because home is a place to hang your hat. Your home can also provide tax savings. I want to focus here on the two most common tax matters related to the family home: the principal residence exemption and moving expenses. Virtually every Canadian homeowner will face these at some point. I cover some other home-related issues elsewhere in the book. See home office expenses in Chapter 4, Tip 39; the "mortgage versus RRSP" debate in Chapter 6, Tip 74; and the Home Buyers' Plan in Chapter 6, Tip 77.

Tim's Tip 13: Change the ownership of a second property to multiply tax savings.

My guess is that unless you've been living under a rock for the last few years you're probably already aware that when you sell your home at a profit it's going to be tax-free. You see, every family unit (which includes you, your spouse or common-law partner, and any unmarried kids under age 18) is entitled to one principal residence exemption. The exemption will shelter any gains on your home from tax. By the way, your home can include a house, condominium, cottage, mobile home, trailer, live-aboard boat, or a foreign property. Sorry, but vacant land or a rental property that you've never lived in won't qualify as your principal residence.

Sheltering Pre-1982 Gains

As I've already mentioned, your family is entitled to only one principal residence exemption. This simply means that, if you own more than one property that has appreciated in value, you may have to pay some tax at some point. There may be some good news for you, however, if you and your family have owned two properties since before 1982. You see, before 1982 your family was entitled to an exemption for each individual. As a result, it may be possible for you to change the ownership of one of those properties today to shelter capital gains that had accrued up to 1982. That's right, our tax law will allow a current change in ownership to retroactively shelter pre-1982 gains from tax.

Jim and Angela are married and own two properties: a home in Fredericton, New Brunswick, and a cottage in Gaspé, Quebec. Both properties were purchased back in 1975, and both properties have been jointly owned by the couple since that time. The home is worth $200,000 more today than when the couple bought it in 1975, and the cottage is worth $100,000 more than what they paid. They are selling the cottage this year. Although they'd like to shelter the $100,000 gain on the cottage from tax, they would rather save their principal residence exemption for the home—which they plan on selling in a couple of years. They can, however, take advantage of two principal residence exemptions for years prior to 1982. This means that they'll be able to shelter the pre-1982 gains on the cottage from tax. To do this, however, they'll have to separate their joint ownership of the cottage. They first paid a visit to a tax professional before arranging for the ownership transfer with their lawyer.

Folks, this is not something to try in the comfort of your living room. The rules surrounding the principal residence exemption are complex! Be sure to visit a tax pro before getting yourself knee-deep into this tax strategy.

Multiplying the Exemption

Don't forget the tax collector's definition of a family unit for purposes of the principal residence exemption: you, your spouse or common-law partner, and any unmarried kids under 18. This means that any children who have reached 18, or are married, will be entitled to their own exemptions. This can be great news for the family!

Consider transferring the ownership of a cottage or other property to a child who is eligible for his or her own exemption. This way, the property can be sold at some point in the future, and any gains after the date of transfer can be sheltered by your child's principal residence exemption.

Of course, there could be some unwanted side effects here. First, when you give the property to your adult child, you will be deemed to have sold it at its fair market

Many Canadians make the mistake of assuming that, just because they are able to sell a principal residence without paying tax on the capital gains, they should pour more and more money into that residence with the intention of enjoying tax-free returns. Folks, think of your home as an investment. If too much of your money is tied up in your home, are you well diversified? Maybe not. Let's face it, while real estate can provide decent returns on investment, it can also provide big losses too. There may be better places to invest your hard-earned money. Be sure to talk to a financial advisor about what investments make the most sense for you.

value at that time. The result? You could end up paying some tax on the gains to date if the property is worth more than your adjusted cost base. This might not be so bad if the gain is small and if you expect the tax savings down the road to be that much greater when your child sells the property. Further, you may be able to use your principal residence exemption here to shelter the gain on the transfer from tax.

Second, keep in mind that when you give your property away to your adult child, the property then legally belongs to your child. The question is, can you trust your child to do with the property as you wish? Maybe. But if you're not comfortable with the idea of handing ownership over, you should consider the use of a family trust. (See Tip 10.) The trust will allow you to maintain control over the property while still effectively passing it to your child for purposes of multiplying the principal residence exemption.

In any event, it's going to be important to do things right, so be sure to visit a tax professional before taking your first step to transfer ownership.

TO MAKE A LONG STORY SHORT:

- Every family is entitled, for 1982 and later years, to one principal residence exemption to shelter from tax the profits on the sale of a home.

- A child who is 18 years or older in the year, or who is married, is entitled to his or her own principal residence exemption.

- Ownership of a second property can be transferred to multiply the available exemptions, but professional tax advice is going to be important here!

Tim's Tip 14: **Plan the family's move carefully to maximize tax benefits.**

If you're going to pack up your bags and move, you might as well do it properly—from a tax point of view.

Why Are You Moving and How Far?

The rules dealing with moving expenses are pretty clear. They say that you're entitled to deduct costs for making a move to start a business, begin working at a new location, or go to school. To boot, you're only entitled to claim expenses when your new residence is at least 40 kilometres closer to your new work location or school than your old residence. By the way, that's 40 kilometres taking the shortest normal route of travel—not as the crow flies, which used to be the test.

Most importantly, you're only entitled to deduct costs up to the amount of income you've earned in the new location. Not to worry, if you can't claim all your moving costs in the year of your move because your income from the new location is too low, you'll be able to carry those expenses forward to claim them in the next year, subject to the same restrictions. The types of expenses you can deduct include:

- travelling costs, including meals and lodging
- moving and storage costs for your household effects
- lease cancellation costs
- selling costs for your old home, including real estate commissions
- legal costs on a new home purchase
- land transfer tax payable on the new home, if you've sold your old one
- costs of maintaining a vacant former residence (including mortgage interest and property taxes to a maximum of $5,000)
- cost of revising legal documents to reflect your new address, replacing driver's licences, auto permits, and utility connections and disconnections

Want to maximize your claim? Here's my advice: Plan your move so that it coincides with a new work or school location, and make sure you meet the 40-kilometre test. If you're a student, don't forget that scholarships, bursaries, and research grants qualify as income in your new location, provided the amounts are taxable.

Action Step

There are two court cases that support the notion that you may be able to move from one residence to the next and claim moving expenses even when you are not moving to take on new employment or to start a new business. Rather, you may be simply maintaining your existing employment or business but are moving because you need additional office space in your home or for other reasons. *See Gary Adamson v. The Queen* (2001) and *Templeton v. The Queen* (1997).

Moving to a New Province?

If you're going to be moving to a new province, keep in mind that you're considered to be a resident of the province where you lived on December 31. Why is this so important? Simple. You're going to pay tax to the province in which you're a resident on December 31. So here's your game plan: If you're moving to a province with lower tax rates, make the move before the end of the year if you can. This way, you'll take advantage of those lower rates sooner. If your new province has higher tax rates, consider waiting until the new year to make the move. You'll enjoy your current lower tax rates for an extra year.

TO MAKE A LONG STORY SHORT:

• You can deduct costs for moving as long as you're moving to a new work location or to school, and your new home is at least 40 kilometres closer than your old home.

• Plan your move so that it coincides with a new work or school location and meets the distance test.

• If you're moving to a new province, time your move to take advantage of lower tax rates.

• Remember that you can pay an adult child to help in the move and then deduct this as an expense. (See Tip 91.)

Claiming Family Care Costs

Tim's Tip 15: Maximize the base for your childcare expenses.

The year 2000 saw my wife give birth to our second child—our daughter, Sarah. And even though Carolyn has decided to stay at home with the kids, I do happen to know a thing or two about childcare expenses—from a tax angle. Let me tell you about them.

Gimme the Facts

Childcare expenses can be claimed when you've incurred them to enable you or your spouse (or common-law partner) to earn an income. In a two-parent family, the lower-income spouse has to claim the expenses in all but a few situations. If you're a single parent, you'll be allowed to make a claim as well. By the way, the tax collector changed the rules in the 1998 federal budget to allow childcare expenses to be deducted where a single parent is in school full- or part-time or where both parents in a two-parent family are in full- or part-time study at a post-secondary school.

You're not necessarily going to be able to deduct every dime of your childcare expenses. There are some restrictions here, although the limits were increased back in the 1998 federal budget. In a nutshell, you'll be able to deduct up to $7,000 of costs for each child under seven on December 31 or who suffers from a less-than-severe physical or mental infirmity. The amount is reduced to $4,000 for kids age 7 to 16 in the year or for those over 16 suffering from a less severe infirmity who are still dependent on you. Costs of up to $10,000 annually to have someone care for a child, of any age, with a severe and prolonged physical or mental infirmity can be deducted. I should mention that the tax collector might further restrict your child-care deductions. The tax collector will calculate two-thirds of your *earned income* for childcare purposes (basically your employment and self-employment income) and, where this figure is less than the limits I've already mentioned, you'll be limited to two-thirds of your earned income.

There has been talk that it's possible to deduct childcare costs as a business expense. While there was some uncertainty around this issue in the past, this isn't the case anymore! A 1993 Supreme Court decision (*Symes v. Canada*) made it clear that you won't be able to deduct these costs as a business expense. Too bad, really. Nevertheless, if you've claimed childcare as a business expense in the past, you can expect a reassessment if the tax collector catches the write-off.

Childcare expenses include payments for babysitters, day nursery services, boarding schools, and camps. You should know that deductions for payments to a boarding school or camp are limited to $175 per week of attendance for kids under 7 years of age and $100 per week for kids 7 to 16. This same dollar restriction applies to parents in full-time attendance at school. (Parents in part-time attendance are limited to $175 per month for kids under 7 and $100 per month for kids 7 to 16.)

So when, exactly, is the higher-income spouse allowed to claim the childcare expenses? When the lower-income spouse was at school full- or part-time, in a prison or similar institution for at least two weeks in the year, certified to be incapable of caring for children, confined to a wheelchair or bed for at least two weeks, or separated due to a marriage breakdown. If you're the higher-income spouse claiming the childcare expenses, you'll be limited to $175 per week for each child under 7 or infirm, and $100 for kids 7 to 16.

CHILDCARE DEDUCTIONS: MAXIMUM CLAIM*			
		Child Is Infirm	
Age of Child on December 31	No Infirmity	Severe and Prolonged	Less than Severe
Under 7	$7,000	$10,000	$7,000
7 to 16	$4,000	$10,000	$4,000
Over 16	None	$10,000	$4,000

* The maximum deduction is two-thirds of earned income, or the amount in the table, whichever is less.

Increasing the Base for Your Claim

The tax collector does not attach specific childcare expenses to specific children. All that matters is that your total expenses deducted for all the kids not exceed the number of kids multiplied by the maximum expenses allowed for each child. Confused? Lindsay, Logan, and Jamie will help to make things clear.

---

*L*indsay is 12 years old. Her brother Logan is nine, and her sister Jamie is six. Their parents spent $13,000 on childcare this year ($8,000 for Jamie, $5,000 for Logan, and none for Lindsay). Their parents figure they can deduct a maximum of $7,000 out of $8,000 spent for Jamie, plus another $4,000 out of $5,000 spent for Logan, for a total of $11,000. They were mistaken. The tax collector doesn't attach costs to specific children. Their parents were actually entitled to claim up to $15,000 ($4,000 for Lindsay, $4,000 for Logan, and $7,000 for Jamie). Since their total costs are just $13,000, they'll be entitled to deduct the full costs incurred in the year!

Here's the moral of the story: Remember to report all your children 16 or under in the year, or those with infirmities, on your tax return—even if you didn't incur expenses for some of them. This will maximize the base for your childcare deduction.

I should mention that the court decision in *Stewart A. Bell v. The Queen* (2000) established that payments for recreational and educational activities may not be deducted as childcare expenses. So, those skating or music lessons won't generally be considered deductible. Unless the primary objective of the expense is to provide for the protection and security of the kids, the expense will be denied, even if the activity takes place while you're at work.

TO MAKE A LONG STORY SHORT:

- Claim childcare expenses where they were incurred to allow you or your spouse to earn income.

- The deductible amount will be based on the age of your child and whether or not he or she has any infirmities.

- Maximize the base for your claim by reporting all your kids 16 or under on your tax return, even if you didn't incur childcare expenses for some of them.

Tim's Tip 16: Challenge the tax collector if a disability credit is disallowed.

You know, there are certain tax breaks available to those who have disabilities. The problem is, it can be like pulling teeth to convince the tax collector that the disability is severe enough to warrant tax help. You're entitled to a federal disability tax credit worth $989 in 2002, plus a federal supplement of up to $577 for children who qualify for the disability tax credit—but only where you have a severe and prolonged impairment which "markedly restricts a basic activity of daily living." Your province will also offer a tax credit for a disability, but the amount of the credit will vary by province. By the way, the impairment must have lasted or be expected to last for one year or more, and your disability will have to be verified by a medical doctor, optometrist, audiologist, occupational therapist, psychologist, or speech pathologist, on Form T2201, which should be filed in the first year you make a claim for the credit.

You might be surprised at what will not qualify. In one case, a gentleman was unable to visit the washroom on his own because of a disability. His disability was viewed by the tax collector as being less than severe, however, and no disability credit was allowed. Fair? Probably not. Especially when you consider that the government already admitted to the severity of his disability by qualifying him for Canada Pension Plan disability payments.

A whole slew of court cases have dealt with the issue of whether or not certain disabilities will qualify for the tax credit. And you'll be glad to know that the courts have found CCRA to be wrong in disallowing the credit in some instances. So, if your claim for a disability credit has been disallowed and you believe you meet the criteria set out in the Income Tax Act, then consider filing a Notice of Objection or appealing to the Tax Court of Canada (see Chapter 1, Tip 7).

Now picture this: Your child is eligible to claim the disability credit but doesn't have enough income to take advantage of it. Not to worry, the disability credit can be claimed by you—the supporting person. And there's more. If you support a dependent child who is over age 18 and suffers from a physical or mental infirmity, you'll be entitled to an additional federal tax credit of $577, which will be reduced by 16 percent of the dependant's income over $5,115.

TO MAKE A LONG STORY SHORT:

- You're entitled to a disability tax credit where you have a severe and prolonged disability that markedly restricts a basic activity of daily living.

- The tax collector has not been generous in allowing these credits.

- Consider filing a Notice of Objection or appealing to the Tax Court of Canada if you disagree with the tax collector's disallowance of your claim (see Chapter 1, Tip 7).

Tim's Tip 17: Choose carefully whether to claim attendant care as a deduction or a credit.

If you're disabled, you'll be entitled to claim attendant care costs that you incur to allow you to earn income. The limit for the deduction is two-thirds of your *earned income*, which generally includes employment and self-employment income (although students may be eligible to claim an amount thanks to the 2000 federal budget, even where the student has no income, subject to certain limits). It used to be that this deduction was limited to two-thirds of your earned income, or $5,000, whichever was less. Thanks to the 1997 federal budget, the $5,000 limit was removed and only the two-thirds test applies.

But before you claim the deduction, you should weigh another option first. You see, you're entitled to claim those attendant care costs as a medical expense credit instead, if you prefer. Recall that we talked about deductions versus credits in Chapter 1, Tip 3. Normally, a deduction will save you at least as much as the credit ever could, and probably more. But in this situation, there's another point to consider: You can claim all the medical expenses on the tax return of either spouse when you claim them as a credit.

You may be better off classifying the attendant costs as a medical expense, particularly when your income is quite low. To figure out which method is better, your best bet is to use a tax software package. If any software package can ensure that you're paying less, it's QuickTax. The folks at Intuit, the makers of QuickTax, know exactly what Canadian taxpayers need. Other packages like TaxWiz or Ufile do a fine job as well. Of course, you can always have a tax professional do the calculations for you.

TO MAKE A LONG STORY SHORT:

- You may be entitled to claim attendant care costs if you're disabled and require the care to earn income.

- Attendant care costs can be claimed as a deduction or as a medical credit. You'll have to do a calculation to figure out which is best for you and your family.

Surviving Separation and Divorce

It's a sad fact, but the truth is that a growing number of Canadian marriages end in divorce each year. In fact, in 1967 there were just 55 divorces for every 100,000 marriages that year. Compare that to the 1998 figures (the most recent stats available), where there were 228 divorces for every 100,000 marriages. This represents

an increase of over 400 percent since 1967. The question
is: How does divorce impact the family financially?

Statistics Canada shows that the average income for a
two-parent family in Canada in 1998 was $70,043. Lone-
parent families fared much worse with an average income
of just $29,887 in 1998. The message is clear: There are no
winners financially (other than the lawyers) when a separation or divorce takes place.

Having said all that, I want to talk to those of you who,
for one reason or another, are separated or divorced. There
will be definite tax advantages to both you and your spouse
or ex-spouse if you can agree to structure your affairs so
that you're paying the least amount of tax possible.

> ### Did You Know?
>
> Under Canadian tax law, it's possible for a taxpayer to have more than one spouse! You may even be eligible to claim spousal credits for each of them. I can't recommend marrying more than one person though—this could land you in prison as a violation of other legislation!

Tim's Tip 18: Claim the equivalent-to-married tax credit, if applicable.

If you're separated or divorced (those who are single and widowed can also claim
this credit) and you're supporting another family member living with you, then you
may be entitled to the equivalent-to-married tax credit. How much tax can you
expect to save? Up to $1,037 federally plus an additional amount from your
province (the provincial average is about $645).

Specifically, you'll be entitled to claim this credit if you are supporting a person
related to you who is living in your residence and who is under 18. You can ignore
the age-18 requirement if the dependent person is your parent or grandparent or
suffers from a physical or mental infirmity.

As a general rule, joint custody will mean that one spouse can claim this credit.
However, a recent technical interpretation dated January 7, 2002 (document
2001-0101105), supports the notion that where there is joint custody over more
than one child, it is possible that each spouse may be able to claim a full equivalent-
to-married credit on the basis that the children would be wholly dependent on both
parents at different times throughout the year. The separation agreement will have

to be structured so that one parent can claim the credit for one child while the other can claim it for a second child. This may require one spouse supporting just one of the children in the agreement. If you don't structure your separation agreement correctly, you may be stuck with just one spouse being entitled to the credit. Speak to a tax pro for more information.

TO MAKE A LONG STORY SHORT:

- Claim the equivalent-to-married credit if you are separated, divorced, or otherwise single, and you support a relative who lives with you.

- The credit could save you over $1,500 in tax.

- Joint custody will generally allow one caregiver to claim the credit, but it may be possible to structure your separation agreement so that both parents can claim a full credit when joint custody over more than one child exists.

Caution!

Upon a marriage breakdown, make sure that any transfers made from one spouse's RRSP, RRIF, or RPP to the other spouse's plan are made directly from one plan to the next to avoid tax on the transfer. That is, the plan assets should never actually pass through the hands (or the bank account) of either spouse, otherwise the tax collector will take a share of those assets as though they were taxable withdrawals from the plan.

Tim's Tip 19: **Avoid a tax hit when splitting retirement plan assets.**

I know that things can get ugly when it comes time to divvy up the assets upon separation or divorce. For a lot of people, much of their net worth is tied up in their RRSP or RRIF. The good news is that the tax collector won't add insult to injury by forcing tax to be paid on RRSP or RRIF assets if they're transferred from one spouse's RRSP or RRIF to the other spouse's plan. As long as the payment is made in accordance with a written separation agreement, or a decree, court order, or judgment, then a tax-free transfer can take place without a problem. I should also mention that transferring assets from a Registered Pension Plan

(RPP) to an RRSP or another RPP can also be done on a tax-free basis in the event of a marriage breakdown.

All of this invites the question: Who is going to pay the tax when the with-drawals are made from the RRSPs later? It's quite simple: The annuitant spouse will. If, for example, you transfer some of your RRSP assets to your spouse's plan upon a marriage breakdown, your spouse will be taxed on the withdrawals from his or her plan, and you'll continue to pay tax on any withdrawals made from your own plan. Make sense?

You'll also be glad to know that the rules that would normally apply to discourage withdrawals from a spousal RRSP (scc Chapter 6, Tip 75) won't apply here.

TO MAKE A LONG STORY SHORT:

- When dividing up the assets after separation or divorce, avoid taxes on the transfer by splitting RRSP or RRIF assets in accordance with a written separation agreement or a decree, court order, or judgment.

Tim's Tip 20: Maximize Child Tax Benefits by applying for one-income status.

If you happen to have kids under the age of 18, you may be entitled to collect Canada Child Tax Benefits from the tax collector. Now these benefits won't make you rich, but they're better than a kick in the pants. Your benefits are based on the combined income of you and your spouse.

Currently, the benefits are $1,151 annually for each child, plus an additional $80 for the third and subsequent children, and $228 per child under seven when no childcare expenses are claimed. Once your family income reaches $32,960, these benefits are phased out.

There could be more in store for you. If your income is low, you may be entitled to a *National Child Benefit Supplement* of $1,293 for the first child, $1,087 for the second child, and $1,009 for the third and additional kids. This benefit is phased out beginning at $22,397 of income.

Since your benefits are based on the combined incomes of you and your spouse, the benefits will be clawed back quite quickly for many Canadians. However, when your marriage breaks down, the parent with whom the kids will be living is able to make a special election—within 11 months following the month of marriage breakdown—to base the benefits on the income of that spouse only. That is, the estranged spouse's income will be ignored in the benefit calculation. Making this election could put hundreds of extra dollars in the pocket of the spouse making the election.

TO MAKE A LONG STORY SHORT:

- Canada Child Tax Benefits are based on the combined incomes of both spouses and, as a result, often quickly disappear.

- Make an election within 11 months of marriage breakdown to have the benefits based on one income only. This may increase the benefits significantly.

Tim's Tip 21: Consider splitting real estate when dividing up assets.

I've already talked about the benefits of the principal residence exemption (see Tip 13). That's the exemption that allows you to sell your home at a profit without paying any tax on the gain. The problem, of course, is that each family is entitled to just one exemption. This is a problem, particularly where the family owns more than one property—perhaps a cottage or other vacation property in addition to the family home. Oddly enough, separation or divorce provides an opportunity to multiply the exemption. You see, once you're separated or divorced, you are considered to be your own "family," and you'll be entitled to your own principal residence exemption.

So, where two properties are owned, it makes a whole lot of sense from a tax point of view to give each spouse one property when splitting the spoils. That way, both properties can eventually be sold with any gains sheltered from tax.

TO MAKE A LONG STORY SHORT:

- Each family is entitled to just one principal residence exemption, but each separated or divorced person is entitled to his or her own exemption.

- Where the family owns more than one property at the time of a separation or divorce, it makes sense from a tax point of view to give each spouse one property, to multiply the number of exemptions that can be claimed.

Tim's Tip 22: **Deduct legal costs incurred to collect support payments.**

If you're like most, you probably enjoy paying legal fees about as much as getting a root canal. And the tax collector doesn't make things any easier because legal fees are not often deductible unless you're running a business. There are certain situations, however, when legal fees can be claimed, and collecting alimony or maintenance payments may be one of those situations.

The rules say that where you've paid out legal fees to enforce the payment of an existing right to alimony, maintenance, or support, you'll be able to deduct those fees. This assumes, by the way, that those payments owing to you will be included in your income. To the extent that they are completely exempt from tax, don't expect the tax collector to allow you the deduction.

You'll be out of luck if you hope to claim legal fees paid in connection with a court application to increase or decrease your alimony or support (Quebec is an exception), or to establish a right to alimony or maintenance. There's an exception here. If you had to sue your spouse or former spouse in a Family Court, or under certain provincial legislation, to establish a right to maintenance, then the legal fees may be deductible.

TO MAKE A LONG STORY SHORT:

- Legal fees are not often deductible, but may be deducted when incurred to enforce your right to receive taxable alimony or maintenance payments.

Tim's Tip 23: Consider preserving pre–May 1997 support agreements.

Here's a situation where you're going to have to work closely with your spouse or ex-spouse to beat the tax collector. I know it might be a tall order when the tension between the two of you might be thick enough to cut with a knife, but do yourselves a favour and work together on this. Let me explain.

The Way It Was

Key changes introduced in the 1996 federal budget have changed the way child support payments are taxed. It used to be that the payor was able to claim a deduction for the payments made and the recipient spouse was taxed on those payments. While the arrangement may have been frowned upon by many who received the child support (because they were taxed on the payments), it had the advantage of reducing the amount of money ending up in the tax collector's coffers. Here's why: The payor spouse usually has a higher marginal tax rate than the recipient. So the deduction that was claimed usually saved the payor more in tax than it cost the recipient spouse.

*H*enry and Rosette are separated. Henry earns $70,000 annually and his marginal tax rate is 42 percent, while Rosette earns about $35,000 and has a marginal tax rate of 35 percent. Last year, Henry paid Rosette $10,000 in child support. He claimed a deduction, which saved him $4,200 in taxes ($10,000 × 42 percent). Rosette, on the other hand, reported the $10,000 as income and paid $3,500 in taxes. Combined, Henry and Rosette beat the tax collector by $700 ($4,200 less $3,500). Since the tax savings were in Henry's hands, he agreed to spend the $700 savings directly on his child.

The Way It Is

Things have changed. For child support agreements entered into after April 30, 1997, the payor is no longer able to deduct the payments made. On the flip side, the recipient is no longer required to report the payments as income. If you had an agreement in place before May 1997 that either provided for the deductibility and taxability of payments made, or was simply an agreement entered into prior to the federal budget of March 6, 1996, then your agreement escapes the new rules that exclude the payments from being deducted by the payor and taxed to the recipient. If, however, you varied the amounts in the agreement after April 30, 1997, then the new rules will apply. Follow me?

Who really wins under the new rules? The tax collector. If we go back to Henry and Rosette's story, the $700 savings enjoyed on a combined basis is gone under the new rules. Consider keeping pre–May 1997 agreements intact to avoid a windfall to the tax collector. The higher-income parent should consider spending the tax savings on the children to convince the lower-income parent to keep the pre–May 1997 agreement in place.

TO MAKE A LONG STORY SHORT:

- Our tax law says that child support agreements made or varied after April 30, 1997, provide for payments that are non-deductible to the payor and non-taxable to the recipient. The tax collector comes out ahead under these rules.

- Consider keeping pre-May 1997 agreements intact to avoid the tax collector's win here.

Getting into the Game

It's time to turn to the Tax Planning Tip Sheet at the front of the book and review the strategies introduced in Chapter 2. Ask yourself, "Can this tip apply to me?" Each *Yes* or *Not Sure* could lead to big tax savings for you and your family.

SIGNING WITH THE TEAM: STRATEGIES FOR EMPLOYEES

I'm not sure, but I think my pay deductions finally caught up with my salary.

3

I f you happen to be one of the millions of employees in Canada today, then you know that the Canada Customs and Revenue Agency (CCRA) is not exactly bending over backward to provide you with tax relief. Sure, I'll be talking to you about the specific deductions that you're entitled to, but here's a tip for those of you who are employees: While it's important to claim all the deductions possible, you need to focus your energy on other tax planning opportunities. Why? Simply put, the deductions available to employees are very limited, except in special situations.

You're going to do yourself a favour by reading this chapter and working with your employer to minimize your tax bill.

Optimizing Employment Benefits

Tim's Tip 24: Take non-taxable benefits as part of your compensation, with smart strategies from A to Z.

You know, I'd have to give most employers a 4 out of 10 on the creativity scale when it comes to compensating employees in Canada. I mean, most employees simply receive a flat salary or hourly wage for the work they perform, with no thought given to the tax bill that the employee is going to face. If employers and employees would give just a little more thought to the way in which compensation is paid, the results could be very tax efficient. I'm talking about non-taxable benefits.

A llison works for a software company, Software Inc. She has one child, age seven, and her childcare costs to enable her to work can be very high— about $6,000 annually after factoring in the tax savings from her childcare deductions. How much additional salary does Allison have to earn just to pay for these childcare costs? Since her marginal tax rate is 50 percent, the answer is $12,000. That is, an additional $12,000 in salary would leave Allison with just $6,000 after taxes—just enough to pay for the childcare. Last year, Software Inc. decided to open a daycare facility right in the building for the benefit of employees. Allison no longer has to pay for daycare services. This benefit to Allison is worth the equivalent of $12,000 in additional salary! The best part, of course, is that Allison is not taxed on the value of the daycare provided to her. This is a non-taxable benefit.

The best part about non-taxable benefits is that they never show up on your personal tax return as income. Now, here's my question: Can you list all the non-taxable benefits you're currently receiving? If the list isn't long, consider negotiating with your employer the next time you take on a new job or are due for a salary review. The following A-to-Z list of non-taxable benefits will help you get started. It's divided into four categories: home benefits, family benefits, individual benefits, and workplace benefits. You'll find more information on many of these in the CCRA's Interpretation Bulletin IT-470R.

Home Benefits

a. Mortgage subsidies

Did you know that your employer can actually pay for part of your mortgage interest, and the benefit can be tax-free? It's true. Here's the deal: As long as your mortgage interest costs remain at or above CCRA's prescribed interest rate each quarter, there will not be a taxable benefit to you. If, for example, your mortgage interest rate is 8 percent, and CCRA's prescribed rate is just 5 percent, then your employer can pick up the tab for the 3-percent difference. Keep in mind that the benefit must generally be available to all employees.

Since 1998, any interest subsidies that your employer provides upon your relocation will now be taxable. I'm talking about situations where you relocate for work and take on a larger mortgage or higher mortgage rate as a result. Any help from your employer will now give rise to a taxable benefit, where it would not have in the past! Sorry for the news.

Caution!

b. Relocation costs

If your employer requires you to relocate and reimburses you for costs associated with making the move, this reimbursement is not taxable in your hands. An allowance is different in that you're not required to provide any receipts to your employer—and a non-accountable allowance of $650 or less is not taxable provided you've certified in writing to your employer that you used the allowance to cover moving costs. A non-accountable allowance over $650 is taxable (although you may be able to deduct your actual moving costs in this case).

c. Loss-on-home reimbursement

A woman I know found a new job last year that required her to move from Toronto to Vancouver. She had paid $250,000 for her home in Toronto, and she sold the place for just $235,000 when she made the move. Her new employer picked up the tab for the $15,000 loss she incurred on the sale. The best part is this: She wasn't taxed on this loss reimbursement. Provided your employer requires you to relocate and doesn't reimburse you for more than $15,000 of losses, you won't face a taxable benefit. Thanks to the 1998 federal budget, you'll face a taxable benefit equal to one-half of any loss reimbursement over $15,000 for relocations after September 30, 1998. Reimbursements for relocations made before this date were tax free as long as they were paid before the year 2001.

d. Fair market value guarantee

Suppose for a minute that an employer asks you to relocate, and you're forced to sell your home fairly quickly for a lower price than you might otherwise receive if you weren't in such a hurry. Well, there's good news for you. Your employer can actually guarantee that you'll receive fair market value for your home—to a maximum of $15,000—and you won't be taxed on this benefit. For example, if it can be established that the true fair market value of your home is $175,000, and you're forced to sell quickly for $160,000, your employer can pay the $15,000 difference to you—tax free. Not a bad deal. If your employer pays you more than $15,000 for a relocation after September 30, 1998, you'll be taxed on one-half of the excess as a result of the 1998 federal budget. For relocations before that date, the payment was tax free as long as you received it before the year 2001.

e. Employer home-purchase

I've seen a number of situations where an employer will buy a home from an employee to enable the employee to relocate to a new workplace. Typically, the company will then turn around and sell the home on the open market. This allows an employee to move right away, rather than wait for the right offer on the home. In this case, the benefit to the employee will be tax free as long as the price paid to the employee does not exceed the fair market value of the home.

Action Step

Looking for a non-taxable benefit? Consider buying from your employer the vehicle that your employer has been providing for use in the business. You'll manage to save a bundle by buying the vehicle used. Your employer may be willing to offer this opportunity if it's time to upgrade the vehicles anyway. And by the way, making this kind of purchase may minimize the tax cost of the dreaded standby charge that applies when an employer's vehicle is made available to you (see Tip 29).

f. Remote location benefits

Do you work in a remote location? A remote location is called a *prescribed area*, and it includes many places far south of the Arctic Circle. There's no need to move to Nunavut to receive these tax-free benefits! If you happen to work in a prescribed area, you may be eligible for tax-free benefits in the form of board and lodging, rent-free or low-rent housing, travel benefits, and allowances for a child's education—all paid for by your employer. Generally, it will have been necessary for you to reside in this prescribed area for at least six months.

g. Assets of personal value

Let's suppose for a minute that you've found a computer or a desk that you would really like to have. And what if your employer were to buy the asset for use in the business and let you make use of the asset for work? This would be a definite benefit to you, but it would be a non-taxable benefit. Here's the best part: After two or three years, you could simply buy the asset from your employer for its fair market value at that time. Chances are pretty good that the asset will have depreciated in value enough to make the purchase very affordable. By the way, your employer doesn't need to buy the asset to make this idea work. Leasing the asset and allowing you to buy it at the end of the lease term can work just as well.

Family Benefits

h. Personal counselling

This is one of the lesser-known benefits that could really lend you a hand—not only financially, but mentally or physically as well. If your employer pays for counselling related to the mental or physical health of you or someone related to you, the benefit is non-taxable. This might include counselling related to stress management or an addiction, for example. Financial counselling related to your re-employment or retirement is also non-taxable, so if you're due for a severance or retirement package, be sure to negotiate a number of counselling sessions with a tax professional or financial advisor.

i. Daycare services

If your employer provides in-house daycare services, this benefit will be tax-free. You should note that this is different from your employer paying for daycare provided by a third party. Third-party daycare paid for by your employer is a taxable benefit to you, although I should mention that, in this case, you may still be entitled to claim a deduction for those childcare expenses included in your income as a taxable benefit. The deduction is claimed under the regular rules for childcare expenses, described in Chapter 2, Tip 15.

j. Transportation passes

If you're an employee of a bus or railway company, you'll be able to accept transportation passes from your employer—tax-free. Things work a bit differently if you're an employee of an airline. In this case, your passes will be tax-free as long as you're not travelling on a space-confirmed basis, and provided you pay at least 50 percent of the economy fare for the flight you're on. There's good news if you're a retired employee of any transportation company at all: You won't be taxed on any passes that you receive.

k. Group plan premiums

Most employees these days are members of a group plan for sickness, disability, or accident insurance. You'll be glad to know that the premiums paid by your employer to this type of plan are tax-free benefits to you. You'll want to make sure, however, that any premiums paid on a disability insurance plan are paid by you and not your employer. You see, if your employer pays these premiums, any benefits that you receive under the policy will be taxable payments to you. Not so if *you* pay the premiums. Check out your plan at work to ensure that your disability payments would be tax-free if you had to collect.

l. Private health services plans

A private health services plan (PHSP) is a plan set up to cover certain costs not covered by public health insurance. I'm referring to costs like prescription drugs, hospital charges, and dental fees. Any contributions to a PHSP will be a non-taxable benefit to you. By the way, the government changed the rules in 1998 to allow self-employed proprietors to deduct PHSP premiums from business income.

m. Disability top-ups

A number of Canadians ran into some difficulty a few years ago when the life insurance company that held their disability policy could no longer make good on disability payments. Where your employer tops up disability payments made to you so that you receive all the benefits you were expecting under your disability policy, those payments will not be taxable to you. This applies to all payments made after August 10, 1994.

n. Death benefits

Next time you're talking to your employer about non-taxable benefits, ask that a death benefit be paid to your heirs if you happen to die while in the employ of the company. You see, a benefit of up to $10,000 can be paid to your heirs tax-free once you're gone. It's not going to make your family rich, but hey, it's going to cover the cost of your funeral! How's that for practical?

Individual Benefits

o. Commissions on sales

Picture this. You're an insurance agent or broker and you purchase a life insurance policy for yourself. The commissions owing on the sale are paid to you, just as though you had sold the policy to a third party. Are you taxed on the commissions you receive? No! In fact, any commissions on merchandise that you acquire for your own personal use will not be taxable. Evidently, commissions on sales of investment products to yourself are *not* tax-free. This hardly seems fair in light of CCRA's position on life insurance sales.

p. Discounts on merchandise

If your employer sells, say, soap or toothpaste, and you're able to buy those items at a discount, the benefit is not taxable to you. But this benefit doesn't apply to personal hygiene products alone. Any discounts offered by any employer to its employees will generally be a non-taxable benefit. The only catch is that these discounts must be generally available to all employees.

q. Membership fees

Perhaps you like to play golf, squash, or tennis—or just hang out at the social club? Membership fees paid by your employer for social or recreational clubs will generally be a non-taxable benefit so long as the membership is principally for your employer's advantage, rather than your own. Generally, your employer will not be able to deduct these fees for tax purposes. But that may not be a concern—particularly if your employer is a non-profit organization where tax deductions are not important.

> **Caution!**
>
> It's an interesting fact that tips paid to a waiter or waitress are not caught under the definition of employment income in our tax law. But beware! This does not mean those tips you've received are tax-free. These are considered to be taxable employment benefits—and you're going to have to report them on your personal tax return every year. CCRA has been targeting this industry in order to collect tax that has often been evaded in the past.

r. Gifts and awards

You're entitled to receive certain non-cash gifts from your employer. CCRA's policy was relaxed in 2001 when it announced that employers can now give up to two non-cash gifts to each employee on a tax free basis provided the aggregate cost of those gifts does not exceed $500 (including GST, HST, and PST). In addition, employers can give up to two non-cash awards to an employee each year, tax free, provided the aggregate cost of the awards does not exceed $500 (including GST, HST, and PST). By the way, some gifts, like air miles, are considered akin to cash and will be taxable.

s. Education costs

Revenue Canada's policy on education benefits changed in 1998. It's now clear that there are three types of education costs: two are tax-free but the third is taxable. (1) First there's *specific employment-related training*, which involves education directly related to the skills you use at work. It's tax-free. (2) Then there's *general employment-related training*, which does not relate directly to your required work skills but may be generally relevant, and could include courses such as stress management or employment equity training. It's also tax-free. (3) Finally, there's *personal interest training* in areas that have nothing to do with your work, like ballroom dancing or furniture recovering (unless you dance or cover furniture for a living, of course). This benefit is taxable.

t. Vacation property use

How would you like a few days away at the company condominium in California? If you're required to spend a few days at the firm's property, in Canada or abroad, the benefit will not be taxable to you to the extent the trip is business related. Be sure to keep an itinerary of scheduled meetings and events as evidence to the tax collector that business activities actually took place.

u. Out-of-town trips

Next time your employer sends you on a business trip, why not extend the trip and turn it into a personal vacation too? Once I was forced to spend a week in Whistler, BC, learning about advanced tax issues. I thoroughly enjoyed extending that trip by another week just to relax. You see, turning a business trip into a personal vacation will mean that costs paid by your employer will be tax-free benefits to the extent the trip is business related. This can really cut the cost of any vacation!

v. Host or hostess trip

I was asked to speak at a financial advisors' conference in Halifax. On that trip, a woman who worked for a financial planning firm was asked to come along to act as a hostess. The majority of her time was spent helping to organize events and generally keeping the event running smoothly. But she shared with me that she did have some time to relax and take in the scenery. While she was still able to enjoy her time there, the trip was a tax-free benefit to her because her hostess duties took up a substantial part of each day. If you happen to take a similar trip, you'll enjoy non-taxable benefits as well.

Workplace Benefits

w. Meal subsidies

Before you get too excited, I'm not talking here about your employer picking up the weekly grocery tab. But where your employer provides subsidized meals—most commonly at a workplace cafeteria—the benefit will be tax-free, provided you're still required to pay a reasonable charge.

x. Recreational and fitness facilities

More and more employers are recognizing the importance of having healthy employees. As a result, it's more common than ever for employers to provide in-house fitness and recreational facilities. I know of some corporations that go so far as to reward employees financially for maintaining a certain level of fitness. If your employer provides these facilities, the benefit is non-taxable.

y. Special clothing and uniforms

Some employers are keen on presenting a certain image or look and, as a result, will provide uniforms or special clothing to their employees. If you're in this boat, you'll be glad to know that the clothing is a non-taxable benefit to you. I met a guy once who really enjoyed wearing his employer-provided pants and jacket out on the town. Let's just say that this guy enjoyed an extra benefit—non-taxable, of course.

Action Step

If your employer already provides a recreational facility at work, ask that a fitness instructor be present at the facility for a certain number of hours each week. It's well accepted that a fitness professional's presence helps to increase the use of the facility at work, which provides for a healthier workforce. Your boss might just be shocked at the increased productivity around the office! More and more companies are hopping on this bandwagon. And the best part is that the cost of the instructor will not generally be a taxable benefit if the instruction is available to all employees.

z. Transportation to work

How would you like it if your boss insisted on sending a stretch limo to pick you up each morning? The truth is, where your employer provides you with transportation to or from work for security or other reasons, the value of that transportation is a non-taxable benefit. This is not the same, however, as your employer giving you an allowance or reimbursement for transportation that you provide yourself: You could be taxed on that type of benefit. (See Tip 30 for more.)

TO MAKE A LONG STORY SHORT:

- Most Canadian employers lack creativity when structuring employment compensation.

- Receiving a non-taxable benefit is the same as receiving salary or wages that will never show up on your tax return.

- Next time you change employers or renegotiate your salary or wages, ask for non-taxable benefits to form part of your compensation package.

Tim's Tip 25: Calculate whether a taxable benefit works to your advantage.

There's no question that most benefits your employer provides to you will be taxable as regular income. Want some examples? If your employer pays the premiums on a life insurance policy for you, provides you with a company car, allows you to keep the frequent-flier air miles earned on business trips, or provides you with many other benefits—you can expect the value of the benefits to show up on your T4 slip at tax time.

Is this a bad thing? Not necessarily. Where the benefit that your employer provides is acquired by your employer for less than you'd have to pay yourself, you'll come out ahead. Further, you'd have to pay your out-of-pocket cost sooner if you were to pay for the item yourself. Consider Floyd's story.

*F*loyd wanted very much to have a new computer system for home. He *priced out the new system at $5,000. Floyd's employer agreed to pay $5,000 this year for the system on his behalf. His employer has two options: (1) pay the computer supplier the $5,000 for the system, or (2) pay Floyd the $5,000 so that he can pay for the system himself. In the first case, a $5,000 taxable benefit is added to Floyd's T4 slip, and this will cost him $2,500 in tax at a marginal tax rate of 50 percent. This $2,500 tax bill will not be owing until April 30 next year when he files his tax return for this year. In the second case, Floyd's employer will pay him the $5,000 directly, and $2,500 in taxes deducted at-source will be withheld immediately. Floyd will have to come up with another $2,500 to bring his available cash to $5,000 in order to buy the computer system. In both cases, the out-of-pocket cost to Floyd is $2,500. The difference is in the timing of that outlay. In the first case, the $2,500 is paid as additional taxes when Floyd files his tax return next April. In the second case, Floyd pays the $2,500 to the computer store today in order to buy the computer. Better to pay that $2,500 next year than this year.*

If you're going to be taxed on a benefit received from your employer, exactly how much will be added to your income? Simple. You'll be taxed on your employer's cost of the benefit. In Floyd's example, the computer system cost his employer $5,000, so Floyd's taxable benefit is $5,000. The good news is that your employer may be able to negotiate lower prices on certain things because of your employer's size and number of employees. If this is the case, the amount of your taxable benefit may be reduced—and your true cost will shrink even further.

TO MAKE A LONG STORY SHORT:

- A taxable benefit will still leave you better off than if you had purchased the item yourself since your out-of-pocket cost will be delayed until you file your tax return for the year you received the benefit.

- In addition, your employer may be able to buy the item at a lower cost than you can on your own. This will reduce your taxable benefit and your true cost will shrink further.

- The value of the benefit added to your income is simply your employer's cost of the item.

Tim's Tip 26: Negotiate a loan from your employer instead of from a bank.

Next time you're thinking of borrowing money from the bank for any reason, why not consider approaching your employer for a loan instead? Loans from your employer should be viewed by you—and your employer—as a perk that forms just another part of any creative and tax-efficient compensation package!

Interest Savings

You see, you could save interest costs if the loan is made at a lower interest rate than you'd pay to the bank. You may have to include a taxable interest benefit in your income, but you're still bound to enjoy savings. How much will your taxable benefit be? Simple. It's calculated as CCRA's (or Revenue Quebec's) prescribed interest rate minus the actual rate of interest you pay. By the way, if you're paying interest to your employer, you've got to make those payments during the year or within 30 days following the end of the year (January 30).

John wanted to buy a new car. He figured it would help him in his work since he is always driving clients here and there. He needed to borrow $10,000 to make the purchase. John approached his employer, who agreed to lend him the $10,000 at an interest rate of 3 percent, although CCRA's prescribed rate throughout the year was 8 percent. What is John's taxable benefit? It amounts to $500, which is simply 5 percent (8 percent minus 3 percent) of $10,000. This taxable interest benefit will appear on John's T4 slip. John's true cost of borrowing is just $550 ($250 in tax on the benefit plus $300 in interest paid to his employer). If John had borrowed from the bank at, say, 8 percent, he would have paid $800 in interest. John saved $250 ($800 minus $550), or 2.5 percent, just by borrowing from his employer.

It's worth mentioning that you won't face any taxable benefit at all if the rate of interest charged by your employer is equal to or greater than commercial rates available from your local bank or other financial institution. This is true even if these commercial rates are lower than CCRA's prescribed rate.

Home Loans

If your employer lends you money to buy or refinance a home, some special rules apply. And these rules will work to your advantage. In this case, the prescribed rate used to calculate your taxable interest benefit will be either the rate in effect at the start of the loan or the current prescribed rate, whichever is less. The loan is deemed to be a new loan every five years. As a result, the prescribed rate in effect at that time will be the maximum rate for the next five years.

There's more good news if the purpose of your loan was to buy a home because of a job relocation (rather than to refinance your existing home). In this case, the tax collector will allow you to claim a deduction for the taxable interest benefit on the first $25,000 of the loan. This interest deduction is available only for the first five years of the loan and, to qualify, your relocation must have moved you at least 40 kilometres closer to your new workplace.

Investment or Automobile Loans

There may be other situations where you'll be entitled to claim a deduction for all or part of the taxable interest benefit. In a nutshell, if you'd be entitled to an interest deduction had you borrowed from the bank instead, you'll also be entitled to a deduction for the interest paid to your employer. And by the way, even where you haven't paid your employer any interest, the amount of the resulting taxable interest benefit is considered by the tax collector to be interest paid by you, and may entitle you to a deduction. So if you borrow from your employer to invest, to buy a car for use in your work, or for some other purpose that normally provides you with the ability to deduct interest, you'll reduce your taxable interest benefit.

If you're going to borrow for both deductible and non-deductible purposes, and your employer isn't willing to lend you money for everything, borrow the non-deductible funds from your employer and the deductible from your bank. Here's why: Your true interest cost when borrowing from your employer is likely to be less than the bank's interest, so borrow the funds from your employer that will otherwise cost you the most—the non-deductible funds. Since borrowing from your bank is going to cost you more interest, you might as well get all the breaks you can through deductions.

TO MAKE A LONG STORY SHORT:

• Borrowing from your employer rather than from a financial institution will normally save you interest costs.

• While you will normally have a taxable interest benefit to include in your income, there may be special relief from this taxable benefit if you are borrowing to buy or refinance a home, or for a purpose that would normally entitle you to deduct interest.

Tim's Tip 27: Opt for stock options or similar tax-efficient compensation.

One of the more creative methods to compensate employees is the good ol' stock option plan. Not sure how this works? Let me explain. A stock option plan will entitle you to buy shares of the company that employs you—or shares of a related company. This purchase will take place at a predetermined price—called the *exercise price*. Normally, you'll exercise your right to buy the shares only when the fair market value of those shares is higher than your exercise price. After all, why would you want to buy company shares for $10 if the shares are only worth $8? If the shares are ripe for the picking because the market value is higher than your exercise price, then your stock options are said to be *in the money*.

If you exercise your stock options for, say, $20,000 while the fair market value of those shares is $30,000, then you've received a benefit from your employment. In fact, you'll face tax on that $10,000 benefit. But here's where stock options can be very attractive. Provided certain conditions are met, you'll be able to claim an offsetting deduction equal to 50 percent of the stock option benefit you've reported as income. Further, the benefit may not be taxable until the year that you actually sell the stocks acquired under the option thanks to the 2000 federal budget (more on this in a minute). In my example, you'd include $10,000 on your tax return as income from employment in the year the option is taxed, but you may be entitled to an offsetting deduction of $5,000. This can make a stock option very tax-efficient.

What conditions have to be met to entitle you to the 50-percent deduction? There are three:

(a) you must deal with the company at arm's length (basically, you and your family members must not control the corporation);

(b) the shares must be common shares, not preferred shares;

(c) the stock options cannot be in the money on the day the option is granted.

That is, the fair market value of the shares on the date the options are granted must be no greater than your exercise price. Otherwise, you could exercise your stock options right away and sell your shares that same day for a profit. This is no different than receiving cash, so the tax collector won't allow the 50-percent deduction.

*C*ary's *employer, Option Corp., set up a stock option plan for its employees. Cary was granted stock options in 2002 at a time when Option Corp. shares were selling for $10 on the stock market. Cary was granted options to purchase 1,000 shares of Option Corp. at a price of $10 per share—his exercise price. In the year 2003, shares of Option Corp. were trading on the stock market for $15, so Cary decided to exercise all his options. Cary paid $10,000 for his Option Corp. shares ($10 × 1,000 shares), but they were worth $15,000 on the date he exercised them ($15 × 1,000 shares). Cary will have to report the $5,000 difference as employment income. In fact, this amount will appear on a T4 slip for him. The good news? Since the conditions for the 50-percent deduction were met, Cary will also be entitled to claim a deduction of $2,500 (50 percent of $5,000) on line 249 of his tax return.*

Things are a bit different if your employer is a Canadian-controlled private corporation (CCPC) and you buy your shares at arm's length from the company. It has been the case for quite a while that you will not have to report your taxable stock option benefit in this situation until the year you actually dispose of your shares.

What's more, you'll be entitled to the 50-percent deduction I've been talking about, even if you haven't met conditions (b) and (c) noted above, as long as you hold the shares for two years before selling them.

New Rules for Options

The Department of Finance had been under pressure over the last few years to help Canadian corporations—particularly high-tech businesses—attract and retain top-notch, talented workers and make our tax treatment of employee stock options more competitive with the United States. The outcome? The 2000 federal budget proposed to allow employees to defer the taxable benefit from exercising employee stock options for publicly listed shares until the disposition of the shares, subject to an annual $100,000 limit, which I'll talk more about in a minute.

Employees who sell their shares will be eligible to claim the 50-percent stock option deduction in the year the benefit is included in income. The new rules also apply to employee options to acquire units of a mutual fund trust. By the way, employee stock options granted by CCPCs are not affected by the proposed measure (we've been able to defer the taxable benefit on these types of options until the year of sale for some time now).

Who is eligible for this deferral? If you're an employee who, at the time the option was granted, dealt with your employer (or any related company) at arm's length and was not a specified shareholder (generally, one who owns 10 percent or more of the company's shares), then you may be eligible.

What options are eligible? An eligible option is one under which the shares to be acquired are ordinary common shares; the shares are of a class of shares traded on a prescribed Canadian or foreign stock exchange, and the total of all amounts payable to acquire the shares, including the exercise price and any amount payable to acquire the options, is not less than the fair market value of the shares at the time the option is granted. Follow me? You should be aware that the new rules apply to eligible options exercised after February 27, 2000, regardless of when the option was granted or became vested (first became exercisable).

Now, back to the $100,000 limit. You'll be limited to exercising $100,000 worth of options *per year of vesting* to enjoy the deferral. If you exercise more than this amount, the taxable benefit arising on the excess options will be taxed in the year you exercise the options (not the year you sell the shares). The $100,000 limit applies to the value of the stock options in the year that they vest (the year that you first have the right to exercise the options under the option agreement), and not the year you exercise the options. The value of a stock option here is simply the fair market value of the underlying share at the time the option was granted, and the $100,000 limit applies across all stock option plans of the employer corporation and related corporations.

Finally, the taxable benefit will be deferred until the time you dispose of the shares acquired under the option or, if earlier, the time you die or become a non-resident of Canada for tax purposes.

What are the reporting requirements? If you exercise stock options that qualify for the deferral, be sure to:

- Notify your employer in writing of the amount of the stock option benefit you want to defer. The deadline for options exercised in 2002 is January 15, 2003. Your stock option benefit could be subject to payroll withholdings unless you submit your notification immediately after exercising your options (some provinces may still levy payroll withholding taxes).
- Designate the options that will provide the greatest tax deferral.
- Consider whether it's beneficial to sell some of your shares within 30 days after exercising your options. (This would allow you to designate those option shares as the specific shares being sold rather than having to blend the cost of these shares with other shares you might already own in the same company. Doing so could reduce your taxable capital gain on the sale.)
- File Form T1212, Statement of Deferred Stock Option Benefits, with your tax return.

Will this deferral really help you? While it may seem like a windfall that the tax collector is willing to defer the taxation of your stock option benefits, you're not likely to take advantage of this provision if you're handling your stock options properly. You see, in most cases you shouldn't exercise your stock options unless you're planning to sell the shares right away. What's the benefit of exercising your stock options if you're going to hold the shares for any length of time beyond that exercise date? "Tim, my shares could go up in value if I hold them; isn't that a good enough reason?" you might ask. My response is this: You can simply hold the options for that same length of time. Your options will go up in value just as the stocks would have. You don't need to hold the shares themselves to benefit from the stock price increasing. In fact, it's preferable simply to hold the options rather than the stock in most cases for two reasons:

> When you acquire shares under a stock option plan, there's always the risk that you could acquire too much stock in one company—your employer. Make sure that your overall investment portfolio remains properly diversified. This may mean selling some of those option shares from time to time and reinvesting in other securities. Speak to your financial advisor about proper diversification.
>
> **Caution!**

- if you hold the shares and they drop in value after exercising your options, you won't be able to apply the capital loss against the taxable employment benefit you faced (or will face) on the stock options; and
- there's ugly paperwork and accounting to look after if you're going to hold your shares after exercising the options and you want to defer the tax under the new rules (see the filing requirements above).

There may be one situation where you may exercise your options and hold the shares beyond that date: When your options would otherwise expire (for example, after a certain length of time or when you leave the company) but you like the future prospects of the company. In this case, the new rules permitting a deferral of tax could come in handy.

Are Stock Options Always a Good Idea?

Do stock options always make sense? Well, not always. You want to be confident of two things. First, you should feel confident that the shares in the company are going to increase in value over time. Only then will you be *in the money*. Second, you want to be confident that you'll be able to sell the shares later. Think back to Cary's example. Cary's purchase may look good on paper, but he won't actually realize a profit unless he sells those shares for a higher value than what he paid. You've got to be able to sell those shares. This can be a problem with private company shares in particular. Before exercising stock options in a private company, you'd better have a way out—in other words, someone to sell the shares to.

Phantom Stock Plans and Stock Appreciation Rights

A phantom stock plan works much like a stock option plan, except that you don't actually acquire shares. Rather, your employer will simply pay, in cash, the difference between your exercise price and the fair market value of the company's shares on the date you exercise your phantom stock options. With a phantom plan, you don't have to worry about raising the money to buy the shares and, best of all, you don't have to worry about how you're going to sell the shares later. The drawback? You're not entitled to the 50-percent deduction against your taxable benefit and you won't be able to defer tax on the benefit.

A stock appreciation right (SAR) is a combination of a phantom plan and a stock option plan. When it comes time to exercise your SARs, you'll have two choices: Buy shares in your employer, or take cash as you would under a phantom plan. Talk about flexibility! The best part of a SAR is this: So long as the employee has the right to choose between shares and cash, and this decision isn't influenced by the employer, then the employee will still be entitled to claim the 50-percent deduction against the taxable benefit reported as income (assuming the usual conditions are met), and to defer the taxable benefit until the year the shares are sold (where you take shares rather than cash). In my mind, this makes SARs a better choice than straight stock options or phantom plans.

TO MAKE A LONG STORY SHORT:

- Stock option plans can be a very tax-efficient source of compensation, since the plan may entitle you to a 50-percent deduction to offset the taxable benefits and the taxable benefit may be deferred until you sell your shares.

- These plans are best when you're confident that your employer's shares will increase in value and you'll be able to sell the shares down the road.

- Phantom plans and stock appreciation rights (SARs) are hybrids of a stock option plan, except that they don't require you to buy shares. SARs are especially attractive, since they still offer the potential for the 50-percent deduction and the tax deferral.

Claiming Employment Deductions

The fact is, employees are provided with very little in the way of deductions. Unless something is specifically allowed as a deduction, then don't count on claiming it. Nevertheless, you certainly don't want to pass up the opportunity to claim what you're entitled to.

Tim's Tip 28: Claim all the employment deductions you're entitled to.

Let's take a look at the things our tax law will specifically allow employees to deduct.

a. Commissioned employee expenses

If you're an employee selling a product or service and you're compensated partially or fully by commissions, you may be able to claim expenses against that commission income. Your employment contract must require you to pay your own expenses, and you must ordinarily be required to carry on your employment duties away from your employer's workplace. The types of expenses you can deduct are as varied as those available to a self-employed person (see Chapter 4), with some exceptions. Most notably, you can only claim expenses up to the limit of your commission income. That is, you can't create a loss with your expenses.

b. Travel expenses

You can count on deducting any travel costs related to your employment if you were required to pay these costs and did not receive a reimbursement or tax-free allowance to cover those costs. I'm talking about costs such as taxis, trains, planes, buses, parking, or hotels. If you work for a transportation company (as a bus or truck driver or as a flight attendant, for example) and you incur costs for meals and lodging, you can deduct those costs if you weren't reimbursed. Just 50 percent of your meals will be deductible in this case.

c. Automobile expenses

If your employer required you to use your own vehicle in your employment and you did not receive a reimbursement or tax-free allowance to cover your automobile costs, you'll be entitled to claim a deduction for a portion of all your car costs. I'll talk more about this in Tips 29 and 30.

d. Aircraft expenses

If you provided your own aircraft for use in your employer's business, and you did not receive a reimbursement or tax-free allowance to cover your costs of flying the aircraft, you'll be able to claim a deduction for a portion of those costs. Your deductible portion is based on the percentage of flying hours that were spent on business in the year.

e. Cost of supplies

Did you incur any costs for supplies consumed directly in your employment activities? If so, you may be able to deduct these costs at tax time. Your employer will have to verify (on Form T2200) that you were required to pay these costs yourself and that you did not receive a reimbursement or tax-free allowance to cover them. By the way, supplies can include cellular phone air time and long distance calls, but won't include connection or monthly service charges, or Internet service fees.

> **Action Step**
>
> Many of the employment deductions I refer to are available only if your employer requires you to pay for certain costs. To ensure that you're entitled to claim the costs, your best bet is to put in writing the requirement that you pay for these things. This is done most easily before you start working for an employer.

f. Assistant's salary

If your employer required you to pay for an assistant, you'll be entitled to deduct the cost of hiring that person. This includes the wages or salary paid plus your share of any Canada Pension Plan and Employment Insurance premiums paid.

g. Home office expenses

In certain situations, you'll be entitled to claim costs for an office in your home. Before you deduct anything, you've got to meet some tests. First, your employer must require you to have an office in your home. Second, your home must either be your principal place of employment (meaning half your work or more is performed there), or it must be used on a regular and continual basis to meet people as part of your work. Employees will generally be restricted to claiming a portion of any rent, utilities, repairs, maintenance, and supplies associated with the office space. Commissioned employees can add a portion of property taxes and home insurance to the list of eligible expenses (note that mortgage interest and property taxes are excluded here). The deductible portion depends on the percentage of your home used as your office. I'll deal with home offices for the self-employed in Chapter 4.

h. Office rent

If your employer required you to pay your own office rent, you'll be able to deduct the cost of that rent. Sorry, this does not include rent for space in your own residence. See my previous point on home office expenses for more information on using your home as your workplace.

i. Attendant costs

When you have a severe and prolonged impairment and you need to hire an attendant in order to perform your duties of employment, you can claim a deduction for the attendant costs, up to a maximum of two-thirds of your earned income. See Tip 17 for more details.

j. Union and professional dues

You can deduct union or professional dues if you had to pay those dues to maintain your membership in a union or to maintain your professional status in an organization recognized by statute. Sorry to disappoint you, but you can't claim a deduction for dues to a voluntary organization: Only the self-employed can write off those costs.

k. Musician's instruments

If you are employed as a musician and are required to provide your own instruments, you'll be able to claim a deduction for the cost of any rental, maintenance, or insurance on the instruments. In addition, if you own the instruments, you'll be entitled to claim capital cost allowance (CCA) (depreciation) on your instruments. Keep in mind that your total deductions cannot exceed your employment income as a musician.

l. Artist's expenses

If you earn employment income from artistic activities, then you'll be entitled to claim a deduction for virtually any unreimbursed costs incurred to earn that employment income. Your total deduction is limited to 20 percent of your income from artistic employment activities, or $1,000, whichever is less. Oh, yeah. I should mention that this $1,000 limit is reduced by any interest or capital cost allowance claimed for work-related use of your automobile or by any claim for musician's instruments.

m. Legal fees

If you had to pay a lawyer to collect or establish a right to salary, wages, retiring allowances, severance payments, private pension plan benefits, alimony, or mainte- nance payments, then those fees will normally be deductible. The general rule is this: If you pay legal fees to recover income that will be taxable to you, you'll very likely be entitled to a deduction for those costs. You'll also be entitled to claim a deduction for legal fees paid to file a Notice of Objection or Appeal against the tax collector. See Tip 7.

> **Did You Know?**
>
> Here's another possible employment deduction for you: If you happen to need an assistant in your work, consider hiring your lower-income spouse. Even if your employer is not willing to pick up the tab, you can hire your spouse yourself. You'll be entitled to a deduction against your employment income, and your lower-income spouse will pay the tax instead. This will reduce your overall family tax bill. To make this work, you'll need to have your employ-ment contract worded so that you're required to provide your own assistant.

n. Clergy deduction

Are you a member of the clergy? If so, you may be entitled to a deduction with respect to your residence. Now, the government changed the rules in 2001, but proper planning can result in continued tax savings for virtually all clergy.

The rules work this way: Where you're a member of the clergy and you provide your own residence (whether you rent or own), your clergy residence deduction will be limited for 2001 and subsequent years to the least of the following two amounts: (a) one-third of your total remuneration from the office or employment or $10,000, whichever is greater, and (b) the fair rental value of the residence (reduced by other amounts deducted in connection with that residence). In addition, you're now required to file a prescribed form with your income tax return that will have to be signed by your employer to verify that you meet the status and function requirements of a clergy member.

Where your employer provides you with a residence, you can deduct all amounts that were included in your income with respect to that accommodation, including utilities. In any event, whether you provide your own residence or it's provided for you, the deduction you claim cannot exceed your income from that employment in the year.

If you're a member of the clergy, speak to your employer about these new rules, and visit the Department of Finance's Web site at **www.fin.gc.ca** for a copy of the December 21, 2000, news release that contains the details, or call the Public Affairs and Operations Division of the Department of Finance at (613) 996-8080.

Last Thoughts

When claiming certain employment expenses, you must file Form T777 (Statement of Employment Expenses). In addition, your employer will have to sign Form T2200 (Declaration of Conditions of Employment), although you don't need to file

Form T2200 with your tax return; keep it on file in case the tax collector wants to see it. Ask your employer for a signed T2200 each January, and if you leave an employer during the year, get a signed T2200 before you go.

I should also mention that, when you make a claim for employment expenses and your employer happens to be registered for GST purposes, you'll generally be able to claim a GST rebate for the GST paid on the expenses you're deducting. To claim this rebate, you'll have to file Form GST370. The GST rebate is taxable in the calendar year in which it's received.

Finally, always be sure to keep the receipts that support any expenses you claim, if the receipts are not filed with your tax return. The tax collector may ask to see them later.

TO MAKE A LONG STORY SHORT:

- Employees aren't given a lot of breaks in the form of deductions.

- Claim all the deductions you're entitled to, and make sure you obtain a signed Form T2200 where necessary and file Form T777 with your tax return.

- Remember to claim a GST rebate where possible, using Form GST370.

- Always keep your receipts on file in case the tax collector wants to see them.

Driving Automobiles on the Job

I was sitting in a restaurant in Red Deer, Alberta, not long ago, and I couldn't help but overhear a rancher bragging to the owner of a small farm from Lloydminster, Saskatchewan. "I can get in my car at six in the morning," he said, "drive for six hours, spend an hour eating lunch, drive for another six hours, and I still wouldn't have reached the end of my property." "Yeah," the farmer said, nodding sympathetically. "I had a car like that once."

Now there's a man using his car—regardless of its condition—for his work. Do you use your car in your employment? Now, I'm not talking about driving from home to work and back again. I'm talking about using your car for other employment activities on a regular basis. Perhaps you're one of the few who has been provided with a car by your employer. What a perk that is! Or is it? Let's talk about automobiles and employment.

Tim's Tip 29: Say "thanks, but no thanks" when offered a company car.

There's a definite misconception that an employer-provided vehicle is a sign that you've "made it." You've arrived. You're loved so much by the company that they insist on showering you with benefits, not the least of which is a luxurious company car.

Yeah, right.

In many cases, it's going to hurt you to have a company car at your disposal. Why? Because the tax collector may require you to pay tax on two separate benefits. The first is called a *standby charge*, and the second is an *operating cost benefit*.

Standby Charge

There's nothing uglier than a standby charge in my estimation. Here's how the rule works: A taxable benefit called a standby charge will be added to your income and reported on your T4 slip just for having a company car at your disposal. The government figures that there's got to be some personal benefit to you, so you ought to be taxed somehow. The standby charge is calculated as 2 percent of the original cost of the car (or two-thirds of the lease payments, if the car is leased) for each month that the car is available to you. That works out to be 24 percent of the original cost of the car each year! You'll be able to reduce this taxable standby charge only if two conditions are met. First, your business use must account for 90 percent or more of the total kilometres driven; and second, your personal use of the car must be less than 1,000 km per month in the year. Don't bother counting those trips straight from home to the office and back again as business kilometres—they won't generally qualify.

By the way, to add insult to injury, the tax collector will also add 7 percent GST to your taxable benefit (15 percent HST in Nova Scotia, New Brunswick, and Newfoundland). In Quebec, the additional tax amounts to 7 percent GST plus 7.5 percent QST.

Operating Cost Benefit

If your employer pays for any operating costs on the car (insurance, gas, repairs, etc.), then you'll face an operating cost benefit. For 2002, the figures are unchanged from 2001. The calculation is 16 cents per kilometre for each kilometre of personal use (13 cents per kilometre for automobile salespeople). If you reimburse your employer for all operating costs within 45 days after the end of the year (that is, by February 14 each year for the previous year's operating costs), then you'll avoid this operating cost benefit altogether.

> If your employer provides you with a company car, your taxable benefit from the standby charge every year could be high enough that, after just four years, you will have effectively paid tax on the original purchase price of the car! How's that for a tax hit? Reduce the tax hit by keeping your personal use to under 12,000 kilometres each year and to less than 10 percent of total time the car is available for use. If you can't manage this, then consider giving up the company car!
>
> **Caution!**

There's another acceptable way to calculate your operating cost benefit where your business use of the car is greater than 50 percent. To take advantage of this second method, you've got to inform your employer in writing before December 31 that you'd rather use the alternative method of calculating the operating cost benefit. This method allows you to simply take 50 percent of your standby charge as your operating cost benefit. Which method is best for you? In a nutshell, you'll prefer this second method if the cost of the car is fairly low and your personal kilometres are close to 50 percent of the total kilometres driven. But remember: Not more than 50 percent is allowed here.

Know Your Options

Should you always say "no thanks" to a company car? Generally, I discourage employees from taking a company car. Here's why: The standby charge you're going to face is always based on the original cost of the car, even as the car depreciates in value over time. This is a bad deal if there ever was one. In most cases, it'll be better for you to provide your own car, and then take an allowance or reimbursement from your employer to cover the costs of using your car for work. I'll talk more about this in a minute.

If you're going to accept a company car, here are three things to keep in mind:

! Consider buying the car from your employer after two or three years to avoid a consistently high standby charge on a vehicle that has depreciated in value.

! Avoid company cars that cost over $30,000. You see, this will lead to a double-tax problem. Your standby charge will be based on the full cost of the car, but your employer will only be entitled to depreciate $30,000 (plus GST and PST) of that car in 2002. The excess over $30,000 is effectively taxed twice.

! Minimize the amount of time the car is available to you for personal use. If, for example, you park the car at your employer's place of business at the end of the workday, you could argue that the car is not available to you for personal use that day. You should be aware, however, that the tax collector will generally take the view that the car is still available to you unless your employer requires you to park it at the office in the evenings or while you're on vacation. At any rate, if the car is only available to you 345 days each year, rather than 365, you'll effectively face a standby charge for just 11 months instead of 12 months because of the way the calculation is done.

TO MAKE A LONG STORY SHORT:

- You may face two different taxable benefits if your company provides you with a car: a standby charge and an operating cost benefit.

- In most cases, you'll be better off providing your own car to avoid these taxable benefits and then taking an allowance or reimbursement from your employer for use of your car at work.

Tim's Tip 30: **Claim automobile expenses that exceed your allowance or reimbursements.**

So, you're convinced that providing your own car for use at work is better than using a company car. Great. Now, how is this use of your car going to save you tax? The rules can be kind of tricky, but I'll walk you through them.

Reimbursements and Allowances

First, you need to understand the difference between a reimbursement and an allowance. A *reimbursement* is never taxable. If, for example, you incurred certain car expenses on the job and you submitted actual receipts to your employer for reimbursement, you would not be required to include that reimbursement in your income.

An *allowance* is different. It's a payment from your employer for which you are not required to provide actual receipts. That is, you're not required to account for the payments received. Is an allowance taxable to you? It all depends. Let me explain.

An allowance paid to you for using your own car for work will be non-taxable if it is considered *reasonable*. The allowance will generally be considered reasonable if it's based on actual kilometres driven for work (CCRA considers a reasonable allowance for 2002 to be $0.41 per kilometre for the first 5,000 kilometres, and $0.35 for each additional kilometre; the rates are 4 cents higher in the Yukon, Northwest Territories, and Nunavut; these amounts are what your employer is permitted to deduct). That means you'll need to keep a daily driver's log showing how many kilometres you've driven and the purpose of the trip. If you meet this test, then the allowance is tax-free. If the allowance is not based on distance driven, then it is not considered to be reasonable, and it must be included in your income. In fact, this type of allowance is supposed to be reported by your employer on your T4 slip each year.

Claim Those Deductions

When do you suppose you're entitled to claim a deduction for automobile expenses? Well, you can forget about a deduction if you were fully reimbursed for your expenses, or if you received a reasonable allowance and you accepted that allowance as tax-free compensation.

WHEN CAN YOU DEDUCT AUTOMOBILE EXPENSES?

	If you received a reimbursement	If you received an allowance
Amount received is reasonable	Reimbursements are always tax-free. You cannot claim a deduction for automobile expenses that have been fully reimbursed.	Allowances are considered reasonable if they are based on kilometres driven. In this case, the allowance is tax-free and you cannot claim a deduction for automobile expenses.
Amount received is not reasonable	If you were not fully reimbursed for your automobile costs, and no allowance was received, you may deduct the costs incurred over and above your reimbursements.	Allowances are not reasonable when they ignore kilometres driven, or when the employee otherwise considers the allowance not reasonable. In this case, the allowance is taxable and you can claim a deduction for actual expenses.

You're entitled to a deduction if you received an allowance that's not reasonable—in other words, an allowance that is not based on distance driven and that is treated as taxable income. In this case, your deductible expenses help to offset the income.

But what if you received an allowance that is based on distance driven, and therefore would normally be considered reasonable, except that you feel the allowance is not reasonable at all because your actual business-related automobile expenses are greater than the allowance? In this case, you have the option of including that "unreasonable" allowance in your income and claiming a deduction for your actual automobile expenses.

Here's the general rule: If your allowance based on distance driven is less than your actual car expenses, then consider the allowance to be unreasonable, include it in your income, and claim a deduction for those actual car expenses. Likewise, if you have not been fully reimbursed for your actual car expenses, claim a deduction.

What to Claim—and How

You're entitled to claim a portion of all your operating costs. These include gas, oil, repairs, insurance, licence fees, cleaning, and auto club fees—to name a few. In addition, you can claim depreciation—called capital cost allowance (CCA)—on the cost of your car if you purchased it. Keep in mind, however, that the maximum cost you can depreciate is $30,000 (plus GST and PST) for 2002. If your car costs more than this, you won't be entitled to any tax relief for the excess.

Interest costs on a loan to buy your car are also deductible. But there are limits here. For 2002, the maximum that can be deducted is $300 per month for loans on vehicles acquired after 2001.

Finally, if you lease your car rather than own it, you'll be entitled to claim a deduction for a portion of your lease costs. The maximum deduction in 2002 is $800 (plus GST and PST) for each month you leased the car.

To determine the portion of your automobile expenses that you can deduct, add up the kilometres driven for work in the year, divide that by the total kilometres driven in the year, and multiply by 100. The result is the percentage of the expenses you can deduct.

As I mentioned at the end of Tip 28, you'll need to file Form T777 with your tax return, and your employer will have to sign Form T2200 to verify that you were required to use your automobile for work. I also talked about the GST rebate that you may be entitled to claim using Form GST370.

> Be sure to maximize the employment use of your car to maximize your deduction. This can be done by visiting clients and suppliers or making other business stops on the way to or from work. This will turn non-business kilometres into business kilometres. Also, consider using one car only for work to simplify your record keeping.

Action Step

TO MAKE A LONG STORY SHORT:

• A reimbursement and an allowance are different things. A reimbursement requires that receipts be provided to your employer, while an allowance does not.

• Reimbursements and reasonable allowances based on kilometres driven are not taxable. Unreasonable allowances are taxable.

• Claim a deduction for automobile expenses if you have not been reimbursed or if your actual expenses are greater than an unreasonable allowance received.

Deferring Compensation

You'll recall from Tip 4 that pushing your tax bill to a future year almost always makes sense. But given today's tax law, it's not so easy to take a portion of your employment income and arrange to pay tax on it a year or two down the road. You see, the *Income Tax Act* has rules to govern these salary deferral arrangements. For example, if you earn $75,000 in 2002 but agree with your employer that you'll take $50,000 in 2002 and $25,000 in 2003, you're going to face tax in 2002 on the full $75,000. Sorry about that. But don't fret. There are some ways you can escape the salary deferral rules. Wherever it's possible and practical, be sure to defer your income to a future year by taking advantage of these ideas. This is especially important given the general decline in tax rates from year to year that we've been experiencing.

Tim's Tip 31: **Defer tax with a Registered Pension Plan (RPP), RRSP, or Deferred Profit Sharing Plan (DPSP).**

Registered Pension Plan (RPP)

A Registered Pension Plan (RPP) at work operates much like your RRSP. Putting money into an RPP, however, will limit your ability to use an RRSP. The government imposes this limitation through something called your *pension adjustment*. You see, the tax collector doesn't want you to have an unfair advantage over those who save through an RRSP alone for retirement. An RPP allows you to defer tax on your employment income by providing a tax deduction for the money you contribute to the plan. You'll face tax when funds are paid to you out of the pension plan, but this won't likely be for a number of years.

I'll make this one comment: I'm not a big fan of company pension plans in many situations. The reason? If you don't plan on staying with the same employer for the better part of your working career, you may actually lose a portion of your retirement savings every time you move from one employer to the next. Since the average Canadian is likely to change jobs a number of times in a lifetime, a lot of people could be short-changed in saving for retirement. I prefer an RRSP alone (since it's portable) in many—but not all—situations. You may want to talk this issue over with a tax professional or a financial advisor.

Registered Retirement Savings Plan (RRSP)

I suppose that Registered Retirement Savings Plans (RRSPs) are one of the more familiar tax-deferral vehicles available today. I won't go into much detail on these now because I've devoted Chapter 6 to retirement savings. Suffice it to say that your RRSP may be the most effective method to push the tax on your employment income to a future year. It's no secret how this works. If you earned $40,000 and had accumulated RRSP contribution room of $10,000, you could contribute the full $10,000 to your RRSP and deduct that amount from your income for the year. In effect, you'd pay tax on only $30,000 of your employment income. And the $10,000 would grow tax-deferred in your RRSP. In fact, you won't pay tax on those funds until you make withdrawals later in life. Can't get a better or more direct deferral than that.

Deferred Profit Sharing Plan (DPSP)

With a Deferred Profit Sharing Plan (DPSP), your employer may contribute up to 18 percent of your income or $6,750 (for 2002), whichever is less. Sorry, but a DPSP is not an option for shareholders or their families who own more than 10 percent of any class of shares of the employer. You can't make contributions to a DPSP—only your employer can. As a result, you're not entitled to a deduction for

DPSP contributions. These contributions are based on your employer's profitability, and so there may not be any contributions in years where the company loses money.

How are these contributions taxed? The funds will grow inside the DPSP tax-deferred, and you'll pay tax on the amounts paid out of the DPSP to you. With most DPSPs, taxable payments can be made to you over a maximum 10-year period, which, by the way, is going to result in a longer deferral of tax than simply paying the funds out in one lump sum. You might even consider rolling some of the payments out of your DPSP into your RRSP, RPP, or a term annuity (with a guarantee period not exceeding 15 years)—just to defer tax even longer. Money contributed to a DPSP will reduce the amount that you can contribute to your RRSP in a manner similar to RPPs. By the way, some of the proceeds out of your DPSP may be tax-free if they represent your pre-1991 contributions made at a time when employees were allowed to contribute to DPSPs.

TO MAKE A LONG STORY SHORT:

- A Registered Pension Plan (RPP) can provide a deferral of tax on your employment income, although in many cases I prefer an RRSP to an RPP when given a choice.

- An RRSP is the most common tax-deferral vehicle in Canada and, like an RPP, provides a direct deferral of tax on employment income.

- A DPSP is a plan to which your employer alone can contribute.

- Contributions to RPPs and DPSPs will reduce the amount you can contribute to your RRSP.

Tim's Tip 32: Push the tax on your bonuses to a future year.

If you're entitled to a bonus for work performed in a given year, you'll be able to defer receipt of that bonus for up to three years, and you won't face tax on the bonus until you actually receive it. How much tax will this save? That depends on the rate of return you can generate on the money you would otherwise use to pay the tax, and your marginal tax rate down the road. If you expect to have a lower marginal tax rate in the near future, deferring your bonus can make sense. Consider Eileen's case.

---

*E*ileen earned a $10,000 bonus from her employer in 2002 and would be due to face a tax bill of $4,600 on that bonus, at her marginal tax rate of 46 percent, if she were to receive the bonus in 2002. Eileen expects to have a lower marginal tax rate in the near future since she'll be retiring in 2005. So, she arranged with her employer to defer receipt of her bonus until December 31, 2005 (three years after earning the bonus). The result? She's going to face tax at her expected marginal tax rate of 35 percent, for a tax bill of $3,500, three years from now when she receives the bonus.

Is there a downside to this idea? Sure. If you're hurting for cash, you may not want to wait for three years to receive your bonus. And your employer won't be able to deduct the bonus until the year it's paid. In addition, if you're concerned about the financial stability of your employer, you may want to take the cash sooner rather than later.

Another good option is this: If you're due to receive a bonus for 2002, ask for payment in January 2003 and contribute that money to your RRSP right away if you have the contribution room. This way, you won't have to wait long to receive the payment from your employer, which gets the money working for you sooner. In addition, you won't face tax on the bonus until 2003 when you receive it, but you'll receive a tax deduction in 2002 for the amount of the bonus thanks to the RRSP contribution. A good deal all around.

TO MAKE A LONG STORY SHORT:

- You're entitled to defer a bonus for up to three years. You won't face tax until the year the bonus is paid.

- Deferring the bonus can make sense when your marginal tax rate is expected to be lower in the future, or where you're only deferring the bonus until early in the new year and you contribute that amount to your RRSP.

Tim's Tip 33: Consider a leave of absence or sabbatical plan to defer tax.

For a deferred-salary leave or sabbatical plan to be accepted by CCRA, you must make sure that your employer documents the plan in writing, and that the main purpose of the plan is to fund a leave of absence and not, for example, to provide retirement benefits. If the tax collector looks at the plan as some kind of attempt to defer tax without really funding a leave of absence, you'll face tax on the full amounts as if they were regular salary.

Who says you have to be a teacher or professor to take advantage of a leave of absence or sabbatical plan? With the help of your employer, you can set up a similar plan. It works this way: You can set aside up to one-third of your salary each year for up to six years. You won't have to pay tax on the portion of your income set aside. Your leave of absence or sabbatical must begin no later than six years after the deferral begins, and must be at least six months long (three months if you are taking the leave to attend an educational institution full-time). For the plan to qualify, you'll have to return to your workplace for at least as long as your leave, and you'll have to pay tax on the deferred income no later than the seventh year whether you take the leave or sabbatical or not.

TO MAKE A LONG STORY SHORT:

- A leave of absence or sabbatical plan will allow you to defer tax on up to one-third of your income for a full six years.

- Certain other conditions must be met for the plan to qualify, and you'll pay tax on the deferred income no later than six years after the deferral begins, whether or not you actually take the leave or sabbatical.

Calling It Quits

There's going to come a day when you won't be working for your employer anymore. Perhaps this is by your own choice—you've put in your dues, and it's time to
start a new chapter in life. Maybe it's by your employer's choice—the company
might be downsizing, right-sizing, or whatever you want to call it. In any event,
you'll do yourself a real favour by working with your employer to make your
departure a tax-efficient one.

Tim's Tip 34: Roll as much as possible of your retiring allowance into your RRSP or RPP.

I met a gentleman about two years ago. After we talked over his financial affairs, it
became evident that he had been given a bum steer. You see, the gentleman had one
thing on his mind: paying down his mortgage with his retiring allowance. When he
retired from his last job, a "counsellor" in his former workplace somehow forgot to

inform this man that he was able to roll a good portion of his retiring allowance into his RRSP or RPP.
It seems that this "counsellor" liked the idea of
paying down the mortgage as well. As a result, this
man took his $60,000 retiring allowance, handed
$30,000 to the tax collector, and used the remaining
$30,000 to pay down his mortgage.

Boy, this type of misguided advice makes me
steam. Remember this: There is no better option for
your retiring allowance than to roll it into your
RRSP where you'll defer tax until you make withdrawals. Yes, this is your best option in virtually
every case, even if you have a mortgage outstanding.
If you don't make this rollover, you're going to face
tax, all at once, on any retiring allowances you
receive. The gentleman in my story could have made

> **Action Step**
>
> When you receive a retiring
> allowance, it's not critical
> that the allowance be trans-
> ferred directly to your RRSP
> when it's paid out. But be
> sure to contribute those
> funds to your RRSP within
> 60 days following the end of
> the year that you received
> the payment—that is, by
> March 1, 2003, for retiring
> allowances received in
> 2002, or March 1, 2004,
> for allowances received in
> 2003. See Tip 71 for more.

regular withdrawals from his RRSP to meet his mortgage payments, and the mortgage still would have been paid off by the time he was 63 years of age. In the meantime, he would have avoided that immediate $30,000 tax hit, and those assets would have grown tax-deferred in his RRSP.

How much of your retiring allowance can you roll to your RRSP? The answer is $2,000 per year or part year of pre-1996 service. In addition, you'll be able to roll $1,500 for each year or part year of service prior to 1989 in which you had no vested interest in any employer's contributions into an RPP or DPSP.

TO MAKE A LONG STORY SHORT:

- Your best option when receiving a retiring allowance from your employer is to roll as much of it as possible into your RRSP or RPP to defer tax as long as possible.

- This rollover must be made within 60 days following the year you receive the payment.

Getting into the Game

Whether you're leaving an old job, starting a new one, or heading into this year's performance review, make sure you know all the ways you can maximize your after-tax employment income. Turn now to the Tax Planning Tip Sheet at the front of this book and review the strategies introduced in Chapter 3. Ask yourself, "Can this tip apply to me?" With a little planning, each *Yes* or *Not Sure* might mean more dollars in your pocket.

BECOMING A FREE AGENT: STRATEGIES FOR SELF-EMPLOYMENT

To be successful:
Rise early, work late,
and strike oil.

4

I can still remember those long hot summers when I was a kid—you know, after school finished at the end of June each year. In those days, two months of carefree living seemed like an eternity. I laugh now. Two months these days feel more like two weeks!

When it got too hot to play outside, my friends and I would retreat to the rec room. And if it was up to me, we'd pull out a game like Monopoly—something with lots of strategy, luck, and money. From the time I was young, I guess I was destined to be an entrepreneur. It's in my blood.

Now, I'm not going to suggest that if you happen to love Monopoly (even the long version) you're destined to be self-employed. But I will say this: If you have the inclination to run your own business—either full time or part time—you will significantly increase your tax planning opportunities. Make no mistake: Self-employment is one of the last great tax shelters.

And, like owning all the yellow, green, and blue properties in Monopoly, winning the tax game through self-employment can leave you feeling on top of the world.

Jumping on the Bandwagon

No doubt about it, a growing number of Canadians are turning to self-employment for their livelihood. Some out of necessity, but many simply because they recognize the benefits—tax and otherwise. In some cases, taxpayers are jumping on the self-employment bandwagon by renegotiating their work arrangements with their employers. This can be an effective strategy *if* you do it properly.

Tim's Tip 35: Structure your work so that you're self-employed, not an employee.

From a tax point of view, it can make a lot of sense to do your work on a contract basis as a self-employed worker, rather than as an employee. You may want to approach your current employer with the idea of resigning and being hired back on this basis. But you'll have to dot your I's and cross your T's here. Just because you call yourself self-employed doesn't mean the tax collector will agree with you. You see, the Canada Customs and Revenue Agency (CCRA) is more concerned about the true substance of your business relationships than whether you call yourself self-employed. Consider Anwar's story.

A nwar worked as a software programmer for Acme Software Inc. for seven years. In order to provide Anwar with more tax breaks, and to save the company certain costs, his employer agreed last year that Anwar would resign and the company would hire him back on a contract basis. Anwar still performs most of the work at Acme's offices, and he's still enrolled in Acme's bene-fits plan. Last year, Anwar claimed a number of expenses against his self-employment income from Acme that he wouldn't have been able to claim as an employee. CCRA took a close look at his relationship with Acme and decided that he's really still an employee of the company. The tax collector has disallowed Anwar's deductions, and reassessed Acme for its share of the CPP and EI premiums that should have been paid. Sadly, the tax collector is likely right in this case.

You see, CCRA looks at four tests to determine whether you're truly self-employed, or just an employee. You'd do well to look at these, too—before the tax collector comes knocking.

- *Control Test.* Do you control when, where, and how you work? If you're in control, this is evidence in your favour that you may be self-employed.
- *Integration or Organization Test.* How vital are you to the organization you're working for? Can it survive without you? The further removed you are from being critical to the company, the easier it will be to convince the tax collector that you're actually self-employed.
- *Economic Reality Test.* Do you assume any financial risks in your work? Do you supply your own tools of the trade? Do you assume any liabilities in your work? Do you perform services for different organizations or at least have the right to do so? If your answers to these questions are generally "yes," this is a stroke in your favour when claiming that you're self-employed.
- *Specific Results Test.* Is there an end in sight to the particular project you've been engaged to work on? Or is your arrangement with the company one where no specific result or end is contemplated? To convince CCRA that you're truly self-employed, you'll need to show that you've been hired to complete a specific task and that your relationship is not simply ongoing.

> **Action Step**
>
> Make sure that you sign a written contract with any organization that you work for as a self-employed individual. The contract should clearly spell out the nature, extent, and duration of your services. Set up the contract so that you pass the four self-employment tests: control, integration, economic reality, and specific results.

TO MAKE A LONG STORY SHORT:

- Arrange your work relationships so that you're considered self-employed rather than an employee.

- You'll need to pass four tests to convince the tax collector that you're truly self-employed and not simply an employee in disguise.

Choosing Your Business Structure

An important question that you'll face when entering the world of self-employment is this: What business structure are you going to choose?

Tim's Tip 36: Understand the three most common business structures.

There are three common business structures available to you: a proprietorship, partnership, or corporation. Let's take a closer look at them.

Proprietorship

A proprietorship is you, in business for yourself. A proprietor may have employees but owns the business alone. Last week I passed some kids at the side of the road selling lemonade, and since I'm always interested in supporting entrepreneurial efforts, I stopped for a drink. Although the kids seemed a little confused when I explained that they were operating a proprietorship, they'll appreciate the education later in life, I'm sure.

The real benefits of a proprietorship are these: There is little or no cost involved to set up your business as a proprietorship; it's as easy as hanging up a shingle or putting up a sign, and there is little government regulation. The only requirement you might have is to register the business name with the provincial government (for example, "John's Heating and Cooling"). And even this requirement can be waived if you simply operate the business under your own name (for example, "John's" or "John Doe's").

Of course, there can be some drawbacks to a proprietorship, too. First, you'll face unlimited liability for the debts and obligations of the business—effectively, you and the business are one and the same. Second, it may be more difficult as a proprietor to raise financing if you need capital to start or expand the business. Third, there's less flexibility when it's time to plan for the succession of your business. Finally, there's the question of image. Is there a risk that others will view your business as a small, unsophisticated operation? Maybe. But in most cases, the fact that you're a proprietorship will have no effect on whether someone retains your services or buys your products.

> Operating as a proprietorship could leave you vulnerable to creditors and lawsuits if your business involves significant financial or other risks to you or other people, including your employees. Protect yourself with business insurance, and consider operating through a corporation to limit your liability.
>
> **Caution!**

If you're a proprietor, the profits of your business are yours personally. You must report all the income and expenses of your business on your personal tax return each year (Form T2124 for business activities or T2032 for professional activities). You don't pay yourself a salary; instead, you simply take cash out of the business for personal use. This is called a *draw*. Of course, if you draw too much, the business may not have enough cash to operate. If you incur losses as a proprietor, those losses are also reported on your tax return, and can be applied against your other sources of income (see Tip 45 for more).

Partnership

A partnership works much like a proprietorship, except that there is more than one business owner. A partnership is really just a group of proprietors joining forces to carry on business together with the idea of generating profits. The benefits to a partnership are these: you're able to share the risks of being in business; you may have greater access to capital; and you can pool your skills.

The truth is, a partnership can also bring new challenges. Think of these as drawbacks if you want. First, you and your partners may not always agree on how the business should be run, and resolving these differences can be tough at times. Second, getting rid of a partner that isn't working out is not exactly an enjoyable task. And finally, a partner is generally liable jointly for the debts and obligations of the partnership (although limited liability partnerships are possible and are often set up by professional accounting and law firms).

If you're a partner, you'll be required to pay tax on your share of the partnership's profits. In fact, as with a proprietor, partners are required to report their profits or losses on their personal tax returns. The partnership itself is required to file a partnership information return annually with CCRA.

If you're going to enter into a partnership, even with family members, be sure to visit a lawyer to write up a partnership agreement. This is critical. The agreement should cover issues such as these: how and when the profits of the partnership will be allocated to each partner; how to handle disputes; what to do when a partner dies or leaves the partnership; and whether insurance will be purchased on the lives of each partner.

Corporation

A corporation is a separate legal entity. In fact, a corporation is considered to be a separate *person* for tax purposes. And, just like you, a corporation has to file its own tax returns and financial statements with the tax collector. You can usually tell which businesses are set up as corporations because you'll see the terms *Inc.*, *Incorporated*, *Corp.*, *Corporation*, *Company*, *Ltd.*, or *Limited* after the name of the business.

There are two key benefits to a corporation, and one of these is tax-related. First, a corporation generally offers limited liability protection to its shareholders (the owners). That is, the debts and obligations of the corporation do not become obligations of the shareholders. I should mention that, in some circumstances, a director of a corporation may be liable for certain obligations of the company.

The other benefit is a *tax deferral*. You see, most small Canadian corporations are entitled to an attractive rate of tax on the first $200,000 of *active business income*. That rate is generally about 20 percent, although this varies slightly by province. Passive income—generally from investments—in that same corporation will face tax at about 50 percent. Quite a difference! It's the low rate of tax on active business income that provides the opportunity to defer tax. Notice that I didn't call this a permanent tax reduction. This is a tax deferral that lets you push taxes to a future year. And this is great tax planning (see Chapter 1, Tip 4). Consider Astrid's case.

*A*strid's corporation expects to generate $150,000 in income this year. Astrid's going to pay herself $100,000 in salary, which keeps her income below the highest marginal tax bracket. If she were to receive any more salary, each additional dollar would face tax at about 46 percent in her hands (see page 286 for actual rates). The remaining $50,000 will be left in her corporation, where it will be taxed at just 20 percent. Her tax deferral in this case is about 26 percent (46 minus 20 percent). Once Astrid pays the remaining $50,000 out of the company, she'll face tax personally and the tax deferral will be over. But until that point, she saves herself tax dollars.

There are two drawbacks to a corporation. The first is the cost of setting it up and maintaining it. For the set-up, you're looking at paying between $500 and $1,500. Usually a lawyer is best for this, although you can do it yourself. There's also the cost of paying an accountant to prepare your corporate financial statements and tax returns each year—a job best left to a professional where corporations are involved. Accounting fees can vary widely, depending on the nature of your business and the neatness of your records.

The second drawback is *trapped losses*. You see, if your business loses money from its operations, it will have *non-capital losses*. These losses can be carried back three years or forward seven to offset taxable income in those years. If losses are incurred by your corporation in its first few years, they will be trapped in the corporation and will only be available to offset income earned by the corporation in the following seven years. Beyond seven years, the losses expire. This is not nearly as good as if you had incurred those losses personally as a proprietor or partner. As a proprietor or partner, the losses could be applied to offset your other personal income, and could even be carried back three years to recover taxes you may have paid personally in those prior years.

TO MAKE A LONG STORY SHORT:

- There are three common business structures. A proprietorship is the simplest and least expensive to establish, but offers the least protection from creditors and fewer tax planning opportunities.

- A partnership is slightly more complex. It's much like a group of proprietors working together and sharing the profits and losses.

- A corporation is the most complex. It requires fees to set up and maintain but can provide limited liability and greater tax planning flexibility.

Tim's Tip 37: Consider incorporation once your business has grown, but not before.

I know, I know. You're looking forward to the day when you can incorporate your business and move to a whole new level of sophistication. Besides, it sounds great to be called a founding shareholder of a corporation. Well, hold your horses for a minute.

Remember what I said earlier about the benefits of a corporation? The two key benefits are these: (1) limited liability for shareholders, and (2) opportunities for tax deferral. There's a good chance that you may not even benefit in these ways if you incorporate too soon. Think about it. Will you benefit significantly from the limited liability offered by a corporation? It depends on the industry and the nature of your business. If, for example, you're in the desktop publishing business, your potential liability is likely much lower than if you're in the construction industry. But as your business grows in size, your need for protection from liability will also grow.

What about the tax-deferral issue? If you're not going to leave any of your business earnings in the company, then you won't benefit from the tax deferral I've been talking about. Refer back to Astrid's story in Tip 36. If she had paid the full $150,000 of corporate earnings to herself rather than leaving $50,000 in the company, she would have lost the benefit of the tax deferral. In many situations, it's not until the business has grown in profitability that the owner is in a position to leave some of the earnings in the corporation and really benefit from a tax deferral.

And remember, as I discussed earlier, setting up a corporation from the start of your business could leave losses trapped inside the corporation that could have been used to recover taxes paid personally in previous years.

The general rule, then, is that you should wait until the business has grown in size and profitability before you incorporate. As with all tax planning, your circumstances will be different from others', and seeking the advice of a tax pro who's familiar with your situation will help you to make the best decision regarding your business structure.

TO MAKE A LONG STORY SHORT:

- The key benefits to setting up your business as a corporation are *limited liability* and the opportunity for *tax deferral* on corporate earnings.

- Normally, you'll experience these benefits most once the business has grown in size and profitability, and so it's often preferable to wait until that time to incorporate.

- Setting up a corporation too soon could result in *trapped losses* in the corporation.

> **Action Step**
>
> If you're operating as a proprietorship or partnership and decide to incorporate your business, visit a tax pro to arrange for your business assets to be transferred to the new company on a tax-free basis. This is normally done under Section 85 of the *Income Tax Act*. In exchange for transferring those assets to the company, you'll receive payment and/or shares from the company.

Tim's Tip 38: Choose the right year-end for your business.

Brace yourself, we're now dealing with a very complex area of tax law—choosing a year-end for your proprietorship or partnership. Before 1995, it was fairly easy to pick a year-end for your business. It used to be that you could effectively defer tax for a full year by choosing a non-calendar year-end. Not so anymore. While you'll generally be able to choose any year-end you want for your business, all proprietorships and partnerships are now required to report income on a calendar-year basis. As a result, if you choose a non-calendar year-end, you'll have to adjust your business income each year to reflect a December 31 year-end. Follow me?

If you changed to a December 31 year-end back in 1995, as so many business owners did because of new rules, you would have calculated your income for the stub period that fell between your former year-end and December 31, 1995. The tax collector has allowed you to report those stub-period earnings over a 10-year period. If you cease or significantly change business operations, give up Canadian residency, or incorporate—watch out—you'll be taxed on the full balance of your stub-period income in that year.

In many cases, since you must report your income as though you have a calendar year-end anyway, it may not be worth the hassle to choose a non-calendar year-end. It'll only mean extra work in preparing your tax returns. There may, however, be an opportunity for you to defer tax. Here's the general rule: If your business is growing and you expect your business income to continue increasing for a number of years, then choosing a non-calendar year-end will provide a tax deferral.

Let's briefly look at how the calculation works. Suppose your proprietorship has an October 31 year-end. On your personal tax return for 2002, you'll have to report your income for the 12 months ended October 31, 2002. But you'll have to convert this to a December 31 year-end. This means you'll have to calculate your income from the business for November and December 2002 as well—called the *stub period*—and add this to your October 31 income. When you do this, you will now be reporting income for a 14-month period (the 12 months ended October 31, 2002, plus income for the 2-month stub period). It hardly seems fair that you should report 14 months of income on your tax return each year. Don't panic. You can now deduct from that 14-month income the stub-period income added in the prior year. This brings your income back to a 12-month figure. Make sense?

By the way, the stub-period income that you add each year is not your actual income for those months. It's based on a formula. In my example, we need to add two months' worth of income, so we'd simply take $\frac{2}{12}$ of the October 31 fiscal year income and call this our stub-period income.

If your business is losing money, either because it's new or because it's simply on the decline, you'll be better off with a December 31 year-end. You're able to change to a December 31 year-end at any time, but once you've made this decision, you can't go back to a non-calendar year-end. As you can see, the rules are confusing, and I've only touched the surface here. Be sure to visit a tax pro before making a decision about which year-end is best for you.

TO MAKE A LONG STORY SHORT:

- It can be a difficult decision to choose between a non-calendar and a calendar year-end.

- Generally, if your business income is expected to rise consistently over the next few years, a non-calendar year-end will offer tax-deferral opportunities.

- Be sure to visit a tax pro before making a final decision on a year-end.

Claiming Business Deductions

Why in the world is self-employment such a great tax shelter anyway? Deductions! In fact, our tax law will allow you to claim a deduction for virtually any costs, so long as the costs were incurred for the purpose of producing income from the business, and provided the expenses are reasonable. Let's take a look at the most common expenses you'll be able to claim.

Tim's Tip 39: **Maximize your deductions for home office expenses.**

There's no getting around it—you've got to pay for a place to live, so why not make a portion of the costs tax deductible? There's nothing like self-employment to make this a reality. However, there are some rules to be aware of. You'll be entitled to claim a deduction for

Did You Know?

As an aside, you might be interested in knowing that in a recent court decision, *Thomas Vanka v. The Queen* (2001), the taxpayer, who was a doctor, was considered to have met the criteria for home office deductions because he met patients regularly from home—but he met them principally by phone. This won't necessarily mean you can do the same, since the facts of your situation may be different, but you should be aware that it may be possible to deduct home office costs as Dr. Vanka did if your facts are substantially the same.

I generally tell folks not to claim capital cost allowance (CCA) on the portion of a home used for business. If you do claim CCA, the tax collector will consider that portion of your home to be a business asset. This will jeopardize your ability to claim the principal residence exemption on that portion of your home—which could leave you open to capital gains tax if you sell your home later at a profit.

home office expenses where you meet one of two criteria: (1) your home is your principal place of business or (2) you use a specific area in your home exclusively for earning income from your business and you meet clients there on a regular and ongoing basis.

Once you've met the criteria, there are a number of expenses to consider deducting. The key here is not to forget deductions that you might otherwise overlook. Here's a list to try on for size:

- rent
- mortgage interest
- property taxes
- utilities (heat, hydro, water)
- home insurance
- repairs and maintenance
- landscaping
- snow plowing
- capital cost allowance (but this is not advisable)
- telephone (100-percent deductible if it's a separate business line)

There are a couple of things to note here. You won't be able to deduct the full cost of these expenses I've listed. Rather, you'll be able to deduct the business portion only. If, for example, your office in the house is 200 square feet in size and your home is 2,000 square feet in total, then 10 percent of these costs would be deductible. By the way, residents of Quebec will find their deductible home office expenses reduced by 50 percent thanks to changes in Quebec's 1996 budget. Be sure to maximize your deductible expenses by maximizing the business percentage of your home. You can do this by including a portion of your hallway and washrooms as business space if they are used in the business, or by excluding certain non-usable space (an unfinished basement, for example) from the calculation of your total square footage of the home.

Telephone expenses are fully deductible if you have a separate business line, and even where you don't have a separate line, a portion of your personal line (based on time usage) will be deductible. Any additional home costs that were incurred solely because you are running your business from home—additional insurance, for example—are fully deductible.

TO MAKE A LONG STORY SHORT:

- Claim a portion of all eligible home costs when your home is your principal place of business or is used to meet clients on a regular and ongoing basis.

- Maximize the business use of your home by choosing carefully the areas to include in the calculation.

Tim's Tip 40: Maximize deductions related to business use of your automobile.

If you're self-employed, you'll be entitled to a deduction for using your car in the business. The rules work basically the same for employees and the self-employed, so I'll refer you to Tip 30 in Chapter 3, where I talk about deducting automobile costs. Keep in mind that you can deduct a portion of a vehicle's costs based on the percentage of your driving that was business-related.

To satisfy the tax collector, you'll need to keep a log book for each trip, and you'd be wise to maximize your business usage. This can be done, for example, by making stops for business on the way home from work or on the way to work. And don't forget about the wide range of expenses to deduct, including auto club costs, car washes, licence fees, and the more obvious: gas, oil, repairs, insurance, loan interest, lease costs, and capital cost allowance.

A little boy once asked his mother: "Mom, what happens to a car when it's too old to run anymore?"

"Someone sells it to your father," the mother replied.

Folks, if this sounds familiar, take this once piece of advice: Use that old jalopy in your business instead of your newer car! Since repair costs may be high, you'll save more tax by making those repairs deductible.

TO MAKE A LONG STORY SHORT:

- Maximize business use of your car by stopping for business reasons on the way home from work, or on the way to work, and keep a log book of distances driven for business during the year.

- Use your jalopy with the most costly expenses for business purposes.

- Refer to Tip 30 in Chapter 3 where I talk about automobiles at greater length.

Tim's Tip 41: Categorize your meals and entertainment expenses to maximize tax savings.

Leave it to CCRA to come up with a way to make any simple subject complex! The rules around meals and entertainment are a perfect example. Generally, 50 percent of any meals and entertainment costs will be deductible if the costs were incurred to earn income from your business.

There are some situations, however, where those costs are 100-percent deductible. In fact, there are six common situations: (1) when the meal or entertainment has been provided to all your employees (a Christmas party, for example, to a maximum of three such occasions each year); (2) when the meal or entertainment costs were incurred by an employee of yours who had to travel out of your metropolitan area to do work and who will be including the allowance or reimbursement in his or her income (in this case, the employee is subject to the 50-percent limitation); (3) when the meal costs were built into the price of a rail, airplane, or bus ticket; (4) when the cost of the meal or entertainment is billed to a client and separately disclosed on your invoice to the client (in this case, your client is subject to the 50-percent restriction); (5) when the cost is incurred as part of a fund-raising event for a registered

Did You Know?

If you're a golfer, you'll be glad to know that CCRA has recently changed its opinion on meals purchased at a golf course. You see, the tax collector used to enforce the policy that those meals were not deductible, forcing many to finish a round of golf and then head elsewhere to eat. Talk about crazy. The policy has now changed. Food purchased at a golf course is now deductible, subject to the usual 50-percent limitation.

charity; and (6) when your primary business is the provision of food, beverages, or entertainment.

Given that some meals and entertainment costs are 50-percent deductible and others are fully deductible, you'd be wise to keep track of the categories separately. If you don't, the tax collector could restrict all meals and entertainment to 50-percent deductibility.

TO MAKE A LONG STORY SHORT:

- Meals and entertainment costs are generally 50-percent deductible when they are incurred to earn business income.

- In some situations, these costs are fully deductible.

- Keep track of the categories separately to ensure maximum deductibility.

Tim's Tip 42: **Maximize your eligibility to claim capital cost allowance.**

You've seen the term capital cost allowance (CCA) now and again as you've browsed the pages of this book. CCA is simply our tax law's term for *depreciation*. And CCA is one of the more attractive tax deductions for any self-employed taxpayer. Here's why: There are a number of things that you have probably purchased which will now become tax deductible in the form of CCA because you're running a business.

Want some common examples? Take your home computer. If that computer is now used in the business, even part-time, then it becomes an asset that you can depreciate through the CCA system. Your printer, software, desk, bookcase, fax machine, car, boat, trailer, and tools are all good examples of depreciable assets—provided they are used in the business.

Did You Know?

CCRA calculates its pre-scribed interest rate each quarter by determining the average rate on 90-day trea-sury bills sold during the first month of the preceding quarter. This figure is then rounded up to the nearest percentage point. The rate charged on overdue taxes is four percentage points above this figure, while interest paid on refunds and overpay-ments is just two percentage points above this figure. (The rates differ in Quebec.)

There are different *classes* of assets for CCA purposes, and each asset used in your business will fall into one class or another. Each class has an opening balance at the start of every business fiscal year, and that balance can be depreciated at the specified rate for that class. For example, your computer hardware is a Class 10 asset in which the undepreciated capital cost (UCC) can be deducted each year at the rate of 30 percent.

In the year you acquire an asset, you're generally entitled to just 50 percent of the CCA you'd otherwise claim. This is called the *half-year rule* because you're only entitled to CCA for half of that first year.

Here are some pointers for dealing with CCA. First, if you're going to acquire new assets, consider buying them before the fiscal year is over and make sure those assets are available for use by the end of the fiscal year. This will provide a CCA claim sooner than if you waited until the start of the next fiscal year. Second, delay the sale of an asset until early in the next fiscal year to permit a CCA claim this year. Third, recognize that CCA is not a mandatory deduction. If you don't want to claim it in a given year, you don't have to. This does not mean you give up that deduction forever. It simply means you're pushing it to a future year. This can make sense, for example, when your business is not yet profitable and you don't need the CCA deduction to bring your taxable income to nil. If you want more information on claiming CCA, CCRA's *Business and Professional Income Tax Guide* can help. So can the Interpretation Bulletins available on CCRA's Web site at **www.ccra-adrc.gc.ca**. Use the site's search function to find the term "capital cost allowance."

TO MAKE A LONG STORY SHORT:

- It's possible to claim CCA on assets that you might already own and are now using in the business.

- Maximize your CCA claim by buying new assets before the end of the fiscal year or by selling old assets after the current fiscal year.

- Your CCA claim is not mandatory each year, and it may make sense to postpone the deduction in certain situations.

Tim's Tip 43: **Pay salaries to family members for a number of tax benefits.**

There's no situation quite like self-employment to allow for effective income splitting between family members. I talked about this strategy briefly in Chapter 2, Tip 9*w*. The idea is this: Your business will be entitled to claim a deduction for any salaries or wages paid to family members, provided the compensation is reasonable for the services provided.

Tai runs his own carpet cleaning business. Last summer, he hired his daughter, Kim, to work in the office booking appointments and doing various other tasks. Tai paid Kim $7,000 for her work last year. Kim used the money to help pay for her college education, but she paid absolutely no tax on the $7,000 since it was her only source of income and it's below her basic personal credit of $7,634. If the $7,000 had not been paid to Kim, it would have been taxed in Tai's hands as business income, and would have cost Tai $3,220 in taxes at his marginal tax rate of 46 percent ($7,000 × 46 percent). These taxes were saved by splitting income through the payment of a salary. In addition, the $7,000 is earned income to Kim, which provides her with Registered Retirement Savings Plan (RRSP) contribution room. A great deal all around.

Did you catch the benefits of paying a salary to family members? First, if the salary is paid to a family member who will face no tax, or less tax than the business would have attracted, there are permanent tax savings. Second, the salary provides RRSP contribution room to the family member on the receiving end. Third, the money stays in the family, as opposed to being paid to an unrelated third party. You'll also notice that this strategy works very well when a child needs money for school. Think about it. Tai was able to support his daughter's education in a manner that was tax-deductible to his business and tax-free to Kim. All that's required is that the salary or wages be reasonable for the services provided.

TO MAKE A LONG STORY SHORT:

- Paying salaries or wages to family members with a lower marginal tax rate can result in permanent tax savings and a perfect splitting of income.

- The compensation will provide RRSP contribution room to your family member but must be reasonable for the services provided.

- This strategy offers a great way to cover education costs for children in school.

Tim's Tip 44: Recognize the special tax treatment for certain expenses.

I'd like to talk briefly about a variety of different expenses that have special tax treatment. This list isn't exhaustive, but it covers the key expenses. In most of these cases, the tax collector has simply restricted the amount that can be deducted, similar to the meals and entertainment expenses we looked at in Tip 41. Here we go.

a. Personal or living expenses

You won't generally be able to deduct any costs that are considered personal in nature, such as food or clothing.

b. Prepaid expenses

Sorry, but you can't deduct costs that you've paid for unless the services have already been provided to you. You can deduct them later though, after you receive the services.

c. Personal services business expenses

If you operate your business through a corporation and the tax collector considers you to be really an employee of another employer (that is, simply an "incorporated employee") then you're operating a *personal services business*. You'll be restricted to deducting only salary, wages, benefits and allowances paid to yourself, plus a few other expenses that would have been deductible personally if you had been working as an employee.

d. Recreational facilities and club dues

Sad to say, but a business is not entitled to deduct costs for using or maintaining a recreational facility (for example, golf fees) or club dues when the main purpose of the club is to provide dining, recreational, or sporting facilities.

e. Private health services plan

Since 1998, self-employed folks have been able to deduct premiums paid for health coverage under a supplementary health plan. To be deductible, your coverage can't exceed the coverage of your non-related employees. If you don't have non-related employees or where they represent fewer than half of all employees in your business, you'll be restricted to deducting premiums of $1,500 for each of yourself, your spouse and children 18 or over in the year, and $750 for each of your minor children.

f. Automobile allowances

If you pay kilometre-based allowances to your employees, including yourself, your business in 2002 is restricted to deducting 41 cents on the first 5,000 kilometres driven by each employee, and 35 cents on the excess. These limits are higher in the Yukon, Northwest Territories, and Nunavut (45 cents on the first 5,000 kilometres and 39 cents thereafter).

g. Conventions

The tax collector will allow you to deduct the costs of attending just two conventions each year that are related to your business. There are some further restrictions if the convention is held on a cruise ship, or in certain other situations.

h. Advertising in certain media

You'll generally have a problem deducting your newspaper, periodical, and broadcast advertising costs when you're aiming at a Canadian market but advertise through foreign media.

i. Life insurance premiums

If a life insurance policy on your life is paid for by your business, the premiums are not generally deductible. There's an exception when the policy is required as collateral on a loan for the business.

If you're not sure about the deductibility of certain business expenses, speak to a tax pro.

TO MAKE A LONG STORY SHORT:

- Some specific expenses are given special tax treatment. You should be aware of the key ones.

- In most cases, the tax rules restrict the deductibility of these expenses.

Action Step

If your business has incurred non-capital losses that will expire in the near future, make sure you visit a tax pro to help you plan to use up these losses. There are several strategies for using losses. These include: delaying discretionary deductions like capital cost allowance (CCA); selling assets at a profit and then buying them back; transferring income-generating assets to the business; and other ideas.

Tim's Tip 45: **Deal properly with losses from your business.**

It's pretty common in the first few years of business for your expenses to exceed your income from the business. The result? Losses. We call these *non-capital losses*. As long as you're not incorporated (refer to Tip 36), non-capital losses can be applied to reduce any other source of income you might have reported on your personal tax return for the year. This is going to save you tax dollars.

Applying Non-Capital Losses

Your non-capital losses have to be used to offset other income in the year they are incurred, if possible. If you don't have other income, the losses can be carried back to offset taxable income in any of the three previous years, or carried forward for up to seven years to offset taxable income in the future. If your losses aren't used up by the end of the seventh year, they expire.

Choosing which years to apply your losses against can be something of an art. Consider this example:

---

*K*evin *reported income of $30,000 in 2000 and $60,000 in 2001. In 2002, he reported non-capital losses of $100,000 after starting up a courier service in the year. Kevin has a few options for using his losses. He can carry back $30,000 of the loss to 2000 and $60,000 to 2001 to recover all the taxes he paid in those years, leaving $10,000 in losses to be carried forward for up to seven years. The problem with this idea, however, is that Kevin doesn't need to carry back losses of $30,000 and $60,000 to 2000 and 2001 respectively in order to wipe out his tax liability for those years. The reason? He's entitled to a basic personal credit for those years, which effectively shelters approximately the first $7,000 of income in those years.*

The moral of the story is simple: Your goal is to apply the losses against dollars that will provide the most tax savings. It never makes sense to bring taxable income for a year below the taxable threshold dictated by your basic personal credit (which is $7,634 in 2002). This would be a waste of losses since your tax bill is nil below this threshold.

Similarly, it can be a bright move to bring taxable income down to the first tax bracket of $31,677 in 2002, but not below, if you expect to earn income well in excess of this amount in the next couple of years. In Kevin's example above, he may want to apply his losses to 2001 only, but not to 2000. If he applies the losses to 2000, he'll bring his taxable income in that year below $30,000, which will save him tax at a rate of about 26 cents for each dollar of loss claimed. If he avoids applying the losses to 2000 and carries forward the unused losses, he might be able to apply them against income in excess of $30,000 in future years, which will save him tax at about 35 cents on the dollar. That is, he'll get more bang for his losses if he expects to earn well over $30,000 of taxable income in the next few years and saves some of his losses for those years.

Reasonable Expectation of Profit

And now for some very good news. In the past, the CCRA often denied losses when business owners had claimed losses for several years in a row. The argument was always that there was no "reasonable expectation of profit" (REOP). Two court decisions handed down by the Supreme Court of Canada on May 23, 2002, may provide relief to business owners in this situation going forward.

In the cases *Brian J. Stewart v. The Queen* and *The Queen v. Jack Walls et al.*, a principle was established: When an activity lacks any personal element to it, then it should be considered a commercial activity and a source of income (whether or not losses have been incurred). The SCC established that there is no opportunity to apply the reasonable expectation of profit test where there is no personal element to the activity being carried on by the taxpayer.

You'll still have to take care not to report losses for consecutive years (three years in a row may raise a flag) where your activity does have a personal element to it (where, for example, your business is clearly a hobby as well). In this case the REOP test may still apply.

TO MAKE A LONG STORY SHORT:

- Non-capital losses from your business can be carried back three years or forward seven years to offset taxable income in those years.

- Never use losses to reduce your income below the taxable threshold set by your basic personal tax credit, and consider saving the losses if you can use them in the next few years to offset dollars taxed at a higher rate.

- Two recent court decisions will support your claim of losses where your business is truly commercial in nature. But where your business has a personal or hobby element to it, make sure you've got a reasonable expectation of profit to support your claim of losses.

Adding Up the Tax Hits

Don't be fooled into thinking that income taxes are your only tax burden as a business owner. In fact, there are a number of different "taxes" that your business will be subject to, and while I'm not going to talk about these in detail here, it's important that you're aware of what they are.

Tim's Tip 46: Understand the various "taxes" affecting your business.

In case the income tax burden you'll face on your business profits is not enough to faze you, try a few of these other "taxes" on for size. I call these taxes and, in most cases, that's precisely what they are. In other cases, these are more akin to premiums owing. There are four categories worth talking about.

Canada/Quebec Pension Plan and Employment Insurance

I've got good news and bad news for you. The good news is that, as a self-employed individual, you won't be required to pay any Employment Insurance (EI) premiums on your own earnings. This will save you $2,059 in 2002 when factoring in both the employee ($858) and employer ($1,201) portions, although you won't be entitled to collect EI if you decide to try. The bad news is that you'll have to make Canada/Quebec Pension Plan (CPP/QPP) contributions on your self-employment earnings, and you'll have to pick up both the employee and employer portions, amounting to a maximum of $3,346 in 2002. And CPP/QPP contributions can only get uglier in the

In a family-run business, it may be possible to consider certain family members exempt from Employment Insurance (EI) premiums. This will save you the cost of the premiums, but it means that these family members won't be eligible to collect EI down the road if they find themselves unemployed. If you choose this route, make sure that the salary paid to these family members is reasonable, since the tax collector is more likely to examine the salaries of persons who are EI-exempt.

Caution!

future. In fact, these contributions are scheduled to rise to 9.9 percent of income in 2003!

Provincial Payroll Taxes

Provincial payroll taxes originated in Manitoba and have spread like wildfire across the country. These payroll taxes normally apply to employment income and in some cases extend to self-employment income. There's good news if you live in Ontario. Ontario's Employer Health Tax (EHT) was eliminated for self-employed individuals in 1999.

Workers' Compensation

Many businesses are required to pay premiums to the Workers' Compensation Board. The amount of the premiums depends on the type of work that is being undertaken. Be sure to look into this when you start your business.

GST and HST

Every consumer knows first-hand about the Goods and Services Tax (GST) or the Harmonized Sales Tax (HST) in Nova Scotia, New Brunswick, and Newfoundland and Labrador. Your business will need to register for the GST/HST if your taxable sales of goods or services exceed $30,000 in a fiscal year. Once your sales reach this level, you'll be required to register for GST/HST and start charging the tax in the following month. You'll be required to file GST/HST returns, normally on an annual basis, although some businesses will be required to file more often. In any event, you may be required to remit quarterly installments of GST/HST.

There's an option for many small businesses to calculate the GST/HST owing under the "Quick Method" provided total sales (including tax) are under $200,000. The Quick Method allows you simply to calculate the GST/HST owing as a percentage of total sales (including GST/HST) rather than tracking the actual GST collected and paid throughout the year. CCRA has a guide on using the Quick Method, which you can obtain online at **www.ccra-adrc.gc.ca** or by contacting your local Tax Services Office. By the way, certain businesses can't use the Quick Method (accountants, bookkeepers, and a number of others are on this list—check it out first).

TO MAKE A LONG STORY SHORT:

- Income taxes are not the only type of tax that your business will have to deal with.

- Take the time to understand your obligations related to CPP, EI, provincial payroll taxes, workers' compensation, and the GST/HST.

Getting into the Game

If self-employment is in your game plan, there's plenty you can do to minimize the taxes you pay. Turn now to the Tax Planning Tip Sheet at the front of the book and review the strategies introduced in Chapter 4. Ask yourself, "Can this tip apply to me?" Every *Yes* or *Not Sure* could add dollars to your bottom line. When you've finished reading this book, take your Tip Sheet to a tax pro for help in setting up your tax-savvy proprietorship, partnership, or corporation.

BULLS, BEARS, AND BASEBALL: STRATEGIES FOR INVESTORS

To become a millionaire: Start with 10 million, then invest in a hot tip.

5

All right, I'll be the first to admit it. My life is a little one-tracked. Here's proof: My career is taxation, and my hobby is investing. Being one-tracked makes me good at what I do, but—according to my wife—something far less than exciting at the dinner table. In fact, my wife Carolyn and I were at a friend's place for dinner once when the conversation turned to investment issues. I was in my element. Evidently, everyone else wished they were in bed.

After dinner, Carolyn said to me privately: "Tim, for the first time in my life, I envied my feet—they were asleep. Why can't you take up another hobby, like insect collecting or something?"

"Insect collecting," I replied. "Great idea! I could liquidate some of my South American holdings, and reassess my short position in that small resource play out west to free up some cash. Then I could undertake a fundamental analysis on any insect-related securities that I can locate in the market. Of course, I'd want to check the price–volume histories and look at other technical analyses. Heck, I could even take a long position in some bug-related futures contracts through my broker in Chicago. Carolyn, you're a genius. We could make millions!"

"Help, I married a financial geek!" my wife replied. "Tim, forget what I said about starting a new hobby."

At this point, I want to talk to those of you who, like me, are investors. And this will include just about everyone. In fact, you can consider yourself an investor for our discussion here if you have any money at all invested outside your Registered Retirement Savings Plan (RRSP), Registered Retirement Income Fund (RRIF), or other tax-deferred plan—or if you expect to have these types of investments down the road. These are called *non-registered assets*, also referred to as your *open money*.

Let's look at some strategies that are sure to keep the tax collector away from your open money. It's time for investors to step up to the plate, because these pages contain some guaranteed home runs.

Investing in a Tax-Smart Manner

Tim's Tip 47: Consider the impact that taxes can have on a non-registered portfolio.

If the truth be known, Canadian investors, financial advisors, and money managers have not focussed enough on the impact that taxes can have on your accumulation of wealth over the long run. Now, don't blame your financial advisor for not paying much attention to after-tax investing if in fact your advisor hasn't been concerned about the issue. You see, there hasn't been much research on the issue of after-tax returns, so most advisors have not been fed the proper information on the subject. As for money managers in Canada today, most grew up in the pension industry where, quite frankly, income taxes don't matter (money in a pension fund isn't subject to taxes annually).

The bottom line? Canadian investors have not been shown that after-tax investing is critical to building wealth. But times are changing. Canadians are starting to recognize the impact taxes can have on a portfolio. I'm here to tell you that focussing on after-tax returns is so important when investing outside an RRSP or RRIF that it could mean the difference between having plenty in retirement, and moving in with the kids or performing on a street corner to make ends meet (and unless you're Wayne Newton, performing on a street corner is not likely to get you far).

There are two things in particular that will determine how much tax you pay annually on your non-registered investments: portfolio make-up and portfolio turnover.

Portfolio Make-Up Matters

When I talk about portfolio make-up, I'm talking about the types of investments you're holding in your portfolio (remember, I'm referring to those investments outside your RRSP or RRIF; there are no taxes annually on income earned inside those registered plans). You see, the types of investments you hold will determine the type of income you earn from your investments, which will impact how much tax you pay each year.

Generally, there are three broad categories that your investments will fall into:

- money market investments
- fixed income investments
- equity investments

Money market investments include cash and near-cash investments like Guaranteed Investment Certificates (GICs), Canada Savings Bonds, or money market mutual funds. Fixed income investments, as the name suggests, provide a steady stream of income to the investor, and generally include corporate bonds, government bonds, mortgage-backed securities, preferred shares, or mutual funds that invest in these and similar types of investments. Equity investments are different in that you're an owner, not a loaner. That is, equity investments provide you with ownership in something, whether it's a business, real estate, natural resources, or something similar. Equity investments include common shares in publicly traded companies, real estate, or mutual funds that invest in these or similar things.

What's the difference between money market, fixed income, and equity investments from a tax point of view? It's a critical question. Money market and fixed income investments will generally provide you with interest income (and perhaps with dividends in the case of preferred shares), with little opportunity to generate capital gains. Equity investments, on the other hand, provide an opportunity for capital gains (or losses!), and perhaps some dividend income in the case of common shares.

Make no mistake, these differences are crucial. You see, interest income is taxed at a much higher rate than dividends from a Canadian company, and capital gains. Flip to page 286 at the back of the book and you'll see the difference in marginal tax rates that apply to these different types of income in each province. If you're in the highest tax bracket, you'll face marginal tax rates on these types of income approximately as follows (these are averages for Canada in 2002):

- Interest income   46.5 percent
- Canadian dividends   32.0 percent
- Capital gains   23.2 percent

The bottom line? Money market and fixed income investments are not generally tax-smart because interest income is downright ugly from a tax perspective. Equities, on the other hand, make more sense from a tax perspective since capital gains are taxed at much lower rates. In fact, just one-half of any capital gains you realize after October 17, 2000, will have to be included in your income. This capital gains inclusion rate used to be 75 percent prior to the 2000 federal budget.

Want proof that portfolio make-up can make a difference in your wealth accumulation? Check out Joel's numbers.

Joel has $100,000 to invest for a 20-year period. He can earn a 10-percent rate of return annually over that time. Joel's marginal tax rate is 46.5 percent. He plans to liquidate the portfolio at the end of 20 years. How much will he have at that time after all taxes have been paid? It depends on the type of income he'll be earning—that is, on the make-up of his portfolio. If Joel were to invest strictly in interest-bearing vehicles, he'd have $283,590 in his pocket after taxes at the end of 20 years. On the other hand, if Joel were to invest exclusively in equity investments that grow in value but are not taxed until he liquidates his portfolio, he would have $539,586 after taxes at the end of that time. That is, Joel would have a full $255,996, or 90.3 percent, more at the end of 20 years by changing the make-up of his portfolio. His after-tax portfolio will nearly double in this case! The following table says it all.

PORTFOLIO MAKE-UP MATTERS				
			$100,000 Invested for 20 Years	
Portfolio Make-Up			**Balance Before Taxes**	**Balance After Taxes**
Money Market	(100% interest income)		$283,590	$283,590
Balanced	(50% interest, 50% deferred capital gains)		$438,831	$387,510
Equity	(100% deferred capital gains)		$672,750	$539,586
Assumptions:	$100,000 invested; 10% pre-tax annual rate of return; portfolio is liquidated after 20 years; marginal tax rate is 46.5%; capital gains inclusion rate is 50%.			

Portfolio Turnover Matters

In addition to portfolio make-up, the turnover of your portfolio is critical as well. Every time you liquidate an investment and then reinvest the money, you've "turned over" that investment. The more selling and buying that goes on in your portfolio, the higher your rate of turnover. The problem with turnover is that each sale is a taxable event when it takes place outside of a registered plan. If taxes are triggered, it leaves you with less money to reinvest. This means that your next investment has to perform better than you might have thought: It has to provide you with the rate of return you're expecting, but must go further, to replace the dollars you paid in taxes from liquidating the previous investment. Sure, taxes may eventually be paid on your gains, but it's better to defer the tax to the future than to prepay tax today—it's a timing issue.

You need to know that turnover can take place at two levels: the investor level, and the money manager level. That is, there are generally two culprits who can be accused of turning over your investments: you, and/or the money manager (typically the mutual fund manager where you're invested in funds). You create turnover every time you choose to sell a security that you hold in your portfolio, whether it's a stock, bond, mutual fund, or some other investment. The money manager creates turnover in the same way by selling securities inside the fund you're holding. In either case, guess who pays the tax on any taxable capital gains realized. You got it: You pay the tax.

Let's look at Don's example. It'll help you to understand the difference turnover can make over the long run.

> **Caution!**
>
> Dividends from Canadian companies are taxed at much lower rates than interest income. As a result, many investors think that they're investing in a tax-smart manner when they're earning these dividends. This may not be true. You see, if you need a cash flow from your investments, then earning dividends from Canadian companies can be a good idea. But if you have no need for this cash flow, then receiving dividends annually is creating a tax bill that you could be avoiding. You could instead be investing for long-term growth so that you'll defer your tax hit until you sell the investments, and you'll face tax at the lower rates that apply to capital gains. Now that's tax-smart.

*D*on has $100,000 to invest for a 20-year time period. He knows that capital gains will be taxed at lower rates than interest or dividends in his hands, so he's chosen to invest in equity mutual funds to generate those gains. Don's marginal tax rate is 46.5 percent. If Don earns a 10-percent rate of return annually, how much will he have, after taxes, at the end of 20 years? The answer depends on the level of turnover in his portfolio over that period. If Don chooses funds with a very low rate of turnover (say, zero turnover in this example), he'll have $539,586 in his hands after taxes in 20 years. If Don instead chooses an equity fund with a higher rate of turnover—say 100 percent (meaning that 100 percent of accrued gains are realized each year)—he'd be left with just $438,831 at the end of that same time. Don will be short-changed by a full $100,755 if he chooses a fund with a high rate of turnover in this example. The following table tells the story.

PORTFOLIO TURNOVER MATTERS			
		$100,000 Invested for 20 Years	
Portfolio Turnover		Balance Before Taxes	Balance After Taxes
0% Turnover	(No capital gains are realized annually)	$672,750	$539,586
50% Turnover	(50% of accrued gains are realized annually)	$543,965	$485,565
100% Turnover	(100% of accrued gains are realized annually)	$438,831	$438,831

Assumptions: $100,000 invested for 20 years; 10% pre-tax annual rate of return; all returns are capital gains; portfolio is liquidated after 20 years; marginal tax rate is 46.5%; capital gains inclusion rate is 50%.

By the way, you might think that a turnover rate of 100 percent is not realistic for a mutual fund in a given year. Think again. In any given year, there will be many funds with rates of turnover in excess of 100 percent. I've seen funds with turnover rates as high as 800 percent in a year! If you're not sure what the rates of turnover are for the funds you're investing in, call the fund companies you're dealing with and ask.

Tax-Smart Rules

Want to minimize the tax you're paying on your investments outside your RRSP or RRIF? You should. We've seen that taxes *do* matter—a lot! After the discussion we've had here, you'll now understand that there are two rules to start with to minimize taxes annually on your investments:

1. Focus on capital gains when investing outside of your registered plans.
2. Keep portfolio turnover to an absolute minimum.

Many mutual funds are available that are designed to keep portfolio turnover to a minimum. AIC Group of Funds is certainly the best-known fund family in Canada for this philosophy. Speak to a trusted financial advisor for details on specific funds available.

TO MAKE A LONG STORY SHORT:

- After-tax investing has been ignored for too long by investors, financial advisors, and money managers alike. Today, Canadians are starting to think about *after-tax* returns, because taxes *do* matter.

- Taxes on a portfolio are affected by two things: portfolio make-up, and portfolio turnover.

- Minimize taxes by focussing on earning capital gains outside your registered plans and by keeping turnover to a minimum.

Tim's Tip 48: Call your profits *capital gains* and your losses *business losses*.

Sometimes you're going to make money on your investments, and sometimes you're going to lose it. But are you going to call your profits *capital gains* or *business income*? Similarly, are you going to call your losses *capital losses* or *business losses*? This issue can be as clear as mud. No doubt about it, this is one of the very gray areas in our tax law. And it can be tough making key decisions on the gray issues, where it often comes down to toss-ups and testosterone.

Saya loves to invest. In fact, she follows the stock market closely. In an average month, Saya makes about eight trades on her brokerage account. Last year, she generated $35,000 in profits from her investing. But investing is not Saya's primary source of income. She works as a technician in an architect's office, and she earns $45,000 each year as an employee there. Should Saya's profits from investing be considered capital gains or business income? She could argue either way.

> **Caution!**
>
> You can make a special election to treat all your gains and losses from trading Canadian securities as capital gains and losses. Those who are considered *traders* cannot make this election (although a trader is not defined in the *Income Tax Act*). Normally, I don't recommend making this election. The reason? It's irrevocable—you'll be stuck with it for life. Besides, your profits and losses from trading securities will almost always be considered capital gains and losses anyway, so there's often no need to make the election. Why tie your hands when you don't need to?

Here's the general rule: Where you have the ability to argue either way, call your profits capital gains. Here's why: Just 50 percent of capital gains are taxable in Canada, while business income is fully taxable. Have you incurred losses? You'll be better off calling these business losses than calling them capital losses. After all, capital losses can only be applied against capital gains to reduce tax, while business losses can be applied against any source of income at all.

Keep in mind that, in many cases, it will be clear whether your profits and losses are capital or income in nature. Consider the analogy of the tree and its fruit. If you bought a tree with the intention of growing and selling fruit, then the tree would be a capital asset to you. So, if you were to sell the tree itself at a profit, that profit would normally be considered a capital gain. The profits from selling the fruit would be considered business income. As far as the tax collector is concerned, your primary intention when you bought the asset will normally determine the proper treatment.

Want a more lifelike example? Suppose you bought a condominium for the purpose of renting it out, and someone offered a good price to buy the condo from you. Because you bought the condo to generate rents (your "fruit" in this case), the condo is a capital asset, and any profit on the sale is likely a capital gain. If, however, you bought the condo largely to sell it at a profit, and not primarily to rent it, then you could argue that the transaction was income in nature. It's what we call an "adventure in the nature of trade." If you had lost money flipping the property in this case, it's arguable that the loss is a business loss.

In any event, it's important to document your reasoning for the position you take when reporting your gains and losses. And be consistent! That is, don't treat your stock profits as capital gains and your losses from similar investments as business losses. The tax collector doesn't really have a sense of humour in this regard.

Here's one last point: Any profits or losses that you generate from short-selling a stock will generally be considered business income or losses. It only makes sense. You see, a short sale doesn't provide the opportunity for any "fruit from the tree" such as interest, dividends, royalties, or rents. No fruit? Then these securities are more akin to an "adventure in the nature of trade" and will be treated as income.

TO MAKE A LONG STORY SHORT:

- It may not always be clear whether you should treat your investment profits and losses as capital or income.

- Where possible, you'll want to argue that your profits are capital gains and your losses are business losses.

- Document your reasoning and be consistent from one transaction to the next.

Tim's Tip 49: Claim a capital gains reserve to spread your tax bill over time.

Ah, yes, one of the mysteries of the universe—how to avoid tax on capital gains when an asset has appreciated in value. It's not an easy question to answer. I wish more magic were available here. Your best bet in this situation is to push the expected tax bill as far off into the future as possible. You can do this simply by not selling the asset. But if you're determined to sell, you can at least minimize the tax hit by spreading it out over a maximum five-year period.

You see, the tax collector will allow you to claim what is called a *capital gains reserve*—a deduction—when you have sold something at a profit but have not yet collected the full amount of your proceeds from the sale.

---

*L*isa decided last year to sell the family cottage. She had bought it for $75,000 and was offered $175,000 for it—a $100,000 profit she couldn't refuse. She wasn't able to shelter this $100,000 capital gain in any way, so she decided to take payment from the purchaser over a five-year period—$35,000 each year. This way, the capital gain was not taxed all at once last year. Rather, Lisa will pay tax on the gain over the five-year period—she'll report just $20,000 each year. She reported the full $100,000 capital gain last year, but claimed a capital gains reserve for 80 percent (four-fifths) of the gain. The gain will be taken into income slowly over five years.

You'll have to take any capital gains into income at a rate not less than 20 percent (one-fifth) each year. If you're not keen on the idea of taking payment over five years because you're giving up use of the proceeds today, there's a simple solution: Build an "interest" charge into the selling price so that you're compensated for the time delay in collecting payment. For example, Lisa could have collected, say, $37,500 each year rather than $35,000—for a total selling price of $187,500. The additional $2,500 each year is like interest income, but the good news is that it will be taxed as a capital gain (only one-half of capital gains realized after October 17, 2000 are taxable) since it's built into the selling price!

TO MAKE A LONG STORY SHORT:

- It's very difficult to avoid paying tax on accrued capital gains on assets you own.

- Your best bet is to push the tax bill as far into the future as possible.

- A taxable capital gain can be spread out for up to five years by taking payment of the proceeds over an extended period. This is called a capital gains reserve.

Tim's Tip 50: **Think about reporting your spouse's dividends on your own tax return where possible.**

Sure, it may sound crazy, but taking income from the lower-income spouse and adding it to the income of the higher-income spouse could actually save you taxes. You see, if your spouse earns dividends from a Canadian company, he or she will be entitled to claim a *dividend tax credit*. This is simply a credit that is deducted from the taxes your spouse would otherwise pay. But what if your spouse isn't going to pay any tax because of not having much income? In this case, the dividend tax credit could go to waste.

The good news? Our tax law will allow you to elect to include *all* (it's all or nothing) of your spouse's Canadian dividends on *your* tax return where you'll be able to claim the dividend tax credit. How can this possibly save you tax? Simple. By removing the dividend income from your spouse's tax return, your spouse's income will be reduced. This will increase the spousal credit you're entitled to claim for having a spouse who is dependent on you. In fact, the tax collector won't allow you to make this election to report your spouse's dividends unless the spousal credit you're entitled to claim is increased as a result of removing the dividends from your spouse's return. Follow me?

In the end, you'll need to calculate your and your spouse's combined tax bills both ways: (1) having your spouse report his or her own dividends, and (2) reporting your spouse's dividends on your tax return instead. This will tell you whether or not you stand to benefit from the transfer. This is where tax software is going to come in handy. It's easy to do these "what if" calculations with software. The other option is to speak to a tax pro or a financial advisor who may be able to do the calculations for you.

TO MAKE A LONG STORY SHORT:

- It may be possible to save tax by reporting Canadian dividends received by your lower-income spouse on your tax return instead.

- This transfer can be made only where doing so will increase the spousal credit that you're able to claim as a result of your spouse being a dependant.

- You'll need to crunch some numbers to see if this transfer will be beneficial for you.

Understanding Tax-Smart Strategies

Tim's Tip 51: Look into corporate mutual funds as a way to defer tax.

Did you know that mutual funds are created in one of two flavours? I'm talking about the legal structure of the fund. You see, mutual funds can be set up as trusts or as corporations. On the surface, there doesn't seem to be a big difference between the two. In fact, most investors don't know or see the difference between a mutual fund trust and a mutual fund corporation. There are differences, however, and these are worth looking at. Why? Two reasons: (1) you could defer taxes through the appropriate use of corporate mutual funds, and (2) inappropriately investing in corporate mutual funds could leave you worse off than investing in a mutual fund trust.

The Tax Deferral

The biggest selling feature of corporate mutual funds is that you can switch from one fund to another within the same corporation without triggering a disposition for tax purposes. You see, a fund company will establish a single corporation with many different classes of shares (Class A, Class B, and so on). Each class represents a different mutual fund. Take AIC Group of Funds as an example. In 2001, AIC established AIC Corporate Fund Inc. The company offers 19 different classes of shares, and each class represents a different mutual fund. So, Class A shares might be the AIC Advantage II fund, Class B could be the AIC Diversified Canada fund, Class C the AIC Global Technology fund, and so on. Other fund companies have also introduced corporate mutual funds.

If you were to invest in one particular fund and then decide down the road that it's time to move to another fund within that corporation, the switch can be done free of tax. Section 51 of our tax law says that there's no disposition for tax purposes here. There won't be any tax to pay until you redeem your shares for cash, or switch to another fund that is outside of that particular corporation. As for your adjusted cost base (ACB), a switch from one fund to another within the corporation will not change your ACB at all. Your ACB of the original fund will become the ACB of the new fund you own after the switch.

One last point. You should be aware that any corporate mutual fund will generally be considered foreign content inside your RRSP or RRIF. The reason? The tax collector will look at the corporation itself to determine its foreign content status. If more than 30 percent of the cost amount of the assets of the corporation is foreign content (aggregating all the funds, or classes, together), then every fund within that corporation will be considered foreign content—even the Canadian funds.

The Capital Gains Refund Mechanism (CGRM)

There's a provision in our tax law called the *capital gains refund mechanism* (CGRM). Thanks to the CGRM, it may be possible for a mutual fund to realize capital gains in a given year without having to distribute the full amount, if any, of those capital gains by way of a T-slip to you, the investor. Basically, it's a provision that helps to avoid a potential double-tax problem that could otherwise arise. The amount of gains realized by a fund that can be sheltered with this CGRM is based on an ugly formula. In a

Did You Know?

Shares of a mutual fund corporation will generally count as foreign content in your RRSP or RRIF. Is this good or bad? It depends. Since a switch between funds within the corporation is not considered a disposition for tax purposes, the switch will not change the cost amount of the foreign property held by your RRSP or RRIF. This will work to your advantage if the shares have increased in value and you're now switching to another fund in the corporation (since the switch won't increase the cost amount of your foreign content and push you over the 30-percent allowable foreign content limit in your plan). If the value of your fund has dropped and you're now making a switch, it could work to your disadvantage.

nutshell, the CGRM works best when: (1) redemptions from a fund are high in the year, and (2) capital gains realized by the fund in the year are small (that is, turnover in the fund is low).

In the case of a mutual fund corporation, switches from one fund to the next do not count as redemptions (remember, switches are not taxable events), which will generally prevent the CGRM formula from working as effectively in a mutual fund corporation as it would in a trust. Theoretically then, it may be possible that a mutual fund corporation could make larger capital gains distributions than the equivalent mutual fund trust in a given year. What can you do as an investor to ensure that the CGRM is working the best that it can in the corporate mutual funds you've chosen? Choose corporate funds with a very low rate of turnover overall. Don't forget, the lower the rate of turnover, the better the CGRM works. Choosing funds with a buy-and-hold philosophy, then, will help the CGRM do its job better. This is particularly important when buying corporate mutual funds where the CGRM may have a tougher time doing its job otherwise.

The Ideal Investor

Are you a good candidate to invest in corporate mutual funds? Virtually any investor can invest in these funds, but I particularly like them for those who meet any one of these criteria:

- You have money to invest outside an RRSP or RRIF (the benefit of switching between funds on a tax-free basis loses its lustre inside a registered plan where all switches can be done tax-free anyway).
- You plan to make regular adjustments to your portfolio that may require switching from one fund to another (for example, moving to different funds as your investment objectives or time horizon changes).
- You hold your investments in a corporation in a province where capital taxes apply (mutual fund corporations generally qualify for the investment allowance in those provinces, which can reduce the amount of capital tax owing by the company).

TO MAKE A LONG STORY SHORT:

- There is a difference between a mutual fund trust and a mutual fund corporation.

- Mutual fund corporations allow you to switch from one fund to another on a tax-free basis as long as you switch among classes of that one corporation.

- Choose a mutual fund corporation that has among its funds a very low rate of turnover overall. This will help to mitigate some of the shortcomings of mutual fund corporations.

- Mutual fund corporations may work particularly well for those who have money to invest outside of a registered plan, who plan to make regular adjustments to their portfolio, or who invest through a corporation.

Tim's Tip 52: Invest in labour-sponsored funds for tax efficiency and good growth potential.

My wife, Carolyn, is at home with our kids these days, and I'm the only bread-winner in the family at the moment. We started talking about money at the dinner table this week.

"Tim, is it true that money talks?"

"That's what they say," I replied.

"Well, I wish you'd leave a little more here to talk to me during the day. I get so lonely."

"Hmmm. How about if I let you have my entire tax refund this year to spend on whatever you want?" I replied.

"How much was your refund last year?" Carolyn asked.

"Uh, $67.50," I said.

"No deal," she said.

"Okay, I'll put some money into labour-sponsored funds this year and that will beef up my refund," I offered.

"It's a deal!" Carolyn announced.

Folks, it's time to visit the concept of labour-sponsored investment funds—technically referred to as Labour-Sponsored Venture Capital Corporations (LSVCCs). These funds have much to offer.

What's an LSVCC?

An LSVCC is a special corporation designed to provide venture capital to, and promote investment in, small and medium-sized Canadian businesses. And most LSVCCs do a good job of searching out companies with good growth potential.

No doubt, an LSVCC is a higher-risk investment than a blue-chip equity mutual fund, but there's a place in most portfolios for them.

To encourage investment in LSVCCs, the federal and provincial governments provide healthy tax credits to investors. And the tax credits are worth writing home about. You'll be entitled to a federal credit equal to 15 percent of your investment, and a provincial credit equal to, in most provinces, another 15 percent. In most provinces, then, your total credits will equal 30 percent of your investment, to a maximum of $1,500. This means that the first $5,000 invested in an LSVCC each year will net you the maximum tax credits being offered. By the way, there's sad news for you folks in Alberta, New Brunswick, and Newfoundland: You won't receive any provincial credits.

I should mention that if you bought your LSVCC shares after March 5, 1996, you'll have to hold those shares for eight years from the date of purchase before selling them—otherwise you'll have to repay the generous tax credits you received. Shares bought before that date had to be held for five years (many

Action Step

If you want to increase the amount of foreign content that you're entitled to hold inside your RRSP or RRIF, consider investing in an LSVCC. Although you're only entitled to hold 30 percent of the cost amount of your plan assets in foreign securities, holding certain small business properties in your plan will allow you to increase that foreign content by $3 for every $1 of small business property owned, to a maximum of 50 percent foreign content inside your plan. The shares of LSVCCs will generally qualify as small business property, and provide you with this three-to-one additional foreign entitlement.

of those shares have been redeemed by now; if you haven't redeemed yours, consider redeeming them and reinvesting in more LSVCC shares to get tax credits all over again).

Returns on LSVCCs

If you contribute to your RRSP and buy your LSVCCs inside the plan, your potential return on investment can be impressive. Check out these numbers: Assume you invest $5,000 in LSVCCs on or before March 1, 2003, by contributing the cash to your RRSP and buying the funds inside your plan. Your tax savings in 2002 will be $1,500 in refundable credits (assuming credits of 30 percent) plus $2,500 in tax savings from the RRSP deduction (assuming a marginal tax rate of 50 percent), for total tax relief of $4,000. Your out-of-pocket cost of the LSVCC will be just $1,000 ($5,000 less $4,000). Let's assume you hold those shares for eight years and the LSVCC grows by an average of 5 percent annually. At the end of eight years, your investment would be worth $7,387 inside your RRSP. Chances are you're going to leave the cash in your plan and reinvest that money, but even if you were to withdraw that $7,387 from your RRSP, you'd be left with $3,694 after taxes paid on the withdrawal. Do the math: $3,694 on a $1,000 investment over eight years works out to be an annual after-tax return of 17.74 percent. Wow.

I know, I know—you would've received the tax savings for the RRSP contribution even if you hadn't chosen to invest in LSVCCs in the plan. Suppose you had made that $5,000 contribution and simply invested in a blue-chip equity fund. You would have received $2,500 in tax savings, so your out-of-pocket cost would be $2,500. Now, let's assume a 10-percent annual return on the equity fund (double the return of the LSVCC). After eight years, the investment would be worth $10,718. Withdrawing that amount from your RRSP would leave you with $5,359 after taxes, which works out to a 9.46-percent annual return after tax. The bottom line? The LSVCC offered a greater annual return—by 8.28 percent—than the equity fund over the eight years, given my assumptions.

Make the Most of LSVCCs

Because LSVCCs are a higher risk than some of your other investment alternatives, keep these strategies in mind:

- Contribute a maximum of $5,000 annually. The attractive tax credits that mitigate some of the risk are only available on the first $5,000 of LSVCCs purchased each year, so don't invest more than this annually.
- Make another RRSP contribution. Use your tax savings from the LSVCC credits to make another RRSP contribution for added tax savings.
- Invest the tax savings in an equity mutual fund. Investing your tax savings in a good quality, lower-risk, equity mutual fund may enhance your returns and mitigate some of the risk attached to the LSVCC.
- Increase the foreign holdings in your registered plan where possible (foreign securities provide geographic diversification and, based on historical performance, may improve your overall returns). You see, holding LSVCCs in your RRSP will boost your foreign content entitlement by $3 for every $1 invested in the LSVCC—to a maximum of 50 percent foreign content.
- Liquidate your LSVCC shares as soon as your eight-year holding period is over, then reinvest in more LSVCCs for more credits! There used to be a three-year "cooling off" period whereby you couldn't receive more tax credits for an LSVCC investment if you had redeemed LSVCC shares in the last three years. This problem was done away with in August 1998.

TO MAKE A LONG STORY SHORT:

- LSVCCs offer generous tax credits to investors, usually worth up to $1,500 annually in most provinces, and are RRSP-eligible.

- Keep your annual LSVCC investment down to $5,000, since you won't receive credits for amounts over this.

- Use your tax savings from an LSVCC investment to make another RRSP contribution or to invest in a good quality equity mutual fund.

- Adjust the amount of foreign content you hold in your registered plan where possible after adding an LSVCC investment and recycle your tax credits by selling your LSVCC shares after the eight-year holding period and reinvesting in an LSVCC again.

Tim's Tip 53: Look at flow-through shares for a tax deduction and diversification.

My friend Paul has a good sense of humour, and an even better nine iron. On the way home from a round of golf last summer, he kept me in stitches in the car as he relayed one joke after another. I don't know how he remembers them all. At one point he proclaimed, "Tim, I need some gas."

Thinking he was trying to be funny, I responded, "Great, let's stop for some spicy Mexican food."

He looked at me, straight-faced, and said, "No, I'm talking about my investment portfolio. I have absolutely no exposure to hard assets, and I've heard there are some tax breaks available in the resource sector. Is it true?" He was serious.

"Well, yeah, flow-through shares can offer some tax breaks," I said.

I spent the next half-hour explaining to Paul the benefits and risks of flow-through shares. Let me give you the highlights.

Flow-Through Share Basics

Flow-through shares can provide attractive investment returns in addition to the direct tax savings that so many Canadians like Paul are looking for. A flow-through share is a creative, but higher-risk, investment issued by Canadian resource companies looking to raise capital for exploration and development. These shares are designed to provide the investor with tax deductions that generally equal the value of the amount invested—or come close to it.

You see, these resource companies are able to renounce certain deductions and flow them through to the individual investor so that the investor can claim the deduction instead. I'm talking primarily about Canadian exploration expenses (CEE), which are 100-percent deductible by the investor, and Canadian

Many investors and financial advisors today are considering whether it makes sense to build up a retirement nest egg outside rather than inside an RRSP. The argument is that withdrawals from a registered plan in retirement are fully taxable, whereas you'll be taxed only on the growth in your assets when investing outside an RRSP or RRIF—and that tax will apply at capital gains tax rates to boot. There is some validity to this argument, although you'll give up an RRSP deduction if you forgo RRSP contributions. Investing a little money in flow-through shares can provide that deduction. See more on the issue of RRSPs versus non-registered investments in Tip 62.

development expenses (CDE), which are 30-percent deductible on a declining balance basis. The fact is, a resource company can renounce these expenditures up to one year before incurring the actual costs. That's right, a company issuing flow-through shares in 2002 is able to renounce its eligible expenditures in calendar 2002 without actually incurring those expenses until the year 2003.

Flow-Through Tax Facts

As I said, flow-through shares provide a tax deduction to the investor that is typically equal to the amount invested in the shares. The deduction doesn't usually come all in one year, but you can expect about 90 percent of it in the first year, with the balance in the second and perhaps the third year. Under Canadian tax law, flow-through shares are automatically given an adjusted cost base of nil. This means that any sale of a flow-through share will give rise to a guaranteed taxable capital gain. But don't let this scare you off. In fact, there may be some tax planning opportunities here. If, for example, you have capital losses to use up, investing in flow-through shares that provide a capital gain down the road will guarantee a way to use some or all of those losses.

Take a look at some of these other tax uses for flow-through shares:

• Minimize the tax hit on RRSP and RRIF withdrawals. The tax deductions available from the flow-through shares can offset the taxable income created by the withdrawal.

• Reduce the clawback of Old Age Security (OAS) or other benefits. The deductions from flow-through shares can help to reduce your net income and minimize the clawback of these social benefits.

- Mitigate the tax impact of receiving a bonus. A taxable bonus from your employer can push your tax bill up significantly, and can even push you into a higher marginal tax bracket. The deduction from the flow-through shares can help to reduce this burden.
- Provide additional deductions once RRSPs have been maximized. Where you haven't got additional RRSP contribution room, flow-through shares can provide the same effect.
- Reduce the tax impact of realized capital gains. Have you sold any of your assets at a profit this year? If so, the tax deduction from flow-through shares can provide some relief from the taxable capital gain.

Risks and Returns

But the question remains: What kind of return can you expect from a flow-through share? The table shows that you can achieve a 25-percent after-tax return on your investment if you sell your shares for the same price you paid. If you sell the shares for a different price, this return will increase or decrease. You might be interested in knowing that flow-through shares also provide some downside protection. You see,

RETURN ON A FLOW-THROUGH SHARE	
Purchase price of shares[1]	$ (10,000)
Tax savings from deductions claimed[2]	$ 5,000
Proceeds received on sale of shares[3]	$ 10,000
Tax on capital gain on sale[4]	$ (2,500)
Dollar return on investment	$ 2,500
Percentage return on investment after taxes	25.0%

Notes:
1. Shares are purchased for $10,000.
2. Tax savings equal $10,000 x 50% marginal tax rate.
3. Shares are sold at the same price for which they were purchased.
4. Tax on capital gain: $10,000 × 50% inclusion rate × 50% tax rate.

even if your shares drop in value by one-third, you'll still break even thanks to the tax savings you enjoy, assuming a marginal tax rate of 50 percent.

There's no doubt that these shares are higher-risk investments and will fluctuate in value with changes in resource prices or interest rates. As resource prices fall, so will the value of your flow-through shares. And a rise in interest rates may cause the same effect as interest-bearing investments become more attractive relative to these shares. The bottom line? You wouldn't want to hold more than 5 to 10 percent of your portfolio in flow-throughs. Nevertheless, oil and gas securities can play an important role in a well diversified portfolio, and flow-through shares offer tax breaks that little else can today. Your best bet may be to take advantage of the diversification and experienced management offered through a limited partnership or mutual fund that invests in flow-through shares.

Speak to a financial advisor to find out more, or to buy flow-through shares.

TO MAKE A LONG STORY SHORT:

- Flow-through shares are shares in resource companies that are undertaking exploration and development. These shares provide a tax deduction that is typically equal to the amount invested.

- Because of the tax deduction, there are many practical uses for flow-through shares in tax planning.

- These are higher-risk investments that should not form more than 5 to 10 percent of your portfolio.

Tim's Tip 54: Understand the new breed of mutual funds designed for capital protection and tax-smart returns.

If one thing can be said about Canadians, it's that we like a sure bet. We're not known around the world as being risk-lovers. And when it comes to investing, we want to protect our capital even more than we want to see our Olympic hockey team win a gold medal—and that's saying a lot. Mutual fund companies recognize this, and some even understand the importance of minimizing taxes annually. The result? New breeds of mutual funds that are designed to protect your capital and offer tax-smart returns at the same time.

Now, the funds that offer capital protection and tax-efficiency come in many shapes and sizes. Not all are alike. I want to focus on two common types.

Money Market Corporate Funds

I spoke about corporate mutual funds in Tip 51. These are simply mutual funds structured as classes of shares of a particular corporation, rather than as trusts. You'll typically find a money market fund (see my talk about money market investments in Tip 47) in any corporate group of funds. These are safe, conservative funds. Unlike money market funds that are structured as trusts, a corporate money market fund provides the opportunity to pay tax on your returns as capital gains, not interest income. Taxes on capital gains are just one-half of taxes on the equivalent amount of interest income.

How do the funds accomplish this? Simple. A mutual fund corporation cannot make distributions of interest income under our tax law. Rather, only capital gains and Canadian dividends are distributed by way of T-slips to investors. Interest income earned inside a mutual fund corporation is taxed in that corporation rather than being distributed. In most cases, the expenses of operating all the funds in the corporation will be used to reduce the tax liability on this interest income to the corporation. It's then possible for the fund company to reinvest that interest income in more assets in the money market fund. The result?

> Beware of mutual funds that make regular distributions of capital gains to you. You can identify these funds since you'll receive a T3 or T5 slip at tax time reporting those gains. A fund that distributes primarily capital gains is likely invested in equities. While capital gains are a tax-smart type of income, *you* should control the timing of those gains, not the fund manager. You may be better off choosing a fund with a buy-and-hold strategy where there are no or low distributions. You can then choose the timing of your capital gains tax hit by selling the units or shares of the fund at your own pace. Take back control of your annual tax liability!

Caution!

The value of shares in the fund will increase over time. When will you be taxed on this increase? When you sell the shares of the corporate money market fund, of course. Here's the best news: The profits on your sale will be taxed as capital gains— not as interest income. And let's not forget that your capital is protected. After all, the money market fund invests your money in cash and near-cash investments.

Capital-Protected Closed-End Funds

A closed-end mutual fund is simply a fund that will be closed to new investment once a predetermined amount of money has been invested in the fund. In recent days, a new breed of closed-end fund has emerged, designed to protect your capital and provide tax-smart cash flow. Here's how this type of fund typically works:

- The money you invest is split into two nearly equal parts: (1) the fixed portion, and (2) the managed portion.
- The fixed portion is typically invested in a number of stocks, but is subject to a forward contract so that the fund is guaranteed, after a 10- or 12-year period, to get back a certain dollar amount (your original capital). Presto, there's your capital protection.
- The managed portion is invested in a diversified portfolio of high quality, large-cap companies. In order to provide you with a stream of income, the money manager will typically then write covered call options on those investments. Writing covered calls provides the fund with income that can then be distributed to you, the investor. Premiums from writing covered calls are generally taxed as capital gains. Presto, there's your tax-smart income.

What are the risks of capital-protected closed-end funds? Consider these:

- Upside gain potential is limited due to the covered call writing.
- The fund may not reach its targeted distributions if the volatility of the options market subsides and premiums from writing covered calls diminish.
- As interest rates rise, other investments could offer higher pre-tax yields, which could cause the value of your investment in the fund to fall.
- To the extent the fund holds non-Canadian securities, there may be a foreign currency exchange risk.

- Closed-end funds have traditionally traded at a discount to their net asset value. This should not be a concern, however, where the fund company agrees to redeem the investment at net asset value (as most are doing today).

Be sure to speak to a trusted financial advisor about the various funds available today that can offer capital protection and tax-smart income.

TO MAKE A LONG STORY SHORT:

- There are a growing number of funds available that offer capital protection and tax-smart income.

- Two common types of funds to consider are money market corporate mutual funds and capital-protected closed-end funds.

Tim's Tip 55: **Consider an investment in a private company in certain situations.**

There are two general types of private companies you might consider investing in: (1) a holding company designed primarily to earn investment income, and (2) an active business corporation. Let's take a look at these separately.

Holding Companies

As a general rule, there has been no use setting up a corporation to hold investments over the last few years because there has been no real opportunity to defer tax by earning income in the corporation as there was in the past. While this is still the case generally (although there will be a slight tax deferral available in Ontario starting in 2003), there are other things that can be accomplished by investing inside a corporation. It's time to think outside the typical tax box.

There are four potential benefits to setting up an investment holding corporation. They are:

- to minimize clawback of Old Age Security benefits
- to minimize taxes on death

- to minimize probate fees
- to provide a source for earned income

Is this idea for everyone? Absolutely not. But if you have significant open money (investments outside your RRSP or RRIF)—generally $300,000 or more—then the idea could be for you. Consider Ruth.

---

*R**uth is 67 years young and makes withdrawals from her RRSP every year, but her main source of income is the interest she earns on $500,000 worth of investments. Because of this interest income, she suffers a clawback of her Old Age Security benefits.*

Here's what she did: Ruth transferred the $500,000 of investments to a new holding company. This was set up as a loan by Ruth to the company. Now, the interest income earned on the investments is no longer reported by Ruth on her personal tax return—it's taxed in the corporation instead. As a result, her clawback problem is minimized. Next, the company is going to declare—but not pay—a dividend to Ruth each year that is equal to the after-tax earnings of the company. Since Ruth needs the investment earnings to meet her costs of living, she withdraws the after-tax income earned by the company each year as a tax-free repayment of the loan the company owes her. Alternatively, she could take a director's fee or salary from the corporation each year, which would count as earned income—providing her with RRSP contribution room.

Upon her death, two things may happen. First, the dividends still owing to her (that were declared but not paid) will be taxed, but may be reported on a separate tax return called a rights or things return—which will save her tax. Finally, Ruth may be able to pass the shares in her private company to her heirs without probate, by way of a separate will, since the family won't require probate on these shares.

Whoa. Did you catch all that? Let's look at the benefits of an investment holding company once again—in slow motion.

First, you may be able to minimize or eliminate a clawback on OAS benefits by removing income from your personal tax return. You see, when you put your assets into the corporation, the company will report the income and pay the tax from that point forward.

Second, you can minimize taxes upon death. By having the company declare but not pay dividends each year equal to the after-tax earnings of the company, you create an asset for yourself—a dividend receivable. Upon your death, this asset can be reported on a separate tax return called a *rights or things* return. This separate return entitles you to the basic personal credit all over again ($7,634 for 2002) and a lower marginal tax rate on the first $31,677 of income.

By the way, if you need cash flow during your lifetime, you can withdraw cash from the company as a repayment of the loan you made when you transferred your investments to the company. Once this loan has been repaid, the company could make good on the dividends it owes to you.

Third, probate fees may be minimized. Here's how: Since family members are shareholders and directors of the company, and heirs of any shares, it may be possible to pass these shares to your heirs through a separate and non-probatable will. After all, who in your family will require probate in this case?

> If you're going to set up an investment holding corporation, keep the following in mind:
> - you won't be able to transfer your RRSP or RRIF assets to the company;
> - the company will pay taxes at about 50 percent on its investment income, so you're not likely to save any income tax on an annual basis, but the other benefits may still make the idea worthwhile;
> - there will be costs to set up the corporation and annual accounting fees for filing tax returns and financial statements.
>
> The moral: Don't try this idea at home. Visit a tax pro!
>
> **Caution!**

Probably no one. But these shares must pass to your heirs outside of your original will, which may have to go through probate. Speak to your lawyer about this idea. It's based on an Ontario court decision in *Granovsky v. The Queen* (1998).

Finally, the corporation can be a source of earned income for you. Earned income is most commonly paid in the form of director's fees or salary and will provide you with RRSP contribution room that will benefit you while you're under age 69—and sometimes beyond (see Chapter 6, Tip 70).

Active Businesses

It's time to take a look at the tax benefits of investing in the shares of a small private company that carries on an active business. Sometimes this type of company

If you haven't yet used up your enhanced capital gains exemption, consider making use of it today. A study on business taxation was undertaken on behalf of our government, and a document known as the *Mintz Report* was released in the spring of 1998, recommending that the exemption be eliminated. Don't delay! Visit a tax pro to determine whether it's worth your while and whether you're able to claim the exemption.

is referred to as a Canadian-controlled private corporation (CCPC). A CCPC is simply a corporation that is not controlled by a public corporation or by non-residents of Canada, and is not listed on a prescribed Canadian stock exchange or certain foreign stock exchanges. Typically, these are small to medium-sized companies and normally include most Canadian businesses—maybe even the one next door, or your own business. There can be a number of tax benefits to owning shares in this type of company. Read on.

Enhanced Capital Gains Exemption

If you own shares in a small business, and those shares increase in value over time, there's a strong possibility that you'll be able to shelter up to $500,000 of that increase from tax—through the $500,000 enhanced capital gains exemption. To be eligible, your small company shares will have to be *qualified small business corporation* (QSBC) shares. Using the full $500,000 exemption could save you $125,000 in taxes if your marginal tax rate is 50 percent.

What in the world are QSBC shares? In general, these are shares that you (or a related person) must have owned for a two-year period. In addition, the company must be a CCPC. Finally, the company must be using 90 percent or more of its assets to carry on an active business primarily in Canada, and the same must hold true for 50 percent or more of its assets throughout the two-year period you've owned the stock. Sound complex? The truth is, the definition has been simplified here. Be sure to have a tax pro review the company's financial statements to determine whether it qualifies for the $500,000 exemption.

Capital Gain Rollover

Thanks to the 2000 federal budget, it may be possible to dispose of your shares in your small private company and to defer the tax on any gain by reinvesting the proceeds in the shares of another small business corporation. In this case, your adjusted cost base of the new shares is simply reduced by the gain that you defer so that, eventually, you'll be taxed on that gain. Certain conditions must be met to qualify for this capital gain rollover, including these: you must acquire newly issued common shares from the treasury of the new small business; you must be an individual (not a trust); only dispositions after February 27, 2000, qualify; and there's a cap of $2 million (by reference to your adjusted cost base) on the number of shares on which you can defer your gain (this cap was $500,000 for dispositions between February 27, 2000, and October 18, 2000). To qualify, the new company you're investing in must have a carrying value for its assets of $50 million or less before and after your investment in the company. (This threshold is $2.5 million before your investment and $10 million after your investment for dispositions between February 27, 2000, and October 18, 2000.) Other requirements must also be met. Talk to a tax pro for more details if you think you qualify.

Allowable Business Investment Losses

Okay, so you're still not convinced that shares in a small business are worth owning—despite the enhanced capital gains exemption and the capital gain rollover. Too risky, right? But consider this: Your investment in that small business could also offer greater downside protection than other investments if the investment goes sour. Again, the company has to be a CCPC, and 90 percent or more of its assets must be used in an active business that operates primarily in Canada.

If it becomes evident that you'll never recover your investment in the small business, you'll be entitled to claim an *allowable business investment loss* (ABIL). This ABIL equals one-half of the invested money you've lost and can be deducted on your tax return against *any* source of income. Normally, when you lose money on shares you own, you've incurred a capital loss that can only be used to offset capital gains. You should also be aware that, where you've lent money to a small business instead of buying shares, you may still be eligible for ABIL treatment.

TSX Venture Exchange Stocks

If you happen to own stocks that trade on the TSX Venture Exchange, you might be interested in knowing that presently Tier 3 stocks trading on that exchange are not considered to be traded on a "prescribed" stock exchange. The result? Those stocks are currently considered to be private company shares for tax purposes. This means that you may be able to shelter gains on those shares with the enhanced capital gains exemption or consider any losses to be ABILs. The company will have to meet certain tests to qualify as a Small Business Corporation for these tax benefits, but a call to the company to determine whether it meets the test could save you some tax.

Qualified Farm Property

I talked about the enhanced capital gains exemption to shelter any gains on qualified small business corporation shares. This exemption is extended to shelter any capital gains on qualified farm property—which normally includes most family farms or farm quotas. There are some conditions that the farm property must meet to be eligible, so visit a tax pro to determine for sure whether you'll be eligible.

TO MAKE A LONG STORY SHORT:

- A private company that you invest in can take two forms: (1) a holding company, or (2) an active business corporation.

- A holding company may be used to reduce clawbacks on OAS, minimize taxes on death, reduce probate fees, and provide a source for earned income.

- An investment in an active business that is a Canadian-controlled private corporation can offer tax benefits in the form of an enhanced capital gains exemption if the shares increase in value, a capital gain rollover if the shares are sold, and an allowable business investment loss if the investment turns sour.

- Companies trading on the TSX Venture Exchange (Tier 3) may qualify for this capital gains exemption or ABIL treatment.

- Gains on qualified farm property can also be sheltered using the enhanced capital gains exemption.

Sheltering Income with Life Insurance

Tim's Tip 56: Consider an exempt life insurance policy for tax-sheltered growth.

There's no doubt about it: Life insurance can be confusing—and downright intimidating. But don't let this stop you from considering life insurance as an investment tool. Is this for everyone? Nope. But it may be worth discussing the strategy with a trusted financial advisor who can crunch the numbers for your specific situation to see if the idea makes sense.

As an investment tool, an exempt life insurance policy can provide a tax shelter offered by little else. You see, under an exempt policy, a portion of each premium that you pay will cover the cost of your insurance, and the balance will be deposited in a growing pool of investments. The policy is called *exempt* because the investment component of the policy grows exempt from tax. That's right, tax-sheltered growth can be yours—much like what you experience with your RRSP. The best part of this is that, upon your death, the face value of the policy, plus the accumulated investments, are paid out on a tax-free basis to your beneficiaries.

I know what you're probably thinking: "Tim, the problem is that I can't enjoy those investments during my lifetime. I have to die for anyone to benefit here." Not true. You'll be able to access those investments in a number of ways.

For example, you can simply make withdrawals of the accumulated investments during your lifetime, although there could be a tax bill to pay when you do this. Alternatively, you could borrow using the investments in the policy as collateral. Upon your death, the life insurance proceeds would be used to pay off the debt. This last idea is called *leveraged life insurance*, and I like it in some cases, but the idea does come with some risks. Provided it's set up properly and conservatively, it can make sense for some.

Where will you find an exempt life insurance policy? Most whole life and universal policies are set up to be exempt, but not all policies are created equal. It's important to find out your investment options. Make sure you're able to invest in equities to maximize your investment growth over the long term. Speak to a financial advisor who is licensed to sell life insurance.

TO MAKE A LONG STORY SHORT:

- An exempt life insurance policy will allow the tax-sheltered growth of investments inside the policy.

- The face value of the policy plus the accumulated investments will be paid out tax-free to your beneficiaries upon your death.

- There are ways of accessing the investments in the policy during your lifetime, although there may be tax or interest costs involved in doing this.

Tim's Tip 57: Learn how to use cascading life insurance to shelter investment growth from tax for years.

Do yourself a favour. Speak to your insurance broker this week. Insurance brokers always have a good story or two about insurance claims. My broker recently shared with me the true story of Arlene Evans. You see, in December 1990, the Kansas Court of Appeals affirmed Arlene Evans' challenge to Provident Life and Accident Insurance Co.'s determination that her husband had committed suicide. Though he was found in his bathtub, clothed and charred, she said it was an accident, that he was a heavy smoker and had often burned himself. Her strongest argument was that he often struck matches after passing gas, to clear the air, and that the fire that killed him was started this way. Hey, accidents happen.

When you speak to your broker, ask about another insurance story: Cascading life insurance. It may not be as interesting as the story about Arlene Evans, but it'll save you more tax.

The Rules

The cascading insurance strategy takes advantage of Subsection 148(8) of our tax law, which will allow you to transfer ownership of a life insurance policy to any of your children, free of tax, where a child of yours is the life that is insured under the policy. (A "child" includes any natural or adopted child, a grandchild, stepchild, or a son- or daughter-in-law.)

On the surface, the idea may seem crazy. I mean, who's going to buy insurance on the life of a child? Glad you asked. Canadians who would like to pass assets to the next generation completely free of tax and probate, and then to subsequent generations in the same manner—hence the cascading effect—should consider the strategy.

The Strategy

The cascading insurance strategy takes advantage of the fact that it's possible to invest money inside a universal life insurance policy on a tax-sheltered basis (see Tip 56), and that the death benefit, along with the accumulated investments in the policy, are all paid out tax-free to the beneficiaries when the insured dies. The best way to understand cascading life insurance is to walk through an example. Consider Barbara.

Barbara is 70 years of age. She has $200,000 of non-registered money that she doesn't need to meet her costs of living. She wants to minimize her tax hit on the income from this money annually. In addition, she wants to shelter the money from tax and probate fees when she passes it to her daughter Allison, who is aged 35, and ultimately to her grandson Mark, Allison's son, who is a minor. Barbara purchased a universal life insurance policy and put the $200,000 into the policy over a five-year period. She named Allison as the contingent owner. The insurance is placed on Allison's life and Barbara's grandson Mark is the beneficiary. When Barbara dies, Allison will become the owner (since she was named the contingent owner) with the result that Allison will then own the accumulated investments inside the policy. The policy will pass to Allison free of tax and probate fees. What are Allison's options? She could make withdrawals from the accumulating investments in the policy (a taxable event), borrow money using the investments in the policy as collateral (providing her with tax-free cash flow), or she could reserve the whole policy for her son Mark (he'll receive the insurance proceeds free of tax and probate fees upon her death).

Cascading life insurance can be a terrific tax shelter strategy, provided you arrange it properly. Make sure that you name a child as the contingent owner on the policy, and another or the same child as the life that is insured. These two details are critical to ensuring a tax-free transfer of the policy at the time of your death under Subsection 148(8) of our tax law. It's also important that the policy transfer for no consideration (that is, free) to your child.

A cascading life insurance strategy allows you to accomplish a few things, including: transferring money to the next generation without giving up control during your lifetime; eliminating current taxes in your hands on the money invested in the policy; eliminating probate fees on the assets in the policy; and providing you with access to the funds in the policy if needed. Not a bad deal.

TO MAKE A LONG STORY SHORT:

• The cascading insurance strategy takes advantage of our tax law, which allows you to transfer ownership of a life insurance policy free of tax to any of your children when a child's life is insured under the policy.

• The strategy will allow you to transfer money to the next generation free of tax and probate fees, minimize annual tax on the investments placed inside the policy, and maintain control of and access to the funds in the policy during your lifetime.

• Your insurance broker may have some great stories to tell about insurance claims.

Tim's Tip 58: Establish a back-to-back prescribed annuity for tax-efficient cash flow.

Here's a clever idea for those of you who rely on interest-bearing investments for an income stream. It's called a back-to-back prescribed annuity, and it could really boost your income. Here's the deal: A back-to-back simply involves buying a prescribed annuity plus term insurance. The best way to understand this tactic is through a couple of examples. Let's look at Howard's situation, then Lily's.

*H*oward is 70 years old and has $100,000 invested in GICs paying 7.5 per-
cent interest, which provide him with $7,500 of income annually.
Howard's marginal tax rate is 50 percent, since he has other income sources too.
The bottom line is that Howard will pay taxes of $3,750 annually on his GIC
income, and will be left with $3,750 each year as disposable income. Howard
would like to leave the $100,000 to his children, so he likes the GICs because he
can use the interest generated without ever touching the $100,000 capital.

It's true that Howard's investment in GICs will successfully preserve his
$100,000 capital, but the interest income is highly taxed, and so he's left with very
little (just $3,750) each year. Lily's financial advisor had a better idea. Here's her
story.

*L*ily is also 70 years of age and has $100,000 that used to be invested in
GICs, providing the same $3,750 after taxes that Howard receives. Lily's
advisor had another plan: to use a back-to-back prescribed annuity. Here's
what Lily did: She bought a prescribed life annuity with the $100,000 she had
sitting in GICs. The annuity will pay her $12,491 a year. Since only a portion
of each annuity payment is taxable, the tax on the annuity will be just $2,077
each year. You see, each annuity payment is made up of interest income plus a
return of capital, and the capital is returned tax-free. The interest portion
attracts some tax—but much less than she was paying with the GICs. After
taxes, Lily is left with $10,414 ($12,491 minus $2,077) which is much higher
than the $3,750 she received annually with the GICs.

The moral of the story is that a prescribed annuity can provide much more cash
than GICs and similar investments, and a smaller tax bill to boot. The drawback?
Each time Lily receives an annuity payment, she's getting back some of her original
$100,000 capital, so that she won't be able to leave her children the $100,000 that
she could have with the GICs. In fact, aside from buying an annuity with a guaranteed payment period, there's no way to leave any of that $100,000 to her kids,
since the insurance company will keep whatever's left of her capital on her death.

But there is a solution. With the extra cash she's receiving, Lily can buy a term-to-100 life insurance policy that will pay her children $100,000 when she dies. The cost of the policy? About $3,281 each year. So follow the numbers here. Lily takes the $10,414 she has been receiving after taxes, pays her insurance premiums of $3,281, and is still left with $7,133 in her pocket each year. This $7,133 is a full $3,383 more than the $3,750 of after-tax income she used to receive on her GICs.

Now you'll understand why this strategy is called a back-to-back prescribed annuity. The idea involves buying both a life annuity and an insurance policy back-to-back.

Did You Know?

A "prescribed" annuity is different from other annuities. Normally, payments in the early years of an annuity are mostly taxable interest income, with only a small portion being a tax-free return of capital. Under a prescribed annuity, the taxable interest portion remains constant from one payment to the next. This means that in the early years of a prescribed annuity, you'll actually report less taxable interest than you would have otherwise. What a great tax deferral!

There's one more twist on this strategy that you might want to consider. It may be a very good idea to take some of the additional cash generated from the back-to-back annuity and invest in good quality equity mutual funds to protect yourself against inflation and provide an emergency fund. You see, when you buy a life annuity, the interest rate is locked in at the start, and it's a very expensive option to arrange for indexed annuity payments that increase each year with inflation. By investing just a portion of your capital in a back-to-back prescribed annuity (enough to beat the cash flow from the GIC), buying term-to-100 insurance, and investing the rest in equity mutual funds, you will have significantly improved your financial health by reducing taxes, providing a hedge against inflation, and setting aside an emergency fund.

To set this idea in motion, just visit a financial advisor who is licensed to sell life insurance.

TO MAKE A LONG STORY SHORT:

- A back-to-back prescribed annuity involves buying a life annuity to provide increased cash flow and then buying a term-to-100 life insurance policy to replace the capital used to buy the annuity.

- Take this a step further by using some of the additional cash to invest in good quality equity mutual funds as a hedge against inflation and to provide an emergency fund.

Borrowing to Invest: Upvesting

Tim's Tip 59: Consider "upvesting" to accelerate wealth creation and provide tax deductions.

First of all, what is this strategy called *upvesting* all about? Upvesting is really nothing more than *prudently* borrowing money to invest. You've heard the strategy referred to as "leveraged investing" in the past. Upvesting is a term that accurately describes what it is that you're trying to accomplish by borrowing to invest: increasing—or "upping"—your effective rate of return and accelerating the wealth creation process.

The Rewards of Upvesting

There are definite potential rewards to upvesting. Consider these five rewards:

- **Reward 1:** Upvesting is a forced investment plan. The money you borrow is invested up front, and you pay for this investment through required monthly loan payments.
- **Reward 2:** You can build wealth using another's resources. Where you've got cash flow, but little in the way of investments, you can use someone else's resources to jump-start the wealth accumulation process.

- **Reward 3:** Upvesting can boost your effective returns. While upvesting won't improve your *actual* returns, it can increase your *effective* returns (see Jack's example below).
- **Reward 4:** You can reach your financial goals faster. Upvesting gets more money working for you sooner than you might otherwise be able to achieve. The result? You may be able to reach your financial goals sooner.
- **Reward 5:** Upvesting can create a tax deduction for interest costs. Let's not forget about tax deductions. Interest costs are generally deductible for tax purposes when you've invested the borrowed money. I'll talk more about this in Tip 60.

Jack borrowed $50,000 to add to his own $50,000 available to invest, for a total portfolio of $100,000. He earned a 10-percent pre-tax return on the total portfolio last year, or $10,000—all in capital growth. Jack is paying interest of 8 percent on the loan, which cost him $4,000 ($50,000 multiplied by 8 percent) last year. After all taxes and interest have been paid, Jack managed to put $5,500 in his pocket last year. This represents an 11-percent after-tax rate of return for Jack ($5,500 as a percentage of his own $50,000 is 11 percent). That's right, his portfolio grew by 10 percent before tax (which is 7.5 percent after tax given our assumptions), but Jack's effective rate of return was 11 percent after tax! That is, if Jack had not borrowed any money, his after-tax return would have been 7.5 percent. His upvesting strategy, however, created an effective return of 11 percent after tax.

Jack's story is spelled out more clearly in the table below.

You'll notice from the table that upvesting can magnify your returns so that your effective return is higher than you could achieve without borrowing money. In Jack's example, a 7.5 percent after-tax return was magnified to 11 percent after taxes.

EFFECTIVE RETURNS FROM UPVESTING				
		No Upvesting: 10-Percent Gain	Upvesting: 10-Percent Gain	Upvesting: 10-Percent Loss
Personal money	(A)	$100,000	$ 50,000	$ 50,000
Borrowed money[1]	(B)		$ 50,000	$ 50,000
Total invested		$100,000	$100,000	$100,000
Return on investment		$ 10,000	$ 10,000	$ (10,000)
Less: Interest costs[2]		$ —	$ (4,000)	$ (4,000)
Add: Tax savings from interest deduction[3]		$ —	$ 2,000	$ 2,000
Less: Tax on capital gain[4]		$ (2,500)	$ (2,500)	$ 2,500
After-tax returns ($)	(C)	$ 7,500	$ 5,500	$ (9,500)
Effective after-tax return (%)[5]		7.50%	11.00%	−19.00%

Notes:
1. Assume a 1:1 loan.
2. Assume interest rate on loan of 8%.
3. Assume interest costs are deductible; marginal tax rate is 50%.
     Tax savings from interest deduction = 50% of interest paid.
4. Tax on capital gain = $10,000 × 50% inclusion rate × 50% MTR = $2,500; assume capital losses can be applied against other gains in the year.
5. Effective after-tax returns = After-tax returns (Line C) divided by Personal money (Line A), multiplied by 100.

The Risks of Upvesting

Now, before you hop on the upvesting bandwagon, you need to understand the downside potential too. Check out the above table one more time. What would have happened if Jack's portfolio had lost 10 percent of its value last year, rather than gaining 10 percent? Jack's effective loss from a 10-percent decline in value would have been 19 percent! And this calculation assumes that Jack would be able to use the capital loss to offset capital gains on other investments. If he were unable to use the capital losses in this manner, his effective loss would have been 24 percent for the year! Yikes.

The concept of *upvesting*, or borrowing to invest, is going to become more widely understood and used by Canadians over the next few years. The reason? More Canadians are preparing for retirement in the next 15 years than we have seen in our history, and many will have to consider upvesting to ensure they have enough money to support themselves. Make sure you understand upvesting before taking part! For more information on the risks, rewards, and rules of upvesting, ask a trusted financial advisor to provide you with a copy of the booklet *Don't Just Invest, Upvest* written by me and published by AIC Limited.

As you can see, upvesting is great when your portfolio is growing in value. But when your investments drop in value, the effective loss can sting. In fact, the risks of upvesting include the following:

• **Risk 1:** Your investments could drop in value. We just discussed this one.

• **Risk 2:** Interest rates could rise. As interest rates rise, the break-even rate of return you'll need in order to make upvesting profitable will also rise.

• **Risk 3:** Your cash flow could suffer. Cash flow is critical. If you run short on cash, you may be forced to sell investments at a bad time to meet loan payments.

• **Risk 4:** Margin calls could be made. Depending on the type of loan you assume, you may be required to come up with more cash, or liquidate investments, in the case of a margin call. A margin call can arise if your investments start dropping in value.

• **Risk 5:** Tax deductions could be disallowed. A deduction for interest costs is generally available when borrowing to invest—but it's not guaranteed. If interest costs are not deductible, the break-even rate of return in order for upvesting to work will increase. I'll talk more about interest deductibility in Tip 60.

• **Risk 6:** You might just get greedy. Getting greedy could cause you to borrow more than you should. You then run the risk of not being able to meet loan payments if interest rates rise or your cash flow suffers.

• **Risk 7:** You could lose sleep at night. Upvesting could keep you up at night if you're not conservative in how much you borrow.

The Rules of Prudent Upvesting

Don't let the risks I've just mentioned scare you too much. As long as you follow the rules of prudent upvesting, you'll largely be able to manage those risks. Here are the eight rules you should follow:

- **Rule 1:** Understand the risks and rewards of upvesting. I've talked briefly about these risks and rewards above.
- **Rule 2:** Borrow only a reasonable amount of money. As a general rule, don't borrow more than 30 percent of your net worth.
- **Rule 3:** Make sure you've got sufficient and stable cash flow. Stay conservative. If you can afford loan payments of, say, $300 monthly, then take out a loan that will cost you $100 monthly—about 30 percent of what you can afford. This leaves room for increases to interest rates or other changes in your circumstances. Upvesting is only for those with a stable source of cash flow.
- **Rule 4:** Upvest for the long term only. Over the long term—10 years or more—there is a greater probability that your investments will have increased in value—which is critical when upvesting. Over the short term, your investments could be up or down—who knows?
- **Rule 5:** Invest in equity mutual funds. Equity funds offer the diversification that is so critical to upvesting prudently. Further, you'll receive the benefit of professional money management and the potential tax benefits offered by the capital gains refund mechanism (CGRM). See Tip 51 for more on the CGRM.
- **Rule 6:** Keep your interest costs deductible. Deductible interest costs will reduce your break-even rate of return required to benefit from upvesting.
- **Rule 7:** Choose the most appropriate type of loan. I like loans that have no potential for margin calls (a home equity loan, for example). An interest-only loan requires payments of interest only each month, which will enable you to borrow more money for a given monthly payment. If your cash flow is stable and sufficient, I prefer this type of loan. Granted, a blended payment of principal and interest is more conservative since the loan balance drops over time.
- **Rule 8:** Work with a trusted financial advisor. This is key. You see, a good advisor will ensure that your emotions don't drive bad investment decisions. Upvesting can be an emotional experience if your investments drop in value. Your advisor is there to help you stick to a proper game plan.

TO MAKE A LONG STORY SHORT:

- Upvesting is the idea of *prudently* borrowing money to invest.

- Upvesting can significantly increase your effective rate of return. It can also magnify your losses.

- Be sure to understand the rewards, risks, and rules of prudent upvesting before trying the strategy.

- Find more information on upvesting in the booklet *Don't Just Invest, Upvest* written by me and published by AIC Limited. Your financial advisor can get you a copy.

Tim's Tip 60: **Deduct as much of your interest cost as possible.**

Generally, the tax collector will allow you a deduction for your interest costs when you've borrowed for business purposes or to make investments. But a deduction is not guaranteed.

The Rules

Our tax law says that you're entitled to claim a deduction for your interest costs if you've used the borrowed money to invest in a business or to earn income from property. Income from property includes interest, dividends, rents, and royalties—but not capital gains. As a result, there's been much debate about whether or not it's possible to invest in equity mutual funds or stocks that are expected to grow in value but are not likely to result in dividend income or interest. I've got good news to share with you. The tax collector's policy is generally to allow an interest deduction, even where you're borrowing to invest in publicly traded growth shares or equity mutual funds. This was confirmed by three technical interpretations issued by the Canada Customs and Revenue Agency (CCRA): Documents 2000-0036435 (July 17, 2000), 1999-0014010 (December 7, 1999) and 9917535 (June 24, 1999). Further, the Supreme Court of Canada decision in *Ludco Enterprises Inc.* v. *The Queen* (2001) supports the notion that an interest deduction should be available, even when your primary objective is to earn capital growth over time.

This policy only makes sense. Where you're investing in publicly traded securities or equity funds, you're going to be taxed on any capital gains realized on those investments. In addition, these investments typically have the potential to generate dividends or interest income. One word of caution: Where you're investing in a specific investment that has absolutely no potential for dividends, interest, rents, or royalties because of the legal structure of the investment, you should expect CCRA to disallow any interest deduction where you've borrowed to make that investment. In addition, CCRA is expected to release new information about the deductibility of interest costs very soon. Speak to a tax pro about these pronouncements.

Keep It Deductible

If you're not careful, you could lose your interest deduction in future years. You see, the tax collector is going to trace your borrowed money to its current use to determine whether the interest remains deductible year after year. Let's say, for argument's sake, that you borrow $100,000 to invest in units of a mutual fund, and your units grow to a total of $150,000. At that time, you sell $50,000 of those units. If your loan remains outstanding after this sale, what portion of your interest will remain deductible? The tax collector will look to where your sale proceeds are today. If you were to reinvest those proceeds of $50,000, you'd be entitled to continue deducting the full amount of the interest on your loan. If, however, you took that $50,000 and used it for personal purposes—to take a vacation, renovate your home, pay down debt, or even pay down interest on your debt—you'd lose the ability to deduct one-third ($50,000 is one-third of $150,000) of your remaining interest costs.

> ## Did You Know?
>
> The Supreme Court of Canada recently heard the case *The Queen v. Singleton*, which confirms your interest deductibility where you've completed a debt swap. A debt swap is a strategy where you liquidate an existing investment, pay off some non-deductible debt (a mortgage, for example) with the proceeds, and then borrow to replace those investments. This strategy allows you to convert non-deductible interest into deductible interest since the newly borrowed money is used for investment. In recent years there was some doubt as to whether or not this strategy would work. On September 28, 2001, the Supreme Court confirmed its validity!

Consider these ideas to keep your interest deductible:

Skim the interest, dividends, or other income from property (but not capital gains) from your leveraged investments before these amounts are reinvested, and spend this income in any way you'd like. This won't jeopardize your interest deduction because you're not dipping into your principal, or invested capital. However, once this income is reinvested in additional units or shares, it forms part of your capital, and you may run into an interest deductibility problem when you make withdrawals later.

Pay down your investment loans with the interest or dividends you've skimmed from your investments or with another source of cash. Do not, however, use a portion of the capital you've invested with borrowed money to pay down the debt or interest on the debt, unless you're willing to lose a portion of your interest deduction on the balance of the loan. Of course, if you liquidate your investments to pay off your investment loan in one shot, the interest deduction is no longer an issue, since the debt is gone.

Beware of certain advice being passed around today that could leave you with a nasty tax surprise. The strategy is this: Take out a home equity loan, invest the money in mutual funds, liquidate some of those mutual fund units monthly to make payments to the bank on that home equity loan, and then claim a deduction at tax time for the full amount of the interest paid on the loan. Sorry, the interest deduction part of the story doesn't work as advertised. You see, you're using the proceeds from the mutual fund redemptions for a non-income-producing purpose—to pay down debt or interest on the debt. The result? You can expect to lose a portion of your interest deduction.

TO MAKE A LONG STORY SHORT:

- Interest is normally deductible when the borrowed money is used for business or investment purposes. CCRA has confirmed that borrowing to invest in growth shares or equity mutual funds will still give rise to interest deductibility.

- The tax collector will look to your current use of borrowed money to determine whether your interest costs will remain deductible. Keep your borrowed money invested to preserve interest deductions.

Getting into the Game

From mutual funds to flow-through shares, investing properly can make you a clear winner in the tax game. Turn now to the Tax Planning Tip Sheet at the front of the book and review the strategies you've read about in Chapter 5. Ask yourself, "Can this tip apply to me?" When you've finished this book, take your Tip Sheet to a tax professional if you'd like more information on each strategy or help in implementing the ideas.

Action Step

If you borrowed to make an investment that subsequently turned sour, then sold this investment at a loss, be sure to continue deducting a portion of your interest costs. You see, Section 20.1 of the *Income Tax Act* says that you'll be able to continue deducting the interest on your *loss portion* of the investment. This applies to dispositions after 1993 (except for sales of real estate or depreciable assets). But the rules are complex enough to leave your head spinning, so visit a tax pro for help.

EARNING THE GOLD GLOVE: STRATEGIES FOR RETIREMENT

"If you don't know where you're going you might not get there."
~Yogi Berra

6

In major league baseball, the Gold Glove is a coveted symbol of achievement. It's awarded to the best fielders in the game—those who rarely make mistakes when the ball comes their way. To earn it, you've got to keep your head up and your errors down. Most important, you've got to know the turf.

You know, retirement planning is a lot like that. If you want to make the most of your golden years, you've got to be alert, keep your mistakes to a minimum, and understand the world of retirement planning. It's going to take some perseverance and good coaching. Tell you what: You provide the perseverance and I'll provide the coaching. Sound good? Great.

Understanding RRSP Basics

A Registered Retirement Savings Plan (RRSP) is a plan registered with the Canada Customs and Revenue Agency (CCRA) that is designed to encourage and help you save for your retirement. While placing some of your retirement savings outside an RRSP can make sense in some situations (which I'll talk about in Tip 62), the general rule is that an RRSP should form an important part of your retirement savings.

Tim's Tip 61: Contribute to an RRSP for tax deferral and tax-free growth.

Your RRSP offers two attractive benefits that can't be ignored: a tax deferral, and tax-free growth of your investments.

A Tax Deferral

Your RRSP contributions offer a deferral of tax because you'll be permitted to push a portion of your taxable income to a future year. No kidding. When you contribute to your RRSP within your contribution limit, the amount of that contribution may be deducted on your tax return, reducing your taxable income. You won't face tax on those funds until they're withdrawn from your RRSP—usually in a much later year.

For example, suppose you contribute $5,000 to your RRSP at age 35. So long as this is within your contribution limit, you'll be able to deduct the full amount from your total income. If your marginal tax rate is 50 percent, your tax saving will be $2,500 in the year you make the contribution. Now let's say you leave the $5,000 to grow in your RRSP until you reach age 65 and then withdraw $5,000 from your plan. In that year—a full 30 years later—you'll face a $2,500 tax bill. Here's what you could do now to pay that $2,500 tax bill 30 years down the road: You could take $578 today, invest it for 30 years at an after-tax return of 5 percent annually, and watch it grow to be worth $2,500 in 30 years. You could then pay your tax bill with that money. Because of the tax deferral resulting from your RRSP deduction, your tax bill would really cost just $578 in today's dollars, not $2,500. Effectively, you would have reduced your tax bill by pushing it to a future year. This is the value of tax deferral.

Tax-Free Growth

Your RRSP offers another significant benefit. I'm talking about tax-free growth inside the plan. Unlike many investments held outside your RRSP (your *open money*), the investments inside your RRSP will not be taxed as they grow each year, regardless of how much you earn inside the plan.

Don't underestimate the value of this tax-free growth! Just look at how much more you could have by investing inside your RRSP rather than outside. If you socked away $200 each month for 30 years and enjoyed annual growth on your money of 10 percent, you'd have $200,900 at the end of that period if you invested outside your RRSP, assuming an effective tax rate of 40 percent. But what if you made those same monthly contributions for the same length of time, earned that same 10 percent, but invested *inside* your RRSP? When all is said and done, your investments would be worth a whopping $452,100— more than double what you'd have outside your RRSP.

I should clarify something here. It may be possible to invest outside your RRSP in a manner that is very tax-efficient as well (more tax-efficient than my example above).

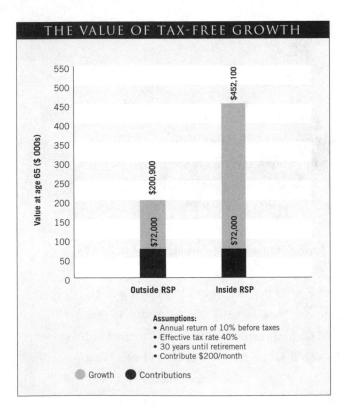

THE VALUE OF TAX-FREE GROWTH

Value at age 65 ($ 000s)

Outside RSP: $200,900 / $72,000
Inside RSP: $452,100 / $72,000

Assumptions:
- Annual return of 10% before taxes
- Effective tax rate 40%
- 30 years until retirement
- Contribute $200/month

Growth   Contributions

For example, investing in certain equity investments can be tax-smart (see Tip 47). In fact, it may be possible to nearly eliminate annual taxable income simply by buying and holding good quality equity investments. There are, for example, mutual funds that do not make significant distributions annually, if any. The AIC Advantage Fund is an example of an equity fund that hasn't made a taxable distribution since 1989 (as of the time of writing); speak to your financial advisor about tax-smart funds available.

The point is this: Investing outside your RRSP can work in addition to your RRSP when it comes to building a retirement nest egg—but only if it's done in a tax-smart manner. More on this in Tip 62.

Now, back to RRSPs. The earlier in life you start your RRSP contributions, the more you'll benefit from the tax-free growth. For example, suppose that you contributed $3,000 to your RRSP each year for 10 years, starting at age 30, and then left those funds to grow at 10 percent each year until you were 65. How much would you have at age 65? The graph shows a value of $518,030. Not bad on total contributions of just $30,000! But what if you waited just five short years until age 35 before making any RRSP contributions, and then contributed $3,000 every year until age 65—a total of $90,000 in contributions? At age 65 you'd have just $493,480. That's right, you'd end up with *less* by waiting five years, even though you would have invested more of your money.

The moral of the story is simple: The earlier you start your RRSP savings, the better off you'll be in retirement.

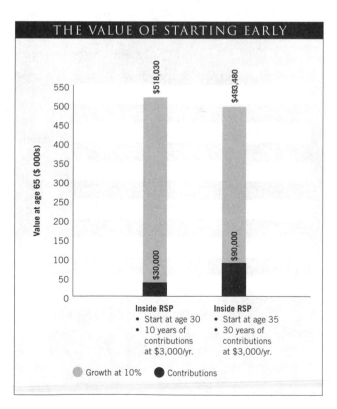

THE VALUE OF STARTING EARLY

Value at age 65 ($ 000s)

$518,030 — $30,000 — Inside RSP • Start at age 30 • 10 years of contributions at $3,000/yr.

$493,480 — $90,000 — Inside RSP • Start at age 35 • 30 years of contributions at $3,000/yr.

Growth at 10%   Contributions

TO MAKE A LONG STORY SHORT:

- An RRSP offers two significant benefits: a deferral of tax and tax-free growth inside the plan.

- The earlier in life that you start, the greater the benefit to you in retirement.

- Having some retirement savings outside an RRSP can make sense in some situations, but only where it's done in a tax-smart manner. More on this in Tip 62.

Tim's Tip 62: Recognize that it's possible to have too much in your RRSP.

I shared with my wife, Carolyn, last week that, at the pace we're going, we'll end up with far too much in our RRSPs in retirement. I nearly pushed her over the edge into the realm of amazement when I told her this. She wasn't so surprised that we'll have enough in retirement, but shocked that I suggested we'd have *too much* in our RRSPs. Like most Canadians, she believes that an RRSP is the cornerstone of any retirement savings program. To suggest that we'll have too much in an RRSP seems crazy to her.

Don't get me wrong here. I believe that having enough in your RRSP is a good thing. Having more in your RRSP than you need to support yourself comfortably in retirement, however, doesn't make sense. And why not? Simple. Every dollar that comes out of your RRSP is fully taxable. With the capital gains inclusion rate now at 50 percent, you can create a pretty tax-smart portfolio outside your RRSP as well.

RRSP Excess

I have met a growing number of Canadians who have too much inside their RRSPs. Some are taking advantage of a strategy called the "RRSP freeze." I believe there's a place for this strategy in some situations. Let's consider Charlie's example.

Charlie is a gentleman who is 50 and plans to retire at 65, just 15 years from now. He expects to live to about age 90 and wants to plan for an income in retirement until that age—a 25-year retirement period. Charlie wants a retirement income of $50,000 after taxes annually (in today's dollars) beginning at age 65. By the way, that $50,000 annually will equal $67,195 after taxes in the year Charlie reaches age 65, assuming a 3-percent inflation rate. The bottom line is that Charlie will need $1,700,500 in his RRSP at age 65 to provide him with the income he needs in retirement (assuming a 10-percent annual return and 3-percent inflation annually). Here's the issue: Charlie already has $490,000 in his RRSP today. Do the math. That $490,000 will turn into about $2,050,000 by the time Charlie reaches age 65— even if he doesn't make another RRSP contribution (assuming a 10-percent annual return). Do you follow? Charlie will have about $2.05 million in his RRSP at age 65, but only needs about $1.7 million. He'll have nearly $350,000 too much in his RRSP at age 65 even without further contributions.

Action Step

How much is enough in your RRSP? How do you know when you've got too much in your plan? First, you need to determine how much income you'd like each year in retirement, in today's dollars. Next, figure out how much money you need sitting in your RRSP on your retirement date to provide that income. You'll have to make assumptions about your rate of return on investments, inflation, tax rates, and perhaps how long you're going to live. Your best bet may be to visit a trusted financial advisor who can crunch the numbers for you.

The problem with having so much in an RRSP is that every dollar in the plan is fully taxable when withdrawn. Compare this to making withdrawals from an investment account outside of a registered plan where you'll face tax on any capital gains only. And just one-half of capital gains are taxable.

RRSP Freeze

What if there were a way for Charlie to remove some of the excess assets in his RRSP without any negative tax implications? Would it make sense? Arguably, it would—particularly when he could then invest those assets outside of his RRSP in a manner that would result in more in his hands after taxes later. Charlie has done that very thing. Here's how: Charlie borrowed $125,000 at 8-percent interest and invested the money in high quality, conservative equity mutual funds. Charlie makes interest-only payments on the loan, and the $10,000 of interest cost annually is deductible on his tax return. Charlie then withdraws $10,000 from his RRSP annually to pay the interest costs. The interest deduction offsets the taxable RRSP withdrawal so that he is effectively not taxed on the RRSP withdrawal.

What has Charlie really accomplished here? He has managed to convert some of his registered money (in his RRSP) into non-registered money on a tax-free basis. Think about it. The $125,000 that Charlie borrowed is invested and growing. It more than replaces the $10,000 withdrawn from the RRSP each year that was used to pay the interest costs on the loan. In fact, Charlie will end up with more after-tax money in retirement through this strategy for two reasons: (1) By borrowing and investing $125,000, Charlie gets more money working for him sooner (compared to simply leaving the $10,000 annually in the RRSP and not borrowing any money), and (2) the withdrawals from the non-registered investments are taxed at much lower rates since capital gains are just 50-percent taxable, and *only the growth* on the $125,000 is taxed. In Charlie's case, his *after-tax* retirement nest egg (dollars he can actually spend!) will be greater by $117,000 assuming a 10-percent investment return both inside and outside the RRSP over that 15-year period until he reaches age 65, and a marginal tax rate of 46.5 percent.

Some people refer to this strategy as the *RRSP meltdown*. I prefer to call it an *RRSP freeze*. To melt down an RRSP (that is, to actually reduce the amount of money in the RRSP over time) you've got to borrow a heckuva lot of money (upwards of twice the value of your RRSP may be necessary). An RRSP freeze is easier to accomplish and this is what Charlie did. A freeze simply caps the amount in the RRSP by making withdrawals annually to limit the growth in the plan.

Drawbacks

Okay, there have got to be some drawbacks to the RRSP freeze or meltdown, right? Right. Consider these.

- You've got to have too much in your RRSP already. Not everyone is in that situation. If you can't crunch the numbers to figure this out, visit a financial advisor who can help.

- Borrowing to invest has to make sense for you—but it's not for everyone. This is the most important issue when deciding whether or not to use the strategy. If you're not a good candidate to borrow money, the strategy is not for you (see Tip 59 for the criteria you should meet before borrowing money to invest).

- Your non-registered investments might be subject to tax annually that could reduce your growth outside the RRSP. You can mitigate against this problem by keeping portfolio turnover very low (see Tip 47 for more on turnover).

- The capital gains inclusion rate could be increased in the future, making non-registered investments less tax-efficient—although I believe that the likelihood of this is slim unless capital gains tax rates in the U.S. increase. And this is just not likely to happen in the foreseeable future.

- You can't turn around and recontribute the money you've withdrawn from the RRSP; the contribution room is lost forever (this generally won't matter to you if you stand to benefit from the strategy).

- There may be a greater temptation to access the money outside your RRSP before you ought to because it's not as highly taxed as withdrawals from an RRSP. In this way, there may be a psychological advantage to RRSPs. Working with a financial advisor who can gently remind you that you're better off leaving your investments untouched until retirement can be a great solution here. Since borrowing to invest is such a significant part of the RRSP freeze or meltdown, you should read Tip 59 before considering this strategy.

TO MAKE A LONG STORY SHORT:

- It's possible to have too much in an RRSP. You may need to visit a trusted financial advisor to determine whether this is the case for you.

- The RRSP freeze or meltdown involves borrowing money to invest and using the interest deduction to offset taxable RRSP withdrawals. The strategy can provide higher after-tax income in retirement.

- There are some drawbacks to the strategy. Most notably, you've got to borrow money, and if this is not prudent for you, the strategy won't work.

Tim's Tip 63: Open a self-directed RRSP once your plan assets reach $20,000.

RRSPs can come in all shapes and sizes. The easiest way to understand the differences is to picture an RRSP as a "basket." When you buy an investment, you can choose to hold the investment inside an RRSP basket or outside the RRSP in your own hands (called your *open money*). Now, RRSP baskets can differ. Some will allow you to hold just one specific type of investment—like a Canada Savings Bond (CSB) or Guaranteed Investment Certificate (GIC)—while others will allow you to hold many and varied investments.

Here are two examples of single-purpose baskets. If you visit your local bank and buy a GIC in any amount, but buy it as an RRSP investment (that is, inside an RRSP basket), the GIC will come in its own RRSP basket. Don't even think about holding other investments in the basket because you won't be able to. Similarly, if you open an RRSP with your favourite mutual fund company, the RRSP basket you receive will hold any mutual funds you buy from that company, but can't generally hold, say, stocks or other investments at the same time.

That's where a self-directed RRSP comes in. A self-directed RRSP is simply an RRSP basket (or account) that can hold virtually any type of investment that qualifies to be held in an RRSP (see Tip 66 for a list). The annual administration fees on a self-directed RRSP are usually higher than with other plans (over $100 in most cases), and so I don't recommend that you move to a self-directed plan until your

RRSP assets reach $20,000. But once you've hit this threshold, a self-directed RRSP makes a lot of sense, for three key reasons.

- **Simplicity.** If you've been living with more than one RRSP account, you'll understand the aggravation of receiving a barrage of paper from each institution each month. It can be confusing trying to track what investments you own and where they are. A self-directed RRSP lets you hold all those investments in one account. You'll get just one monthly statement rather than the pile you've been used to getting. By the way, this will make it much easier for your financial advisor (where you use an advisor) to make sure your total retirement portfolio is properly balanced and diversified.

- **Flexibility.** With a self-directed RRSP, your investment options are wide open and can include any investments that are eligible for RRSPs in general. Don't underestimate the value of this. As you age and your circumstances change, you may want to adjust the overall asset mix in your portfolio, and having all your retirement assets in one place will make this job much easier.

- **Diversification.** In order to maximize your investment returns, it's important to diversify globally. After all, Canada represents under 3 percent of markets worldwide. This means that 97 percent of all investment choices fall outside Canada. There is, however, a restriction that the foreign content inside your RRSP cannot exceed 30 percent of the cost amount of the plan. This 30-percent restriction applies to each RRSP account you own. If, for example, you have two RRSP accounts—one with $70,000 (cost amount) in Canadian investments and one with $30,000 (cost amount) in foreign investments—your total foreign content would be 30 percent ($30,000 as a percentage of $100,000 in total investments). The problem? You'd face penalties in this scenario on the one account that holds

Action Step

If you were to open a self-directed RRSP of $10,000 and pay an annual fee of $100, the fee would represent 1 percent of your total assets in the plan. That is, your investment returns would be reduced by 1 percent just because of the fee. With $20,000 in the plan, a $100 fee represents just 0.5 percent of the assets—a more tolerable ratio. This is why a self-directed plan makes the most sense once you've reached $20,000 in assets. Of course, if you can find a self-directed plan that doesn't charge a fee, you may be smart to opt for that account right away.

nothing but foreign content because each account must have at least 70 percent Canadian content. By combining these two RRSPs into a single self-directed plan, you would face no penalties at all since your overall foreign content would be just 30 percent. A self-directed plan can provide for easier international diversification.

TO MAKE A LONG STORY SHORT:

- A self-directed RRSP is a "basket" (an account) that can hold a wide variety of investments. It should be considered once RRSP assets reach $20,000.

- The benefits of a self-directed RRSP include simplicity, flexibility, and diversification.

Tim's Tip 64: Pay your RRSP fees from outside your plan up to age 69.

Talk about confusing. I need two hands and a foot to count the number of times the tax collector has changed opinions on how your RRSP and Registered Retirement Income Fund (RRIF) fees will be treated for tax purposes. You may recall that, back in 1996, the rules were changed to disallow any kind of deduction for RRSP or RRIF fees. This rule still holds today. Regardless of whether it's your annual administration fee (typically between $40 and $125), or investment management fees (often a percentage of your assets), the fees are not deductible.

If these fees happen to be paid from inside your RRSP or RRIF (that is, paid using assets inside your plan), these payments *will not* be considered taxable withdrawals by you, which is great news. Likewise, if you pay these fees from outside your plan, the payments *will not* be considered a contribution to the plan. This, too, is great news.

Here's the game plan: Pay these fees from outside your plan up to age 69. This will allow your plan assets to grow untouched, and will result in more assets in your plan at retirement. However, once you've reached age 69, start paying these annual fees from inside your plan. This makes sense because, at age 69, you've got to start making withdrawals on a regular basis, and each fee payment is like a tax-free withdrawal from the plan.

TO MAKE A LONG STORY SHORT:

- Administration and investment management fees for your RRSP or RRIF are not deductible for tax purposes.

- Pay these fees from outside your plan up to age 69 to preserve the growth of your plan assets. From age 69 onward, pay the fees from inside the plan as a way to make tax-free withdrawals from the plan.

Contributing to Your RRSP

Tim's Tip 65: **Know your RRSP contribution limit each year, then avoid an accumulation of contribution room.**

Action Step

If you pay a single fee (sometimes called a *wrap fee*) to your financial advisor each year for managing your investment accounts, keep in mind that the fee will be deductible if the account is non-registered. You'll have no such luck deducting the fee for your RRSP or RRIF. If your advisor can make a reasonable allocation of the fee to one account or the other, you'll come out ahead if the greater portion of the fee is allocated to the non-registered account, since this fee will be deductible.

How much are you entitled to contribute to your RRSP each year? Well, that depends on your earned income in the previous year. You're entitled to contribute up to 18 percent of your earned income from the previous year, to a yearly maximum amount. If, for example, you had $75,000 of earned income in 2002, you'd be entitled to $13,500 ($75,000 multiplied by 18 percent) of RRSP contribution room in 2003.

What is *earned income*? Basically, it includes employment income, rental income (minus losses), self-employment income (minus losses), royalties if you're an author or inventor, and alimony or separation payments received (subtract these payments if you made them). But the following don't qualify: investment income, pension income, RRSP or RRIF income, Old Age Security (OAS) or Canada Pension Plan (CPP) income, retiring allowances or death benefits, scholarships or bursaries, or income from limited partnerships.

The most obvious place to find out how much you're entitled to contribute to an RRSP is your Notice of Assessment—that form you get in the mail each year after filing your tax return. Your assessment will detail the amount of your contribution room and is usually accurate. But if you disagree with yours, don't hesitate to get a tax pro involved to check it, since you don't want to rob yourself of contribution room.

By the way, if you don't make the maximum contribution to your RRSP in a given year, your contribution room will be carried forward for use in any future year. But don't get in the habit of allowing that room to accumulate for too long. After all, if you had trouble making a $5,000 contribution this year, it's going to be that much harder to make an even larger contribution next year! Besides, you could be enjoying a deferral of tax and that tax-free growth I spoke about earlier.

There's an exception to this general rule. Where you already have enough in an RRSP and you've opted for the RRSP freeze strategy I spoke about in Tip 62, then you may be willing to allow your RRSP room to accumulate.

MAXIMUM RRSP CONTRIBUTIONS	
Year	18% of earned income from the prior year, to a maximum of:
1999 to 2003	$13,500
2004	$14,500
2005	$15,500
2006	indexed to inflation

TO MAKE A LONG STORY SHORT:

- You're entitled to contribute 18 percent of your earned income from the prior year to an RRSP, to a yearly maximum.

- Even though unused contribution room can be carried forward, don't let this happen, since you'll be giving up a valuable tax deferral and tax-free growth of your money.

- The exception to this rule is where you've opted for the RRSP freeze strategy I spoke about in Tip 62.

Tim's Tip 66: **Make a contribution *in kind* to your RRSP if you're low on cash.**

Who says that your RRSP contributions have to be in the form of cash? It's just not true. In fact, you'll be able to contribute a whole host of qualifying assets to your RRSP, including:

- cash
- Guaranteed Investment Certificates
- most mutual funds
- government-guaranteed debt obligations
- corporate bonds or other debt obligations
- shares listed on a prescribed stock exchange (Canadian and foreign)
- shares of certain private corporations
- mortgages secured by real property in Canada
- certain annuities
- certain life insurance policies
- certain rights and warrants
- other less common investments

Make sure that you don't contribute a non-qualifying asset to your RRSP—the effect could be ugly. In fact, you could face tax on some of the earnings inside your RRSP, tax on the value of those non-qualifying assets, or deregistration of your plan. Do you know what deregistration means? It means you could pay tax on the full amount of your RRSP assets in a single year! While this is not likely to happen, it's a possibility.

Caution!

If you're going to contribute *in kind* rather than in cash, there are two tax consequences:

First, you'll be entitled to a deduction just as you would with any RRSP contribution in cash. The value of the contribution simply equals the fair market value of the assets being contributed to your plan.

! Second, you'll be deemed to have sold those assets when you contribute them to the plan. So, where those assets have gone up in value, you might face a taxable capital gain. Of course, the RRSP deduction will always offset any taxable gain provided you've got enough contribution room. On the flip side, if the asset you're contributing has gone down in value, the tax collector won't let you claim a capital loss on this transfer to your RRSP. Sorry. In this case, sell your investment at a loss outside your RRSP, then contribute the cash to your plan. This way, you can utilize the loss.

Make sure you've got enough RRSP contribution room available before making any contribution, including one in-kind. By the way, you'll generally have to set up a self-directed RRSP in order to make a contribution in kind.

TO MAKE A LONG STORY SHORT:

- If you haven't got the cash, contribute in kind to your RRSP.

- You'll be deemed to have sold any investment that is contributed in kind, which could mean a taxable capital gain, but you'll also be entitled to a deduction for your contribution in kind, within your contribution limits.

- Set up a self-directed RRSP to make a contribution in kind.

Tim's Tip 67: Consider borrowing to make RRSP contributions if you haven't got the cash.

Truthfully, in most situations you'll be better off borrowing to make your RRSP contribution than not contributing at all or making that contribution two or three years down the road. You won't be entitled to claim a deduction for the interest on your RRSP loan, but don't worry—it still works to your benefit to borrow because that money is working for you by growing tax-free. If you have investments outside your RRSP, you may be better off to contribute those to your RRSP and then borrow to replace the non-registered investments. That way, the interest will be deductible. This is a contribution in-kind, as I discussed in Tip 66.

TO MAKE A LONG STORY SHORT:

- Borrowing to contribute to your RRSP makes sense when your other choices are to make no contribution or to delay the contribution for even two or three years.

- The interest on your RRSP loan will not be deductible.

Tim's Tip 68: **Have your employer contribute directly to your RRSP.**

What if I told you that there's a way to nearly double your ability to contribute to your RRSP? Arranging for your employer to send a portion of your pay directly to your RRSP could accomplish this. These are called *employer-direct contributions*. All that's necessary is enough contribution room and some cooperation from the boss.

Action Step

Let me buck a trend here. It's been commonly held that you should borrow for your RRSP and pay back that loan over a period of no more than one year. I don't buy this advice. Even a 5- or 10-year loan can leave you better off in the long run when it lets you use up more of your contribution room. Besides, many Canadians have accumulated so much room that it would be impossible to borrow and pay back the loan over one year. The general rule? Keep your loan interest rate 2 percent below your rate of return inside your RRSP, and your loan term 10 years or less.

*R*ob's employer was due to pay him a bonus of $10,000 at the end of last year. If the bonus had been paid directly to Rob, his employer would have been required to deduct withholding tax for remittance to CCRA. This would have left Rob with about $5,400, which he planned to contribute to his RRSP. But Rob managed to contribute much more. Rather than taking payment of the $10,000 bonus in his own hands, Rob arranged for his employer to send the amount directly to his RRSP carrier. As a result, his employer was not required to deduct the withholding tax; only Canada Pension Plan (CPP) and Employment Insurance (EI) contributions were required. Because almost all of *the $10,000 was contributed to his RRSP, Rob effectively doubled his RRSP contribution without even borrowing to make it happen!*

Your employer may wonder how in the world an employer-direct RRSP contribution works. It's really quite simple. Your employer will write a cheque to your RRSP carrier for a portion of your pay. That portion of your pay must still be reported on your T4 slip, but there's no need for your employer to withhold income tax on the amount. Regulation 100(3) of our tax law says so. There is no special form to fill out or special permission required from CCRA to allow a bypass of income tax withholdings in this case.

Maybe your situation is a little different from Rob's. He received a bonus. But if you're not slated to receive a bonus of any kind, the employer-direct idea still works well where your employer deducts a set amount from each pay, or simply sends one or two paycheques each year to your RRSP. I like the idea better than most group RRSPs because it will give you more flexibility.

If you do receive a bonus from your employer, there's one other trick you can play. It worked well for Rob. He arranged for his employer to send his 2002 bonus directly to his RRSP carrier, but also arranged for this to happen in the first 60 days of 2003. The result? Rob gets a deduction on his 2002 tax return for the RRSP contribution, but he won't be taxed on the bonus until 2003, since it wasn't paid out until 2003. In short, he has managed to defer tax on the bonus for a year *and* claim a deduction for the amount of that income a year earlier.

TO MAKE A LONG STORY SHORT:

- Employer-direct RRSP contributions can significantly increase the amount you're able to contribute to your RRSP without borrowing.

- Your employer will simply send a portion of your pay directly to your RRSP carrier and will avoid income tax withholdings (although CPP and EI will still be payable).

Tim's Tip 69: **Avoid over-contributing to your RRSP and invest any excess outside the plan.**

For the most part, you can expect to face some penalties if you contribute too much to your RRSP. In fact, this penalty equals 1 percent of the excess amount per month. You should know, however, that the tax collector will allow you a $2,000 cushion. That is, the first $2,000 of over-contributions to your RRSP will not attract a penalty. You won't be entitled to claim a deduction for this over-contribution, although the money will still grow tax-free while it's in the plan.

Some argue that the over-contribution doesn't make sense because you're going to be taxed on that $2,000 when you eventually withdraw it from your RRSP, without having ever received a deduction when you put it into the plan. In other words, you'll face double tax here. While this is true, this is not the real reason I believe that you should skip the $2,000 over-contribution. You see, if you've got 10 years or more before you start making withdrawals from your RRSP, then the growth on that money inside the plan will outweigh any double-tax problem you might face.

The reason you should skip the $2,000 over-contribution is that you can invest that same $2,000 in a non-registered account and accomplish the following: You'll have no restrictions on the types of investments (including foreign content) that you can hold when you invest this money outside an RRSP, and withdrawals from a non-registered account are much more tax-efficient than withdrawals from an RRSP since only the growth will be taxed, and at capital gains tax rates to boot (just 50 percent of capital gains are taxable).

If you've read previous editions of this book (2000 and prior years), you'll note that this advice is a departure from what I have said in the past. Since the federal mini-budget of October 18, 2000, reduced the tax rate on capital gains, however, I believe that this new advice makes more sense provided that: (1) you already have a non-registered investment account or are committed to building some assets outside your RRSP, and (2) you're going to invest this money outside your RRSP in tax-smart investments (generating capital gains and keeping turnover low—see Tip 47).

TO MAKE A LONG STORY SHORT:

- Excess contributions to an RRSP attract a monthly penalty of 1 percent of the excess amount.

- You're entitled to a $2,000 over-contribution but you should skip the opportunity to make this contribution. Instead, invest that $2,000 in tax-smart investments in a non-registered account.

Tim's Tip 70: Over-contribute to your RRSP just before winding up the plan at age 69, if you have earned income.

While an RRSP is going to help you save for retirement, you won't be able to keep your plan forever. Because of changes introduced in the 1996 federal budget, you're going to have to wind up your RRSP by December 31 of the year you turn 69. Wouldn't it be nice if you could somehow contribute to an RRSP even beyond age 69? Well, you can. One option is a spousal RRSP, which I'll talk about in Tip 75. Your other option is known as the *senior's over-contribution*.

Pavel turned 69 in July 2003, and so he's going to have to wind up his RRSP by the end of 2003. But he has earned income for RRSP purposes in 2003 of $80,555. The result? Pavel is entitled to $14,500 (18 percent of $80,555) of RRSP contribution room in the year 2004. The problem, however, is that Pavel won't be able to contribute to an RRSP in the year 2004 since his RRSP must be wound up by the end of 2003. Does he lose the ability to make an RRSP contribution for the year 2004? No!

Pavel is going to take advantage of his 2004 contribution room by making his 2004 RRSP contribution in December 2003, before he winds up his RRSP forever. Provided that Pavel has already maximized his RRSP contributions for 2003, making an additional contribution of $14,500 in December will result in an over-contribution to his RRSP, and will mean a penalty of $125 for that month. Effective January 1, 2004, Pavel's over-contribution problem disappears, because he's entitled to new contribution room of $14,500 on that date *(due to his 2003 earned income). The over-contribution made in December 2003 will provide Pavel with a $14,500 RRSP deduction in the year 2004, saving him $6,670 in taxes at a marginal tax rate of 46 percent. Even a tax accountant can see that $6,670 in tax savings is greater than a $125 penalty!*

The key here is that you're going to need earned income for RRSP purposes in the year you turn 69 for this to work. With some active tax planning, it may be possible to generate earned income for yourself to allow you to use this tactic. Your tax pro or financial advisor can help.

TO MAKE A LONG STORY SHORT:

- You'll have to wind up your RRSP by December 31 of the year you turn 69.

- You may be able to take advantage of RRSP deductions beyond age 69 through the senior's over-contribution, which involves making one last over-contribution to your RRSP just before winding up the plan at age 69.

- The tax savings from the future RRSP deduction will outweigh any penalties owing from the over-contribution.

Tim's Tip 71: **Boost the value of your RRSP with tax-free rollovers.**

If the name of the game is saving for retirement, and you're committed to using your RRSP to do this, then you need to be aware of the opportunities to transfer potentially large sums to your RRSP, tax-free. These are called *tax-free rollovers*. I want to tell you about six rollover scenarios.

Transfers from One RRSP to the Next

I have a friend named Pat. He's always been the kind of guy who is never really satisfied with the return on his investments. So, Pat has jumped from one mutual fund RRSP account to the next at least five times in the last six years. Good thing

Action Step

By making large lump-sum transfers to your RRSP, you may significantly boost the level of the assets in your plan. While an RRSP is a great retirement vehicle, large lump-sum transfers may leave you with more in your RRSP than you need to provide a comfortable income in retirement. If this is the case, consider an RRSP freeze or meltdown strategy, which can leave you with more after-tax income in retirement than otherwise. The strategy is not for everyone. See Tip 62 for more.

for Pat that assets can be transferred tax-free among RRSP accounts. I, on the other hand, have changed RRSP accounts only once. I moved from an account at my bank where I held mutual funds to a self-directed RRSP. A self-directed plan let me continue holding those mutual funds I owned, but I'm now able to hold many other kinds of investments as well. I like the flexibility. Whatever your reasons for changing, rest assured that the tax collector doesn't mind a move from one RRSP account to the next. Too bad Martin didn't know that. Here's his story.

*S*ince *Martin has not been thrilled with his RRSP's investment performance, he has decided to switch from one RRSP to another with different investment options. Last week, he withdrew the full $30,000 sitting in his original RRSP and then wrote a cheque for $30,000 to his new RRSP carrier. In doing this, Martin made a mistake that cost him nearly $10,000 in tax! You see, Martin only has $10,000 of RRSP contribution room available. Because he made a $30,000 withdrawal, he has to report this amount as income this year. But he's only entitled to contribute $10,000 this year to an RRSP and claim a deduction for it. The remaining $20,000 will be exposed to tax this year. Yikes—bad move by Martin. He could have avoided any tax on the $30,000 by arranging for a direct transfer of his RRSP assets to the new account.*

Retiring Allowance Rollovers

It could be that you're entitled to receive a retiring allowance when you leave your current job. A retiring allowance could include any number of payments received by you or your loved ones after your death in recognition of your service. These payments might also include early retirement incentives or even damages received as a result of wrongful dismissal. At any rate, a retiring allowance can be rolled to your RRSP tax-free—up to certain limits.

The maximum that can be rolled into an RRSP tax-free is $2,000 for each year or part-year of pre-1996 service, plus an extra $1,500 for each year before 1989 in which you had no vested interest in any employer's contributions to a Registered Pension Plan (RPP) or Deferred Profit Sharing Plan (DPSP). You'll be glad to know that this rollover does not have to be direct from your employer to your RRSP. That is, you'll be able to take the money into your hands personally and still roll those funds to an RRSP as long as you make that contribution within 60 days after the end of the year in which you received the payment. This rollover is made over and above your available contribution room.

Here's one last point: The 1998 federal budget improved things for those who transfer retiring allowances to RRSPs. This rollover often creates a sizeable RRSP deduction for the individual in the year the rollover is made. This used to create an Alternative Minimum Tax (AMT) problem in some cases. AMT is simply an amount of tax that CCRA will require you to pay, as a minimum, if you claim certain large deductions. This is no longer an issue. The feds have said that RRSP deductions will no longer be factored into the calculation of AMT.

RPP Assets to an RRSP

While most Registered Pension Plans (RPPs) discourage or prohibit some transfers from the RPP to an RRSP, there are four situations where this can be done. Keep in mind that transfers from an RPP to an RRSP have to be made directly—you can't take these funds into your own hands first.

- **If you leave your job** for any reason, you may be entitled to take with you certain funds in the company pension plan that are earmarked for you. The amount you can take is generally called the *commuted value* of your pension. Before you get too excited about walking away with thousands of pension dollars at your disposal, be aware that a portion of the commuted value can generally be transferred to a locked-in RRSP only, while the balance is generally taxable. You won't be able to make any old withdrawal from a locked-in plan. Locked-in RRSPs will restrict your withdrawals in a way that is consistent with the payments you would have received under the terms of your pension plan. The benefit of a locked-in plan is that, unlike your pension plan, you have complete control over your investments and could quite possibly generate a greater return on those assets than your pension plan would have offered you. This could spell greater income in retirement.

- **If you die** while still a member of your company pension plan, a tax-free transfer can be made to the RRSP or RPP of a surviving spouse.
- **If you separate or divorce,** and you have a written separation agreement or court order, a lump-sum amount can be transferred from your RPP to the RRSP or RPP of your spouse or ex-spouse.
- **If your pension plan has been amended** to retroactively reduce or remove the requirement for you to make contributions to your company's registered pension plan, you may be entitled to receive a return of your pre-1991 contributions plus accumulated interest. If you transfer this money directly to your RRSP, the transfer will be tax-free.

Inherited RRSP Assets

Your RRSP could cause you some grief as you try to come up with a way to avoid a tax hit on those assets when you die. In many cases, RRSP assets will be taxed on the deceased's final tax return, and whatever is left will pass to the heirs. There are two ways to transfer RRSP assets from the deceased's plan to another RRSP, RRIF, or annuity to defer tax a little longer. The first is to leave your plan assets to your spouse or common-law partner. The second is to transfer the plan's assets for the benefit of a dependant. Check out Chapter 9, Tip 97, for all the details.

Transfers upon Marriage Breakdown

If you're planning to make an equalization payment to your spouse after separating or divorcing, you can use your RRSP assets to do it. You see, any payments transferred directly from your RRSP to your spouse's RRSP, RRIF, or RPP as a result of a marriage breakdown can be transferred tax-free. Before making a transfer, keep in mind that this rollover must follow a written separation agreement, or a decree, order, or judgment by a competent tribunal. I dealt with tax issues around separation and divorce in Chapter 2.

U.S. IRA to an RRSP

You'd be surprised how often I'm asked whether or not it's possible to transfer assets to an RRSP from a U.S. Individual Retirement Account (IRA), which is effectively the U.S. version of an RRSP. The short answer is yes. Our tax law will allow a tax-free transfer to take place—and so I'm including this item in my list of tax-free rollovers. Here's the problem: You won't be able to avoid the long arm of the IRS on withdrawals from an IRA. You'll face tax at graduated U.S. tax rates, plus you'll face a 10-percent early withdrawal penalty if the withdrawal is made before age 59 and a half. The bottom line? Unless the U.S. tax hit is minimal, I usually advise that an IRA be kept intact, although each case deserves its own look. I'll deal with other U.S. tax issues in Chapter 7.

TO MAKE A LONG STORY SHORT:

- There are a few ways to boost the assets in your RRSP through tax-free transfers of other assets to your plan.

- Most of these transfers will require a direct transfer from the original plan to your RRSP, while retiring allowances can be received directly in your hands and then contributed within certain time limits.

Tim's Tip 72: Ensure that your child files a tax return to maximize RRSP contribution room.

Several years ago, when I told my cousin Erik that he should file a tax return, he gave me that I-dunno-what-you're-talking-about-and-sounds-like-a-grown-up-kind-of-thing-to-do sort of look. Erik was 15 years old at the time. But he took my advice, and today he's reaping the benefits. If that special child in your life has earned any income at all, make sure he or she files a tax return. In fact, there's no requirement to file a return in most cases, unless the child's income exceeds the basic personal amount of $7,634 in 2002, or if the child has capital gains to report, in which case CCRA expects a return to be filed. But the benefits of filing a tax return when your child has earned income can't be ignored.

*W*hen *Erik was 15 years old, he started his own lawncare service. It didn't make him rich, but it gave him some spending money and later helped to pay for his university education. Even though his income each summer was well under $6,000, he filed tax returns anyway. The income he reported qualified as earned income and created RRSP contribution room. By the time Erik finished university, he had $5,000 worth of contribution room. This year, in his first year of full-time work after graduation, Erik is going to make that $5,000 contribution to his RRSP. This is going to save him about $2,000 in tax.*

Filing a tax return will benefit your child in two important ways. First, it's going to create valuable RRSP contribution room, which will save your child taxes down the road and provide a good head start in saving for retirement. Second, it will teach your child something about money and taxes if you keep him or her involved in the process.

TO MAKE A LONG STORY SHORT:

- There's no requirement to file a tax return unless income is over $7,634 in 2002 or there are capital gains to report.

- Even if it's not required, helping your child file a tax return can be worthwhile because it will create valuable RRSP contribution room that will save your child tax down the road and provide a good head start in saving for retirement.

Tim's Tip 73: Claim your RRSP deduction in the right year.

Patience, my friend, patience. It's so tempting to make a contribution to an RRSP and claim the deduction on your tax return as soon as possible. But this doesn't always make sense. You see, you're not required to claim a deduction for your RRSP contribution in the year you make the contribution. Did you know that? In fact, you're able to claim that deduction in any future year. I'll admit, there are few things harder in life than forgoing a tax deduction when you know you could be claiming it today. The only thing harder is opening a bag of potato chips and eating just one. It takes willpower. Nevertheless, I'm going to suggest that in certain situations it makes a whole lot of sense to exercise some of that willpower and put off your RRSP deduction to a future year.

Picture this. You make a $5,000 contribution to your RRSP in February of 2003. The RRSP rules actually say that you can make your RRSP contribution for a particular year as late as 60 days following the end of that year (your 2002 contribution can be made as late as March 1, 2003).

> **Action Step**
>
> If you're in your early sixties and you're concerned about the clawback of Old Age Security benefits, consider making contributions to your RRSP but saving the deduction for a future year when the clawback might be an issue.

As a result, the $5,000 contribution you make in February 2003 will entitle you to a deduction in 2002 or any future year. If your marginal tax rate in 2002 is, say, 25 percent, then you'll save $1,250 ($5,000 x 25 percent) through the RRSP deduction. But suppose for a minute that your income in 2003 is expected to be significantly higher, pushing you into a 46-percent marginal tax bracket. By saving your RRSP deduction for just one year, you'll manage to increase your tax savings from that deduction. At a 46-percent marginal tax rate, your savings on a $5,000 contribution will be $2,300. Any financial advisor worth his or her salt will tell you that $2,300 in tax savings next year is better than $1,250 in savings today.

TO MAKE A LONG STORY SHORT:

- Your RRSP contributions will entitle you to a deduction on your tax return, but that deduction may be put off and claimed in any future year.

- Delaying the deduction may make sense when you expect to face a higher marginal tax rate in the next couple of years.

Tim's Tip 74: Contribute to your RRSP instead of paying down your mortgage.

Canadians love real estate. Canadians also love to pay down the mortgage on that real estate as quickly as possible. I can understand why. On a $100,000 mortgage amortized over 25 years with an interest rate of 8 percent, you're on course to pay over $128,000 in interest alone over 25 years. Scary, isn't it? But hold on a minute. When you've got to make a decision between paying down the mortgage or contributing to an RRSP, many Canadians make the wrong move. Your best bet, in almost every case, is to contribute to your RRSP. If you took the time to do the math, you'd agree with me.

Only in very rare circumstances does it actually make sense to pay down the mortgage first. If the following two conditions are *both* met, then by all means pay down the mortgage as your first priority:

- the interest rate on your mortgage is 3 percent higher than the rate of return of your RRSP, and
- you're committed to contributing two-thirds of your annual mortgage payments to your RRSP once the mortgage is paid off.

Meeting the first of these conditions is going to be unlikely, so your best option will generally be contributing to your RRSP first. But why not have your cake and eat it too? Here's how: Contribute to your RRSP each year, and use the tax savings to pay down the mortgage.

TO MAKE A LONG STORY SHORT:

- Except in very rare situations, you'll be better off making contributions to your RRSP than paying down the mortgage.

- Get the best of both worlds by contributing to your RRSP and then using the tax savings to pay down the mortgage.

Tim's Tip 75: **Contribute to a spousal RRSP to equalize incomes in retirement.**

Share and share alike. I think that the soul who first spoke these words was actually a Canadian looking to keep a lid on the family tax bill. I'm talking about one very effective strategy: splitting income with your spouse or common-law partner. You see, in an ideal situation, you and your spouse should have equal incomes during retirement (and prior to retirement for that matter). This keeps the total family tax bill at a minimum. The most practical tool for accomplishing this splitting of income is a spousal RRSP. A spousal RRSP is simply one that you will contribute to, but that your spouse will make withdrawals from. You'll get a deduction for making the contribution, but your spouse, being the annuitant, will pay the tax on any withdrawals. How's that for moving income directly from one spouse to the next? Let me share with you a few facts and strategies surrounding spousal RRSPs.

> **Caution!**
>
> Keep in mind that you won't be entitled to additional RRSP contribution room to contribute to a spousal RRSP. That is, the total contributions to your own RRSP and to a spousal RRSP combined must be within your annual contribution limits. If you exceed your limit, you'll generally be able to withdraw the excess tax-free, but you'll face a penalty of 1 percent per month on the excess contribution until you withdraw it.

Avoiding Attribution on Withdrawals

Our tax law has been designed to avoid abuses of spousal RRSPs. To this end, any withdrawals your spouse makes from a spousal RRSP will actually be taxed in your hands to the extent you made contributions to a spousal RRSP in the year of withdrawal or in the previous two years. For example, if your last contribution to a spousal RRSP was $5,000 in 2001, and your spouse withdraws $7,000 from a spousal plan in 2003, the first $5,000 of that withdrawal will be taxed in your hands since that's the amount of the withdrawal that can be attributed to contributions you made in the year of the withdrawal or the previous two years. To avoid this attribution, the withdrawals will have to wait until the third calendar year after you make your last contribution.

Contributing by December 31

You can effectively reduce the waiting period for withdrawals from a spousal RRSP to just two years—and still avoid attribution—by making spousal RRSP contributions by December 31 each year.

*D*ave *has been contributing to a spousal RRSP for his wife, Andrea. His last contribution was on December 31, 2000. Dave and Andrea had a child in 2002, and Andrea decided to stay home with the new baby for a couple of years. Since Andrea's income will be quite low during this time, she has decided to withdraw $7,000 from the spousal RRSP in the year 2003. The $7,000 will be taxed in Andrea's hands, not Dave's, since Dave will not have made a contribution to the spousal RRSP in the year of the withdrawal (2003), or in the prior two years (2001 and 2002). The good news is that the funds inside the spousal RRSP were really tied up for just two years plus a day (December 31, 2000, to January 1, 2003). If Dave had made his last contribution to the spousal plan just one day later, in 2001, Andrea would have to wait a whole extra year before she could make withdrawals and avoid attribution of the income back to Dave. As an aside, since Andrea will have no other income in the year 2003, she won't face any tax on the $7,000 withdrawal because this is less than her basic personal credit (which is $7,634 in 2002 and will be even higher in 2003).*

Contributing beyond Age 69

A spousal RRSP is a great tool for making contributions to an RRSP even when you pass age 69 and have wound up your own RRSP. You see, as long as your spouse is still 69 or under in the year, you'll be able to make a contribution to a spousal RRSP in the year, regardless of your own age. Of course, you'll need to have RRSP contribution room available before making any contributions.

Contributing with a Deceased's Assets

Here's a little-known tactic that could save you a bundle of tax when you die. I'm referring to one final RRSP contribution that your executor is permitted to make. If you have RRSP contribution room available at the time of your death, your executor will be able to use your assets to make a contribution to a spousal RRSP. The deduction will be claimed on your final tax return. Your spouse will have to be aged 69 or under in the year of your death to allow for this contribution. See Chapter 9, Tip 98, for more.

TO MAKE A LONG STORY SHORT:

- A spousal RRSP is a plan that you contribute to but your spouse or common-law partner makes withdrawals from.

- You're entitled to a deduction and your spouse will be taxed on any withdrawals, which accomplishes a perfect splitting of income.

- Watch out for attribution rules, which could tax some of the withdrawals in the hands of the contributor.

- A spousal plan can be used to make RRSP contributions beyond age 69, and to reduce taxes upon your death through a contribution by the executor.

Withdrawing from Your RRSP

You've worked hard to put money aside in your RRSP. At some point, those funds are going to be withdrawn from the plan. Most commonly, you'll withdraw them once you've decided to retire and you need a steady income from those investments. But there may be times in life when you decide that you need to make RRSP withdrawals sooner.

Before jumping at the chance to pull money out of your RRSP for reasons other than retirement, stop and think twice. You stand to give up plenty of growth in your RRSP by making withdrawals early. Want proof? Consider the cost of RRSP

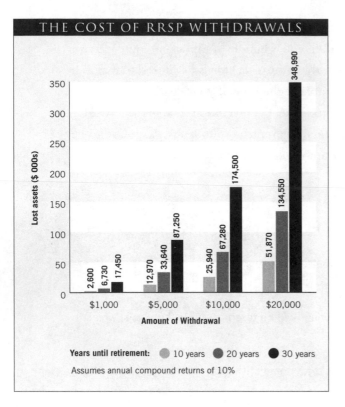

THE COST OF RRSP WITHDRAWALS

Lost assets ($ 000s)

Amount of Withdrawal

Years until retirement: ● 10 years ● 20 years ● 30 years

Assumes annual compound returns of 10%

withdrawals shown in the graph. If you make a $5,000 withdrawal from your RRSP and you have 30 years to go before retirement, you'll give up $87,250 in retirement savings because of your withdrawal, assuming a 10-percent return on your money. A $20,000 withdrawal with 20 years to go before retirement will cost you $134,550!

In some cases it may make sense to withdraw money from your RRSP when you're undertaking an RRSP freeze (see Tip 62), but in this case you're building up investments outside of your RRSP, so you're not giving up growth of your assets. Making withdrawals to meet your costs of living or to make a special purchase can often be a bad idea.

If you still plan to make withdrawals from your RRSP, there are some tax-efficient ways to do this. Let's take a look at them.

Tim's Tip 76: Make RRSP withdrawals during periods of no or low income.

There's no doubt that at certain times in your life you might find yourself strapped for cash. During these times, your RRSP can act as a source of income if need be. It could be that you're unemployed, on disability leave, or on maternity or parental leave. Perhaps you're launching a new business and haven't started generating any income yet. In any event, these times of no or low income may allow you to make very tax-efficient withdrawals from your RRSP.

You see, every Canadian resident is entitled to the basic personal amount that effectively shelters your first $7,634 of income from any tax in 2002. The bottom line is that, if you have no other income, you'll be able to withdraw $7,634 from your RRSP and not pay a cent of tax on that income. Even if your income is over $7,634, you'll still enjoy Canada's lowest marginal tax rate, about 25 percent, on taxable income below $31,677.

You should realize that you're going to face withholding taxes when you make withdrawals from your RRSP. The federal withholding tax is 10 percent on withdrawals of $5,000 or less, 20 percent on withdrawals of $5,001 to $15,000, and 30 percent on withdrawals over $15,000. The percentages in Quebec are 25, 33, and 38 percent respectively. Think of these withholdings as installments on your taxes. In most cases these withholdings won't be enough to satisfy your full tax bill on the RRSP withdrawal, and you'll have to make up the difference when you file your tax return for the year of the withdrawal. In other cases, if your income is low enough, you may get back some of those withholdings as a refund when you file your return. If you want to keep these withholdings to a minimum, be sure to limit each withdrawal to $5,000 or less.

> **Caution!**
>
> If you make withdrawals from your RRSP, the tax collector will not give back contribution room for you to make up that withdrawal later. That is, you'll lose that contribution room forever! This has to be considered a cost of making withdrawals over and above the tax you might pay on any withdrawals.

TO MAKE A LONG STORY SHORT:

- Withdrawing funds from your RRSP can be done tax-efficiently if your income is low, thanks to the basic personal amount of $7,634 for 2002.

- Withdrawals will be subject to withholding taxes, which are simply installments toward your eventual tax bill.

Tim's Tip 77: **Consider the impact of using RRSP assets to buy a home.**

If you're thinking of buying a home but are not sure where to find a down payment, your RRSP may be one option. In 1992 the Department of Finance introduced the Home Buyers' Plan (HBP), which was designed to help certain Canadians use RRSP money tax-free in order to buy a home.

Is this idea for everyone? Not really. The younger you are, the less sense the HBP makes. You see, if you take money out of your RRSP at a young age, even for a home purchase, you give up more growth inside your RRSP than someone who has, say, just 10 years to go before retirement. As a general rule, if you have 35 years or more to go before it's time to retire, then the HBP quite likely does not make sense on paper. Having said this, I'm not going to spoil the dreams of any young person intent on owning a home. So, do what your heart desires. But learn how the HBP works first!

Making Withdrawals

You'll be entitled to withdraw up to $20,000 from your RRSP tax-free for buying or building a home, as long as you haven't owned a home in the five calendar years leading up to and including the current year (you can use the plan in the current year up to 30 days after you've purchased your home). If you're married, then you and your spouse will each be entitled to a $20,000 withdrawal, provided neither of you has owned a home in the last five calendar years (including this year) and you're buying the new home jointly. Even if your spouse has owned a home in that time, you're entitled to make a withdrawal under the HBP, provided it was not your principal residence while you were married or living as common-law partners (same sex or otherwise).

It used to be that the tax collector would only let you make withdrawals in a single calendar year under the HBP. This was changed in 1998 and now you can make withdrawals in a year subsequent to your previous withdrawals provided those previous withdrawals are paid back first. Second, if you are disabled or support a disabled person, you may be eligible to make withdrawals under the HBP even if you have owned a home recently.

Once you've made a withdrawal under the HBP, you've got to close the purchase of a home by October 1 of the following year—called the *completion date*. So, if you make a withdrawal in 2002, your purchase will have to close by October 1, 2003. Can't manage to close the deal that quickly? The tax collector may be willing to provide a one-year extension to that October 1 deadline, and in most cases you have the option of putting the funds back into your RRSP by December 31 following the completion date—without a penalty. Keep in mind, too, that the rules require you to occupy your new home as your principal residence within 12 months after buying the place. Make sure you use Form T1036 (available from your RRSP carrier) when making withdrawals; this will allow the RRSP carrier to bypass tax withholdings on your withdrawal under the HBP.

If you were hoping to buy that boat you've been dreaming of, and call it your home under the HBP, you'll find yourself out of luck. The home must be located on solid ground in Canada, but other than this, most homes will qualify, including: detached and semi-detached homes, townhouses, condominiums, mobile homes, apartment units, and even a share in a cooperative housing corporation.

Making Repayments

If you make withdrawals under the HBP, you've got to pay that money back to your RRSP. You won't get a deduction for these repayments. At a minimum, the repayments must be made in equal annual installments over a 15-year period, and your first payment will have to be made in the second calendar year after the year of your withdrawal. If, for example, you withdrew $20,000 on July 31, 2002, you'd have to make your first repayment in the year 2004, and this repayment could be made within the usual RRSP deadlines for that year. That is, you could make your first repayment in the first 60 days of 2005, for the 2004 year. If you happen to miss a repayment, or repay less than you should, the deficient payment is added to your taxable income—just as any RRSP withdrawal would be.

Don't be afraid to speed up your repayments to your RRSP. In fact, the sooner you repay those borrowed funds, the better. If you do accelerate your repayments, this will reduce the amount of each payment for the balance of the 15-year term.

Timing Your RRSP Contributions

When you're getting involved with the HBP, you've got to carefully plan out your RRSP contributions to ensure you'll be entitled to claim a deduction for them. Here's the deal: If you contribute to your RRSP and then withdraw those same funds within 90 days under the HBP, you won't be able to claim a deduction for that contribution. Any money that was already in your RRSP will be considered withdrawn first, before the new contribution is considered withdrawn. The bottom line is this: Always allow your contributions to sit for 91 days or more before withdrawing them under the HBP.

For more information, get a copy of CCRA's booklet No. RC4135 on the Home Buyer's Plan (get it online at **www.ccra-adrc.gc.ca**).

TO MAKE A LONG STORY SHORT:

- Under the Home Buyers' Plan (HBP), you may be eligible to make tax-free withdrawals from your RRSP in order to buy a home.

- The younger you are, the more it will cost you in lost RRSP growth to use the HBP.

- Money borrowed from your RRSP under the HBP must be paid back over 15 years.

- The rules are many and complex, so take the time to learn how the HBP works first.

Tim's Tip 78: Consider the impact of using RRSP money for full-time education for you or your spouse.

When I first read about the Lifelong Learning Plan (LLP) introduced in the 1998 federal budget, it seemed to me like a waste of effort on the part of the Department of Finance. Since that time, however, I've run into a number of Canadians who are taking advantage of this program, which became effective in 1999. I'm talking about using RRSP assets to finance full-time training or education for you or your spouse or common-law partner. This plan works much like the Home Buyers' Plan I talked about in the last tip, and complements the other education strategies I presented in Chapter 2.

Making Withdrawals

The feds have now made it possible for Canadian residents to withdraw money tax-free from RRSPs for full-time training or education. You'll be able to take up to $10,000 each year, over a four-year period, to a maximum of $20,000 in total from your RRSP for education for you or your spouse. You'll be glad to know that "full-time" doesn't have to mean four years of schooling. It can simply mean a three-month enrollment in a qualifying educational program at an eligible institution. If you're disabled, even full-time isn't a requirement—part-time will also make you eligible for the LLP.

Once you've made a withdrawal from your RRSP under this plan, you'll have to enroll in a qualifying program no later than January of the following calendar year. Sorry, but you won't be able to make any education withdrawals from your RRSP for your spouse if you still have a balance outstanding from withdrawals for yourself. However, your spouse can use his or her own plan to make withdrawals.

Action Step

Making a withdrawal from your RRSP for education may be ideal if you're 40-plus and aren't quite sure what to do with the balance of your career, or if you have a real desire to build on your existing skills to increase your marketability. And if you received a retiring allowance from your former employer that was rolled into your RRSP, then any withdrawal you make won't hurt your RRSP as much—after all, you've just added a few thousand to your RRSP because of the retiring allowance.

Dropping Out

If you don't quite make it through your full-time program, you'll generally face tax on the amount of your RRSP withdrawals made under this plan. But don't panic. There are ways to avoid this tax hit. First, if you meet even *one* of three conditions, you'll manage to sidestep the tax collector:

- You withdraw from the educational program more than three months after the year of your RRSP withdrawal.
- Less than 75 percent of your tuition costs are refundable when you withdraw from the educational program.
- You enroll in another qualifying program on a timely basis.

Second, you can bypass the ugly tax hit by repaying the amount withdrawn by December 31 of the year following the year of withdrawal. Send a copy of the RRSP receipt proving repayment, along with a letter explaining why you are cancelling your withdrawals under the LLP, to the Ottawa Tax Centre, Room 362, 875 Heron Road, Ottawa, ON K1A 1A2.

Making Repayments

You'll have to repay your RRSP withdrawals in equal installments over a 10-year period, and you—not your spouse—must be the annuitant of the RRSP. Your first payment back to your RRSP must be made no later than the first 60 days of the sixth year after your first withdrawal. So, if you make a withdrawal in 2002, your first payment will be due in the first 60 days of 2008. You may have to start your repayments sooner if, after your first withdrawal, you fail to qualify for the full-time education credit for three months in two consecutive years. In this case, you'll have to start your payments in the first 60 days of the year following the second of the two consecutive years. Special rules apply in the year of your death or if you give up Canadian residency.

Kind of confusing, isn't it? Not to worry. CCRA will send you notices to explain how much you have to repay and when. By the way, if you fail to make the proper repayments in any given year, you'll face tax on the deficient payments.

Timing Your RRSP Contributions

As with the Home Buyers' Plan, if you make a contribution to your RRSP and then withdraw those funds within 90 days under this plan, you won't be entitled to an RRSP deduction for the contributions. For more information, refer back to Tip 77 dealing with the Home Buyers' Plan. Also, get a copy of CCRA's booklet No. RC4112 on the Lifelong Learning Plan (you can get it online at **www.ccra-adrc.gc.ca**).

TO MAKE A LONG STORY SHORT:

- The 1998 federal budget opened a door to make tax-free withdrawals from an RRSP for full-time training or education under the Lifelong Learning Plan.

- You can withdraw up to $10,000 each year, over four years, to a maximum of $20,000 in total withdrawals.

- The plan is similar to the Home Buyers' Plan in many ways, and the rules can be complex. Take the time to understand the impact on your retirement savings before withdrawing RRSP money.

Tim's Tip 79: Take three steps to minimize the tax hit on RRSP withdrawals if you're planning to leave the country.

If you're thinking of leaving Canada, perhaps to live it up down south in your retirement, make sure that you leave your RRSP intact when you go. You see, regardless of where you move, you're likely to be better off in the long run by making RRSP withdrawals after you've given up Canadian residency, and not before.

Mark and his wife Karen decided to move to the U.S. at the end of 2002. They liked the thought of spending their retirement in the warmth of Arizona. Before leaving, they visited their tax advisor and took her advice before packing their bags. As a result, Mark and Karen decided to keep their RRSPs intact, so they simply informed the various mutual fund companies and financial institutions holding their investments that they would be non-residents of Canada from 2003 onward. In addition, they sold all the assets inside their RRSPs and reinvested those proceeds just before leaving. Finally, they took great pains to make sure that they gave up Canadian residency properly. The result of all this? Mark and Karen will enjoy extremely tax-efficient withdrawals from their RRSPs.

Did you catch the three steps taken by Mark and Karen? Let's look at them again.

Step 1: Leave the RRSP intact.

If you were to collapse your RRSP before leaving Canada, you'd face a significant tax hit because that withdrawal would be fully taxable in the year of your leaving. Mark and Karen avoided this by leaving their RRSPs intact until they had given up Canadian residency. If you wait until you're a resident of the U.S. or another country for that matter, the only tax you'll pay to CCRA will be a 25-percent withholding tax on any withdrawals from your RRSP. Further, the 25-percent rate will generally be reduced to just 15 percent on *periodic* withdrawals, as opposed to *lump-sum* withdrawals from your plan—provided Canada has a tax treaty with your new country of residence.

By the way, to ensure that your withdrawals are considered *periodic* and eligible for the 15-percent withholding tax rate, you'll have to convert your RRSP to a RRIF first. This conversion can be done before or after you leave Canada. Once you're making withdrawals from your RRIF, be sure not to withdraw more than twice the minimum amount each year, or 10 percent of the fair market value of the plan assets at the start of the year, whichever is greater. Otherwise the withdrawals will be considered lump sum, and you'll face the higher 25-percent withholding tax rate.

Step 2: Step up the cost amount.

If you've taken up residency in the U.S., any withdrawals from your RRSP will be taxed by the U.S. (in addition to the Canadian withholding tax), but Uncle Sam won't tax the full amount of your withdrawals. Rather, you'll be entitled to withdraw from your plan, tax-free, the cost amount of your RRSP investments as calculated on the day you took up residency in the U.S. So, if you can maximize that cost amount, you'll be entitled to greater tax-free withdrawals in the U.S. Mark and Karen accomplished this by selling and repurchasing their RRSP assets—otherwise known as *stepping up* the cost amount of their RRSPs. You see, if you have investments in your RRSP worth $300,000 but you only paid $100,000 for them, your cost amount is $100,000. If you sell those investments and reinvest the proceeds, your new cost amount will be $300,000. This is a step-up in your cost amount. If an investment inside your plan has dropped in value, selling it and reinvesting the proceeds will cause your cost amount to drop—so it doesn't make sense to sell those investments.

Keep in mind that you won't face a tax bill in Canada on the sale since it all takes place inside your RRSP where gains are sheltered from the Canadian tax collector. The only drawback is that you may face some commissions or charges on the sale of your plan assets, so consider this cost first.

Some are under the impression that simply moving RRSP assets from one financial institution or advisor to another will result in a step-up of the cost amount of your investments. Sorry, it won't work. While your new RRSP carrier may not have a record of your true original cost amount, you can bet the U.S. tax authorities will take the time to determine this figure if they decide to look into your RRSP withdrawals.

Caution!

Step 3: Give up residency properly.

Mark and Karen took great pains to make sure they gave up Canadian residency properly. And if you plan on taking up residency outside Canada, you should do the same. If CCRA considers you to be a resident of Canada still, even after you've left the country, you'll face tax on your RRSP withdrawals at full Canadian tax rates, not the lower withholding rates.

Although no single factor will determine whether you're truly a non-resident, the tax collector will consider a number of things, and in particular:

- the permanence and purpose of your stay abroad
- your residential ties within Canada (your primary ties include your dwelling place, spouse and dependants, personal property, and social ties)
- your residential ties elsewhere (the courts have said that you must be a resident somewhere, and you can be a resident in more than one country at the same time)
- the regularity and length of your visits to Canada

To avoid an unpleasant tax hit on RRSP withdrawals once you're gone, be sure to follow all three steps outlined here. Why? Because in this game, it's not three strikes and you're out. Strike out on even one of these steps, and you could cost yourself significant tax dollars. Always visit a tax pro when you're thinking of giving up Canadian residency.

TO MAKE A LONG STORY SHORT:

- If you're planning to leave Canada, leave your RRSP intact and make withdrawals once you're gone. The only tax you'll face in Canada will be a maximum withholding tax of 25 percent, which could be reduced to just 15 percent.

- Be sure to follow these three steps to minimize the tax hit on your RRSP if you plan to leave the country: (1) leave your RRSP intact; (2) step up the cost amount of your plan assets; and (3) give up residency properly (visit a tax pro for help).

Benefiting from RRIFs and Annuities

What would a discussion of retirement be without talking about Registered Retirement Income Funds (call 'em *riffs*) and annuities?

Tim's Tip 80: Roll your RRSP into a RRIF or annuity to defer tax well beyond age 69.

I've said it before: There's going to come a day when your RRSP just won't be around anymore. In fact, your RRSP will mature at the end of the year in which you turn 69. By that date, you'll have to wind up your RRSP and do something with the assets inside your plan. You'll have three options at that time:

- make a lump-sum withdrawal from your RRSP
- buy an annuity with the proceeds of your RRSP
- transfer your RRSP assets to a RRIF

You don't have to choose just one of these options. You can actually do all three without a problem. But which option is your best choice?

Make a Lump-Sum Withdrawal

Now here's an option for the high-flying, fast-living senior. If you want to take your life savings, pay tax on the entire proceeds all in one year, then travel around the world for a year or two until your money runs out, you might like this option. But make no mistake, there is absolutely nothing tax-smart about taking a lump-sum withdrawal from your RRSP when you wind up the plan. This option is, in my view, no option at all. Don't even think about it. You see, you can always make withdrawals at a later date from your RRIF if you want more cash—don't make the withdrawal at age 69 when your RRSP matures. Read on for better alternatives.

Buy an Annuity

The name of this game is deferring taxes. A lump-sum withdrawal won't do it, but an annuity can help. When you buy an annuity you are simply entering into a contract where you pay a sum of money to a company (usually a life insurance company) that agrees to pay to you a guaranteed sum of money each month for a period of time—usually your lifetime. Each annuity payment you receive will be fully taxed—but not until you receive the payment. There are two common types of annuities. The first is a *term-certain* annuity that will pay you a sum each month for a fixed period of years. The second is a *life* annuity that will pay you a sum each month for as long as you live. A life annuity can also be set up so that it's a *joint life* annuity that will make monthly payments to you and your spouse as long as one of you is alive. For additional cost, you can also add other features to your annuity, such as indexation to inflation, or a guaranteed term attached to a life annuity.

Annuities may be for you if you have no interest in investing your own money, and all you want is a guaranteed income for life. One of the drawbacks of an annuity is that once you and your spouse are gone, so is the annuity. That is, you shouldn't expect to leave your annuity to the kids, because they generally won't get anything. Another drawback to annuities is that the amount of your payments is determined by interest rates in effect at the time you buy the annuity. If rates are currently low, you might not end up with as high an income in retirement as you could achieve with a RRIF. Finally, if you choose the annuity option, don't wait until December 31 of the year you turn age 69 to make the purchase—after all, you'll be at the whim of current interest rates if you do this.

Roll into a RRIF

A RRIF is a great retirement plan. It works much like your RRSP. In fact, you can hold all the same investments in a RRIF that you could in your RRSP. However, there are two key differences between a RRIF and your RRSP. First, you can't make contributions to a RRIF. Second, you've got to make withdrawals from a RRIF each year. The amount of your withdrawals will depend on your age or the age of your spouse. A RRIF also works like your RRSP in that any assets in your plan will grow tax-free until they're withdrawn. If you want to transfer assets from one RRIF to the next, you'll be able to do this tax-free.

A RRIF is different from an annuity in that you control the investments that are made. If you're not comfortable with this task, the RRIF can still be a real hands-off option if you link up with a trusted financial advisor who can help with the investment decisions. Further, a RRIF can provide for a more flexible income in retirement because you can control the timing and the amount of your withdrawals, although you must make at least the minimum withdrawal each year (see the table on page 295). With an annuity, your annual income is basically fixed from the start. Another advantage of the RRIF is that it doesn't disappear upon your death or the death of your spouse. Your kids will actually receive the balance of your RRIF, albeit after taxes, once you're gone.

The key drawback to the RRIF is that, if you're not careful, you could make big enough withdrawals in the early years of the RRIF to leave you with very little income in your later years. Proper planning should put this concern to rest, however.

In the end, you'll need to decide which of these three options is best for you. I believe that in most cases the RRIF is the way to go, but speak to a trusted financial advisor before making this final decision—you may have to live with your choice for a lifetime.

TO MAKE A LONG STORY SHORT:

- When your RRSP matures in December of the year you turn 69, you've got three choices for those assets: make a lump-sum withdrawal, buy an annuity, or roll the assets to a RRIF.

- The annuity and RRIF options will allow you to defer tax, while the lump-sum option won't.

- In most cases, the RRIF option will be best, but speak to a trusted financial advisor about which is best for you before making a decision that you may have to live with for a lifetime.

Tim's Tip 81: **Defer tax on your RRIF withdrawals as long as possible.**

The longer you defer withdrawals from your RRIF, the longer you'll enjoy a tax deferral. There are two ways to minimize your RRIF withdrawals.

Base Withdrawals on the Younger Spouse

I remember reading one time about a 70-year-old man from Toronto who married a young woman aged 22. Someone had asked him: "Aren't you concerned about marrying a woman so much younger than you?" "Why should I be?" he said, "she's in great health." If I didn't know that they married for true love, I would suspect that maybe he had some tax planning in mind.

You see, the required minimum withdrawals from your RRIF each year will equal the balance in your RRIF at the start of the year multiplied by a percentage based on your age or the age of your spouse or common-law partner. If your spouse is younger, then the percentage that you've got to withdraw each year will be less if you use your spouse's age in the calculation. And the tax collector will let you use the younger age.

*W*hen Ken set up his RRIF last year at age 69, he decided to base his RRIF withdrawals on the age of his spouse, Leslie, who was just 63 at the time. Ken had $100,000 in his RRIF at the beginning of this year, and because he was 69 at the start of the year, he would have to withdraw 4.76 percent of his RRIF assets ($4,760) from his plan this year if he based those withdrawals on his own age. However, if he based the withdrawals on Leslie's age, he would only have to withdraw $3,700. As the couple gets older, the savings from using Leslie's age will become more pronounced.

Action Step If you keep your annual RRIF withdrawals to the minimum amount, you'll avoid having taxes withheld by your financial institution. This will give you more money up front to meet your daily living needs. Keep in mind that the withdrawals are still taxable, so the fact that no withholding taxes are paid may mean you'll face a tax bill next April when you file your tax return, and you may be required to make installments to the tax collector quarterly.

See the table on page 295 for minimum annual RRIF withdrawals based on your age or the age of your spouse.

Delay Your First Withdrawal

You'll be glad to know that you don't actually have to make any withdrawals from your RRIF in the year you set up the plan. For example, if you set up your RRIF in January 2003, you won't have to make any withdrawals until the year 2004. And when in the year 2004 do you suppose you'll have to make those withdrawals? Right—not until December 31! By leaving your assets to grow untouched in your RRIF as long as possible, you'll maximize the growth inside your plan and defer tax as well.

TO MAKE A LONG STORY SHORT:

- Defer tax as long as possible by minimizing how much you take out of your RRIF and by delaying those withdrawals until absolutely necessary.

- You can minimize your withdrawals by basing them on the age of the younger spouse, and you can delay your withdrawals until the end of the year following the year you set up the plan.

Understanding Registered Pension Plans

Registered Pension Plans (RPPs) are declining in popularity. More and more employers are letting employees fend for themselves in the world of retirement savings. Nevertheless, thousands of Canadians are still members of RPPs, or will become members, and there are strategies to consider here. But first, let's look at the two basic types of RPPs:

- With a **defined benefit plan,** you can expect to receive pension benefits based on a formula—often a percentage of your last few years' salary. Your employer bears some risk in this type of plan since a promise is being made to you that a certain level of benefits will be paid out when you retire.
- With a **defined contribution plan** (also called a *money purchase* plan), both you and your employer may make contributions, but there's no guarantee about how much will be sitting there for you at retirement. The contributions will be paid to you, plus accumulated growth on those assets, but no promises are made beyond that.

If you're a member of an RPP, you've no doubt noticed that the tax collector is not going to let you contribute as much to your RRSP as your neighbour who is not a member of a pension plan. Enter the *pension adjustment* (PA). Your PA is an amount that, in a nutshell, equals the total of your contributions plus your employer's contributions to an RPP each year. The amount of your RRSP contribution room will be reduced by the amount of this PA each year. This keeps all Canadians on a level playing field when saving for retirement. That is, in theory, pension plan members will not have an advantage over those saving for retirement through an RRSP alone.

Tim's Tip 82: Consider opting out of your company pension plan if you have the choice.

I know this sounds radical, but if you have a choice of taking part in the pension plan or not, you should give serious thought to opting out. Let me explain. One thing that can really hurt your retirement savings is to move from one employer with a pension plan to another without a plan. You see, if you stop your membership in a company pension plan, the chances are very high that you will not walk away from that pension plan with all the money that you and your employer contributed to that plan for you. This is particularly true if you've only been in the plan a short time—say three years or less.

Now, let me ask you this. What is the probability that you'll change employers between today and the time you retire? There's a darn high probability of that, I would say. In fact, it's not unusual today to find employees who have worked for five or more employers by age 45. If you take part in a pension plan and move to another employer who may or may not have a pension plan, my bet is that you'll walk away with much less than you figured you would.

Thanks to changes introduced in the 1997 federal budget, you may be entitled to a *pension adjustment reversal* that effectively gives you back some of that lost RRSP contribution room that arose from the pension adjustment over the years while you were in the plan. But this is a far cry from actually giving you all the cash that was earmarked for you in the RPP. You'll still have to find the cash somewhere to make a contribution to use up that room.

Consider this also: If you leave a company pension plan and move to an employer without a plan, you could lose the ability to contribute to any kind of retirement plan for a full year. For example, if you were a member of an RPP in 2002 and $13,500 of contributions were made to that plan on your behalf in 2002, then you'd have a pension adjustment reported on your 2002 T4 slip that would prevent you from making contributions to your RRSP in the following year—2003. If you were to leave your employer on January 1, 2003, and join another employer without a pension plan, you would be in a tough spot. You would not be able to make contributions to an RPP since you're no longer a member of one, nor could you make RRSP contributions because of your PA from 2002. Talk about a rip-off—a full year without contributions to a tax-deferred retirement savings plan.

The bottom line is this: An RRSP is portable, meaning that you can change employers and not worry about losing a beat in your retirement savings. The same cannot be said for RPPs in every situation. You have to weigh this fact against the benefits of a pension plan, which could include a guaranteed income in retirement (under a defined benefit plan) and significant contributions by your employer to the plan. If you're quite sure you'll be with your employer for a significant period of time, then a company pension plan can make sense.

TO MAKE A LONG STORY SHORT:

- When you leave a company pension plan you could very likely be short-changed on the benefits you take with you, particularly when you haven't been a member of the pension plan for long.

- When you leave a pension plan and don't join another, you could lose the ability to use a tax-deferred retirement savings plan for a full year.

- An RRSP is much more portable than a pension plan, but each situation should be evaluated separately.

Tim's Tip 83: Look into an Individual Pension Plan (IPP) to avoid a big tax hit when leaving your company pension plan.

This tip may not apply to everyone, but it's great when it works—as it did in Greer's case. She came to my office very recently to talk about her pension options.

*G*reer is a teacher and has chosen to take an early retirement. The RPP *that she's a member of sent her a statement explaining her options. Option 1: She can take a pension starting the month she leaves the school board. Since she's only 54, this pension is significantly reduced compared to the amount she would receive if she retired at age 65. Option 2: She can take her pension starting at age 65. Option 3: She can take the value of her pension benefits in one lump-sum amount (called her commuted value) and transfer most of this commuted value to a locked-in RRSP, with the balance being taxable in her hands. What's her best bet?*

The Most Common Option

Greer wanted to take the commuted value of her pension—option 3. I don't blame her. It's a popular option. You see, in Greer's case, this commuted value amounts to $450,000. If she's able to invest this money properly, she could provide herself with a better retirement income than the RPP was promising her. Her biggest concern is that, of the $450,000, just $350,000 can be transferred to a locked-in RRSP for her. Under our tax law, there will always be a limit to how much can be rolled tax-free from your RPP to a locked-in RRSP. The remaining $100,000 in Greer's case will face tax in her hands. That's no small tax bill.

The IPP Solution

When I asked Greer what she planned to do after leaving the school board, she told me that she wants to start a business working with children with learning disabilities. "Terrific," I said. I suggested to Greer that it might make sense for her to become the shareholder and employee of a corporation set up to provide these services. The corporation could then sponsor a pension plan specifically for Greer—called an Individual Pension Plan (IPP). An IPP is really a type of RPP. With an IPP set up, it will be possible in Greer's case to transfer the full $450,000 commuted value from her school board pension to her new company pension plan. She'll manage to defer tax on the $100,000 she otherwise would have paid tax on. She was thrilled.

TO MAKE A LONG STORY SHORT:

- You might have two or three options available when you leave a pension plan. It's quite common to take the commuted value of the plan when this is an option.

- Consider setting up an IPP if you will be running a business. This may allow a tax-free transfer of your commuted value to the new plan.

- Speak to a tax pro who is experienced in IPPs to set this plan in motion.

Getting into the Game

With careful planning, you can look forward to a golden future. And the sooner you start your plan in motion, the brighter your financial picture will be. Turn now to the Tax Planning Tip Sheet at the front of the book and review the strategies that you read about in Chapter 6. Check *Yes* or *Not Sure* for each strategy that you are willing to consider implementing. When you're finished this book, take your Tip Sheet to a tax professional for more information or help in implementing the strategies.

AMERICAN LEAGUE RULES: UNITED STATES' CONNECTIONS

In the United States you might get away with murder, but never tax evasion. Just ask Al Capone.

7

Stepping up to the plate when it comes to dealing with the U.S. tax system is going to take a keen eye. And, like Canadian tax law, the U.S. tax system can throw you a wicked knuckle ball when you least expect it. With some helpful tips from this chapter, and a little planning and preparation, you'll have the tools needed to beat the tax collector in the U.S. This chapter will speak to Canadians who invest in the U.S., as well as snowbirds, part-time U.S. residents, and others with U.S. connections. If you're a citizen of the U.S., these rules may not apply to you—a visit to a tax pro is important.

Reporting Your U.S. Income

Tim's Tip 84: Claim a foreign tax credit when you've paid withholding taxes to Uncle Sam.

The fact is, certain types of income received from U.S. sources are subject to taxes in the U.S. If you live in Canada, these taxes usually take the form of withholding taxes of 5 to 30 percent, payable to the Internal Revenue Service (IRS). For the most part, Canadian residents won't find any advantage to earning U.S. source income from a tax point of view. Here's why: You'll have to report the full amount of your U.S. income on your Canadian tax return since Canadian residents are taxed in Canada on worldwide income.

But the story's not over. You'll be entitled to claim a foreign tax credit on Schedule 1 of your Canadian tax return for any U.S. or other foreign taxes paid. This credit prevents a double-tax problem where you're paying tax on the same income in more than one country. Seems fair, doesn't it?

Here's the bottom line: You'll end up paying tax at Canadian tax rates, but you'll send a portion of the tax to the IRS (the withholding tax) and the rest to CCRA. A variety of income types give rise to a foreign tax credit. Let's take a look at the most common sources.

Interest Income

Interest income earned on bonds or other debt instruments will attract a 10-percent withholding tax that will be collected by the company that pays the interest. The major exception to this rule is interest earned on deposits in U.S. banks. This interest is generally tax-free if paid to a non-resident. If your U.S. bank has been withholding tax at source, give them a completed Certificate of Foreign Status (which they should be able to provide) to avoid those withholdings. There's no need

If you're a U.S. citizen living in Canada, you'll be treated differently for U.S. tax purposes than Canadian citizens are. All U.S. citizens, regardless of where they live, must file a full-blown tax return in the U.S. And this means you'll have to report your worldwide income to Uncle Sam. As a result, you won't be subject to withholding taxes in the U.S. If you're a U.S. citizen who has been neglecting to file in the U.S., be warned that you could face civil and criminal penalties.

to file a U.S. tax return to pay taxes on interest income when the correct amount of withholding taxes was applied.

Dividends

The withholding rate applied to dividends is currently 15 percent under the Canada–U.S. tax treaty. Again, you don't have to file a U.S. tax return to report U.S. dividend income when the correct amount of withholding tax was deducted at the source.

Pension Payments

Periodic payments from a U.S. source pension will be subject to withholding taxes at 15 percent. If the payment is in the form of a lump sum, it will attract a withholding tax of 30 percent, which approximates the regular U.S. tax rate. Again, no need to file a U.S. tax return when the proper withholding taxes were applied.

Capital Gains

There's good news for those of you investing in U.S. securities. A sale of U.S. stocks and bonds that generates a capital gain will not normally be taxed in the U.S. as long as you're a resident of Canada—the tax treaty will protect you. The exception is the rare circumstance where you own a U.S. real property holding corporation. This is a corporation whose majority of assets are U.S. real estate. The sale of these shares will be treated the same way as the sale of U.S. real estate by an individual— and I'll talk more about real estate in a minute.

Social Security

The rules around social security have flip-flopped twice in the last few years. Here's how the current rules work: A Canadian-resident who receives U.S. social security reports the income in Canada only, and just 85 percent of the benefits are taxable in

Canada. The U.S. no longer withholds any tax. These new rules were made retroactive to 1996. By the way, the rules work the same for Canada Pension Plan (CPP) recipients resident in the U.S. That is, tax will be paid in the U.S. alone, and not in Canada. Don't forget, U.S. citizens should get the advice of a tax pro since the rules are different for you.

Other Payments

Alimony and maintenance are exempt from U.S. withholding taxes. And if you happen to earn employment income in the U.S., that income will not be subject to withholding or other taxes in the U.S. as long as the income amounts to $10,000 (U.S.) or less in the year. Even if the income is over $10,000 (U.S.), it will still be tax-free in the U.S. if you were present in the U.S. for fewer than 184 days, and if you were paid by a Canadian-resident employer (but not a U.S.-resident employer or a permanent establishment in the U.S. that your Canadian-resident employer might operate).

> **Did You Know?**
>
> Provided you've been resident in Canada for at least 40 years after you reached the age of 18, you'll be entitled to full Old Age Security (OAS) benefits at age 65, even if you leave Canada. If you were resident in Canada for less than 20 years after you reached 18, and you leave Canada, your OAS benefits will cease after six months.

TO MAKE A LONG STORY SHORT:

- Certain types of income from the U.S. will be subject to withholding taxes down south.

- As a Canadian resident you'll be entitled to a foreign tax credit in Canada for U.S. or other foreign taxes you pay.

- Be sure to claim the tax credit to ensure that you're not double-taxed on the same income in different countries. The calculation is done on Schedule 1 of your tax return.

Profiting from U.S. Real Estate

Last summer, Carolyn and I spent a week visiting her brother and his family in Alabama. We spent a good part of the week at the family's cottage (they call them lake houses down south), not far from Birmingham. It was beautiful. While we were there, we met some fellow Canadians at the lake. Turns out they own a lake house and rent it out most of the year. I had a good talk with them about the tax rules affecting their U.S. property.

Tim's Tip 85: Use the *net rental income method* on your U.S. rental property in most cases.

The U.S. will normally impose a 30-percent withholding tax on your gross rental revenue. You can avoid this by filing IRS Form 4224 with the individual collecting and remitting the tax (the person renting the property from you) and electing to use the *net rental income method*.

---

*L*ucy and Silvio own a rental property in Alabama, and they rented it to Nadia for six months at $1,000 per month. Unless Nadia is given Form 4224, she is obliged to withhold 30 percent of the rent ($300 each month) and remit it to the IRS. If the election is made and the form is filed, then Lucy and Silvio will escape the 30-percent withholding tax, but they will be obliged to file a U.S. tax return each year to report the actual income and expenses from the rental property. Turns out that Lucy and Silvio's tax bill is much lower using this method—the net rental income method—than remitting a full 30 percent of the gross rents.

Under the net rental income method, you'll deduct from income all the property taxes, interest, maintenance, insurance, and other costs associated with the property—including depreciation, which is mandatory in the U.S.

Before deciding on the net rental income method, keep these points in mind:

- Not all expenses will be deductible under this method. Generally, you'll need to allocate your expenses between the personal-use portion and the rental portion based on days the property was rented.

- When a property is used personally for less than 15 days each year or 10 percent of the time available (whichever is greater), you won't need to allocate expenses as personal use.
- When a property is rented out for less than 15 days each year, there's no need to report any rental income and no expenses are deductible.
- When you elect to use the net rental income method, the election is generally irrevocable, and this method will apply to all your U.S. rental properties if you have more than one.
- If you want to use the net rental income method, the deadline for the 2002 year is October 15, 2004 (an 18-month deadline is imposed on "foreign nationals" by the IRS). Meet this deadline or the IRS won't allow any deductions!

TO MAKE A LONG STORY SHORT:

- When you own a rental property in the U.S., there are two ways of paying tax on the rents you earn: a withholding tax, or the net rental income method of reporting.

- The net rental income method will generally provide the greatest tax savings.

Tim's Tip 86: Take two steps to minimize the tax hit on the sale of your U.S. real estate.

Let's hope that the U.S. real estate you bought turns out to be a good investment. And if it does, this could mean some tax to pay to the IRS later when you sell the property at a profit. You can minimize your tax hit in a couple of ways.

Minimize Withholding Tax

Normally, the sale of your U.S. real estate is going to attract a 10-percent withholding tax that is remitted by the buyer or the buyer's agent to the IRS. The tax is calculated as 10 percent of the actual sale price of the property and not the gain on the sale. Keep in mind that this withholding tax doesn't remove your obligation to file a U.S. tax return to report the sale of your property. No sir. You'll have to

Action Step

If you want to avoid the 10-percent withholding tax that is normally due when a Canadian citizen and resident sells U.S. real estate, sell the property to an individual who plans to occupy it as a principal residence, and keep the selling price below $300,000 (U.S.). In this case, the IRS will waive the requirement for the buyer to withhold that 10 percent.

report that sale—normally on IRS Form 1040NR if you're a Canadian citizen and resident—and you may have to hand over more tax to the IRS. The 10-percent withholding tax is simply treated as an installment on the taxes owing. If you sell the property for little or no profit, then you might actually recover some or all of that 10-percent tax withheld.

You can apply to the IRS for a "withholding certificate" based on your expectation that the U.S. tax owed will be less than 10 percent of the sale price. This certificate will tell the buyer how much money to withhold, if any. But remember, this exception applies only to the withholding tax. The gain on the sale will still attract tax, and you will still need to file a tax return reporting the gain or loss to the U.S. government.

Minimize Your Taxable Gain

Calculating your gain or loss on the sale of your U.S. property is not rocket science, but you'll want to do it right to minimize the tax bill you could face. In a nutshell, here's the formula to calculate your gain or loss:

	Net proceeds on sale
Minus	Cost base
Equals	Gain or loss on sale

Seems simple enough, right? Well, hold on. You need to make some adjustments to these figures to make sure you're not paying too much tax. Consider this: The net proceeds are calculated by taking the selling price minus all selling expenses—including commissions, fees, and similar expenses (most of these appear on your closing statement). If you forget these additional costs, you could be paying too much tax.

As for your cost base, be sure to take the original cost and add the cost of any major improvements—also called capital improvements. If the property is a rental, then these capital improvements would not have been deductible; rather, they increase your cost base when selling the property. Further, on a rental property, you've got to deduct from the cost base the amount of any depreciation on the property—whether you previously claimed that depreciation or not. This is going to increase your capital gain. If you owned the property solely for personal use, then no depreciation need be taken and your cost base is not adjusted.

Make sense so far? Once the gain has been determined, you can now deduct all the accumulated rental losses that you've been claiming over the years, if any.

> **Action Step**
>
> Make sure you visit a tax pro if you owned your U.S. property before September 27, 1980, and it has been exclusively for personal use. You see, special rules exist for Canadian residents in this boat. Under the Canada–U.S. tax treaty, only the gain since January 1, 1985, might be taxed. To take advantage of this provision, you'll need a valuation of the property at January 1, 1985.

*G*race owns a home in Florida, which she rents out half of the year. She has owned the house for three years and has had rental losses averaging $3,000 (U.S.) each year. The house originally cost $100,000 (U.S.) and Grace has spent $25,000 (U.S.) over the years renovating the house. All the required tax returns have been filed over the three years. This year, Grace sold the house for $150,000 (U.S.) to a person who intends to use the house as his principal residence. What do you suppose Grace's gain on the sale is, if her real estate commissions were $6,000 (U.S.), and depreciation on the home was $13,000 (U.S.) over the three years? Time to crunch a few numbers. Here is Grace's gain:

Net proceeds on sale ($150,000 − $6,000)	$ 144,000
Cost base ($100,000 + $25,000 − $13,000)	($ 112,000)
Gain on sale	$ 32,000
Net rental losses from prior years (3 years × $3,000)	($ 9,000)
Net gain on sale	$ 23,000

Don't forget that any gain or loss on the sale of your U.S. property will also have to be reported on your Canadian tax return if you are resident in Canada. Don't worry about paying tax on the same gains in both Canada and the U.S.—the foreign tax credit I talked about earlier will protect you from this. Alternatively, you might be able to call your U.S. property your principal residence, which could save you a bundle in Canadian tax.

TO MAKE A LONG STORY SHORT:

- When you sell your U.S. real estate, you'll be subject to a 10-percent withholding tax that the buyer will have to remit to the IRS.

- Minimize this tax by selling to someone who plans to use the property as a principal residence or by applying to the U.S. for a withholding certificate.

- Minimize your taxable gain on the sale by making appropriate adjustments to your sale proceeds and your cost base.

Cutting Your Gambling Losses

Tax is definitely a game I can help you to win. As for roulette, blackjack, craps, the ponies, and the rest—you're on your own, I'm afraid. There's not much I can do to help you win in games of chance! But if you walk away from the casino or race track poorer than when you arrived, there may be some consolation.

Tim's Tip 87: Register at a casino or hotel to track gambling losses for tax savings.

Recent changes to the Canada–U.S. tax treaty will now treat Canadian residents in the same way as U.S. citizens and residents with regard to gambling. Specifically, Canadian residents can now deduct gambling losses from gambling winnings in the same year.

As in the past, gambling and lottery winnings will be subject to a 30-percent withholding tax at the time of winning, although winnings from blackjack, baccarat, craps, roulette, and the Big-6 wheel are exempt from tax. If you're hoping to carry your losses back to previous years, or ahead to future years, don't get your hopes up. Winnings and losses cannot be carried back and forth and offset against other years. If you've received winnings that have had tax withheld and you can substantiate losses, you should consider filing a tax return—Form 1040NR—to claim some of these losses back. Keep in mind, you cannot claim a refund for tax withheld on gambling winnings prior to 1996. Also, if you've received tax-exempt winnings or you have no substantiated losses, don't bother filing a 1040NR tax return—you're not going to get any tax back.

The easiest way to provide the IRS with the information required to substantiate gambling losses is to register at one of the hotels or casinos and establish an account. As money is withdrawn from the account, a record is produced showing all your cash withdrawals. In the past, this has been accepted by the IRS as proof of gambling losses.

When filing your return, include the W-2G withholding slip the casino gave you, showing your winnings and the amount withheld plus the official record indicating your withdrawals from the casino account. This return should be filed by the regular deadline for Form 1040NR, which is June 15 for the previous year.

> **Did You Know?**
>
> If you buy that lotto ticket and strike it rich, you'll be glad to know that your lottery winnings are tax-free in Canada. Not so in the U.S.—the IRS will be right by your side waiting to collect some of those winnings. By the way, the expected value of lottery winnings is, on average, six cents for every dollar spent in a lifetime on tickets.

TO MAKE A LONG STORY SHORT:

- Canadian residents can now claim U.S. gambling losses to offset winnings.

- Register at a casino or hotel and establish an account to substantiate your gambling losses.

- File a tax return, Form 1040NR, to claim your losses and recover any withholding tax.

Staying Canadian

If you're planning to spend time in the U.S. each year, there are some things you should keep in mind to avoid the long arm of Uncle Sam.

Tim's Tip 88: Understand the implications of becoming a resident of the U.S.

Becoming a resident of the U.S. for tax purposes can add a whole world of complexity to your tax affairs. If you inadvertently become a resident south of the border, you'll be required to file a U.S. tax return and pay U.S. tax on your worldwide income.

The IRS will consider you to be a U.S. resident for tax purposes if you hold a green card or if you meet the *substantial presence test*. How does it work? If the following formula adds up to 183 days or more, then you've met the substantial presence test and you'll be deemed a U.S. resident.

As a general rule, if you were physically present in the U.S. for 122 days (four months) a year over the last three years, you'll meet this test and be deemed a U.S. resident.

THE SUBSTANTIAL PRESENCE TEST	
Add	The total days you are present in the U.S. in the current year.
	(It must be at least 31 days or you will not be caught by this test.)
Plus	One-third of the days you were present in the U.S. in the prior year.
Plus	One-sixth of the days you were present in the U.S. in the second prior year.
If the total of these is 183 days or more, then you have met the substantial presence test.	

How Do You Spell Relief?

If you meet the substantial presence test, there are still three avenues of relief that could allow you to escape having to file a full-blown tax return in the U.S.

1. **Closer Connection**. If you truly have a closer connection to Canada than the U.S., despite meeting the dreaded substantial presence test, then you can file a Closer Connection Statement with the IRS, Form 8840, telling the IRS about this closer connection. Filing this form will get you out of the obligation to report your worldwide income to Uncle Sam. To claim a closer connection to Canada, you must be present in the U.S. fewer than 183 days in the current year and file Form 8840 by June 15 of the following year (that is, file by June 15, 2003, for the year 2002).

2. **Exempt Person**. Generally, you won't be treated as being present in the U.S. on any day in which you're temporarily present in the U.S. as a foreign government–related individual, a teacher or trainee who holds a J visa, a student holding either an F, J, or M visa, or a professional athlete temporarily in the U.S. to compete in a charitable sporting event. If you're an exempt individual, you're required to file a form with the IRS stating why you're exempt from U.S. taxation.

3. **Tie-Breaker Rules**. It's possible you might be considered a resident of both Canada and the U.S. at the same time under the tax laws in each country. In this case, the Canada–U.S. tax treaty provides relief from being considered a resident of both countries by applying some "tie-breaker" rules. Now, if you hold a U.S. permanent resident visa (a green card) you should be careful about claiming to be a non-resident of the U.S. under the treaty. This could jeopardize your ability to maintain that U.S. residency permit. You should get advice from an immigration lawyer before claiming non-resident status in this case.

TO MAKE A LONG STORY SHORT:

- Avoid becoming a U.S. resident for tax purposes if you hope to keep your tax affairs from becoming a complex quagmire.

- If you spend, on average, more than 122 days each year in the U.S., you might meet the substantial presence test, which will deem you to be a resident of the U.S.

> Don't assume, just because you're considered a resident of Canada for Canadian tax purposes, that the IRS will agree with you. You might also be considered a U.S. resident for U.S. tax purposes! Being a resident of both Canada and the U.S. at the same time will do nothing but complicate your tax affairs.

Caution!

- If you meet the substantial presence test and are deemed to be a resident of the U.S., filing Form 8840 could solve your problem. You may also avoid filing a full-blown U.S. tax return if you're an "exempt person," or you claim protection under the tax treaty's "tie-breaker" rules.

Considering U.S. Estate Taxes

Tim's Tip 89: Determine whether you're a candidate for U.S. estate taxes.

While Canada does not levy estate taxes upon death, the U.S. does. And if you're a Canadian citizen or resident living in Canada, but you own U.S. property, you could be hit with a U.S. estate tax bill upon your death. The kinds of U.S. properties that I'm talking about include: U.S. real estate; shares of U.S. public or private corporations; debt obligations issued by U.S. residents; personal property in the U.S.; and more. The tax bill you can expect is based on the fair market value of those U.S. assets on the date of your death.

> **Caution!**
>
> If you don't calculate carefully, you might just count too many days of presence in the U.S., which could cause you to meet the substantial presence test. In your calculations, be sure to exclude any days in which you were in the U.S. as a student, teacher or trainee, professional athlete temporarily in the U.S. to compete in a charitable event, or diplomat with full-time diplomatic or consular status. If these exceptions apply to you, they also automatically apply to your immediate family.

By the way, I should mention that, even if you're considered a resident of Canada for Canadian tax purposes, you might still be considered to be domiciled in the United States. I know it may sound confusing, but domicile in the U.S. is something different than residency in either Canada or the U.S. And if you're considered to be domiciled in the U.S., you'll be liable for U.S. estate tax on all your assets—not simply on those U.S. assets that I talked about in the preceding paragraph. In most cases, a little planning will let you avoid being considered domiciled in the U.S., and you'll have nothing to worry about. I won't go into the definition of U.S. domicile here, but you should check with your tax pro if you're spending lots of time in the U.S., just to make sure you won't be caught.

Once you recognize that you're a candidate for a U.S. estate tax bill, you should consider a number of planning strategies to minimize these taxes. See Tip 103 in Chapter 9 for all the details.

TO MAKE A LONG STORY SHORT:

- You could be liable to pay U.S. estate tax if you own U.S. assets or are considered domiciled in the U.S.

- If you think you're a candidate for U.S. estate taxes, refer to Tip 103 in Chapter 9 for details on how to minimize this tax bill.

Getting into the Game

You could be well on your way to tax savings on both sides of the border. Turn now to the Tax Planning Tip Sheet at the front of the book and review the strategies introduced in Chapter 7. Check *Yes* or *Not Sure* if you are willing to consider implementing a tip. When you've finished this book, take your Tip Sheet to a tax pro if you want more information or help in implementing your plan.

A LEAGUE OF THEIR OWN: PROVINCIAL TAX ISSUES

If a man does not keep pace with his companions, perhaps it is because he hears a different drummer.

8

W hile it's true that tax rates have been coming down a little over the last couple of years, one thing still remains the same: Our tax system is as complicated as ever! In fact, it's only getting more complex. The reason? Each province now levies an income tax based on your income. You see, it used to be that each province (with the exception of Quebec) simply calculated your tax bill by multiplying your federal tax by a certain percentage. This was a "tax on tax" type of system, and it was pretty simple to calculate your provincial taxes.

No longer. Your province now calculates your taxes based on taxable income. For now, the provinces have agreed to use the same taxable income figure that appears on your federal tax return, which simplifies things. But don't expect this to last forever! The feds will continue to collect the tax for your province (except Quebec), but make no mistake, your province has more control over the calculation of the taxes collected on its behalf. The bottom line is this: Calculating your taxes annually will only get more complex over time. This chapter will help you understand where the calculation of your provincial taxes may differ from your federal taxes. By the way, you'll find the marginal tax rates for each province and territory at the back of the book, beginning on page 286.

Walking to a Different Drummer

Tim's Tip 90: **Understand the various tax rates and credits that apply specifically to your province.**

I've got news to share with you about each of the provinces and territories, so let's start from the west and work our way east, shall we? You'll notice that Quebec is not listed in this Tip since I'll be dealing with Quebec in the next Tip.

British Columbia

Gary Collins, Minister of Finance, released British Columbia's 2002 budget on February 19, 2002. There were no significant changes to personal taxes. Taxable income in BC mirrors federal taxable income for 2002, and the tax rates and credits that apply for 2002 are as follows:

Did You Know?

The federal and provincial governments entered into Tax Collection Agreements back in 1962 that saw the feds collect the taxes for each province and territory. In December 1997 at a meeting of Canada's finance ministers, the federal government agreed to change the system to allow each province to calculate its taxes based on taxable income, rather than as a percentage of basic federal tax. The new system still maintains a common definition of taxable income both federally and provincially, along with a number of other common definitions.

Taxable Income	Tax Rates: 2002	Tax Rates: 2003[1]
$0 to $31,124	6.05%	6.05%
$31,125 to $62,249	9.15%	9.15%
$62,250 to $71,470	11.7%	11.7%
$71,471 to $86,785	13.7%	13.7%
$86,786 and over	14.7%	14.7%

[1] Tax rates for 2003 were announced in 2001 but may be changed in a budget or other announcement made subsequent to the time of writing. Tax brackets listed are for 2002 and will be indexed for 2003.

- The basic personal tax credit amount for 2002 is $8,168, and the spousal credit amount is $6,994. Your tax credit is equal to 6.05 percent of these amounts.
- Other tax credits are calculated at 6.05 percent of the applicable amounts and include: Age amount, dependant amount, CPP contributions, EI contributions, pension income amount, disability amount, disability supplement, tuition and education amounts, medical expenses, caregiver amount, and interest on student loans.
- Tax credits for charitable donations are 6.05 percent on the first $200 of eligible donations and 14.7 percent on amounts over $200.
- The dividend tax credit is 5.1 percent of the grossed-up amount of Canadian dividends.
- Surtaxes are no longer levied in B.C.

Alberta

On March 19, 2002, Patricia Nelson presented her second budget as minister of finance. There were no new income tax measures in the budget. Taxable income in Alberta mirrors federal taxable income for 2002, and the tax rate and credits that apply for 2002 are as follows:

Taxable Income	Tax Rate: 2002	Tax Rate: 2003[1]
All taxable income	10.0%	10.0%

[1] The tax rate for 2003 is assumed to be the same as it is for 2002 since no announcement to the contrary has been made. This rate may be changed in a budget or other announcement made subsequent to the time of writing.

- The basic personal tax credit amount for 2002 is $13,339, and the spousal credit amount is $13,339. Your tax credit is equal to 10.0 percent of these amounts.
- Other tax credits are calculated at 10.0 percent of the applicable amounts for 2002 and include: Age amount, dependant amount, CPP contributions, EI contributions, pension income amount, disability amount, disability supplement, tuition amount, education amount, medical expenses, caregiver amount, and interest on student loans.
- Tax credits for charitable donations are 10.0 percent on the first $200 of eligible donations and 12.75 percent on amounts over $200.
- The dividend tax credit is 6.4 percent of the grossed-up amount of Canadian dividends.
- Surtaxes are no longer levied in Alberta.

Saskatchewan

The Saskatchewan budget for 2002 was presented by Eric Cline, minister of finance, on March 27, 2002. No significant personal tax changes were introduced. Taxable income in Saskatchewan mirrors federal taxable income for 2002, and the tax rates and credits that apply for 2002 are as follows:

Taxable Income	Tax Rates: 2002	Tax Rates: 2003[1]
$0 to $30,000	11.25%	11.0%
$30,001 to $60,000	13.25%	13.0%
$60,001 and over	15.5%	15.0%

[1] Tax rates for 2003 were announced in the 2001 budget but may be changed in a budget or other announcement made subsequent to the time of writing. Tax brackets listed are for 2002. In 2003, the tax brackets are expected to be; $35,000, $100,000, and over $100,000, respectively.

- The basic personal tax credit amount for 2002 is $8,000, and the spousal credit amount is $8,000. Your tax credit is equal to 11.25 percent of these amounts.
- Other tax credits are calculated at 11.25 percent of the applicable amounts and include: Age amount, dependant amount, CPP contributions, EI contributions, pension income amount, disability amount, disability supplement, tuition and education amounts, medical expenses, caregiver amount, and interest on student loans.

- Tax credits for charitable donations are 11.25 percent on the first $200 of eligible donations and 15.5 percent on amounts over $200.
- The dividend tax credit is 8.0 percent of the grossed-up amount of Canadian dividends.
- There is no longer a flat tax, surtax, or debt-reduction surtax levied in Saskatchewan.
- Saskatchewan announced that for 2001 and subsequent years, qualified farm property and small business corporation shares exceeding the $500,000 enhanced capital gains exemption will be taxed at the lowest tax rate for the province (11.25 percent for 2002 and 11.0 percent for 2003).

Manitoba

Finance Minister Greg Selinger's budget of April 22, 2002, did not introduce any significant tax cuts, but did do away with the Learning Tax Credit. Taxable income in Manitoba mirrors federal taxable income for 2002, and the tax rates and credits that apply for 2002 are as follows:

Taxable Income	Tax Rates: 2002	Tax Rates: 2003[1]
$0 to $30,544	10.9%	10.9%
$30,545 to $65,000	15.4%	14.9%
$65,001 and over	17.4%	17.4%

[1] Tax rates for 2003 were amended in the 2001 budget but may be changed in a budget or other announcement made subsequent to the time of writing. Tax brackets listed are for 2002 and will be indexed for 2003.

- The basic personal tax credit amount for 2002 is $7,634, and the spousal credit amount is $6,482. Your tax credit is equal to 10.9 percent of these amounts.
- Other tax credits are calculated at 10.9 percent of the applicable amounts and include: Age amount, dependant amount, CPP contributions, EI contributions, pension income amount, disability amount, disability supplement, tuition and education amounts, medical expenses, caregiver amount, and interest on student loans.
- Tax credits for charitable donations are 10.9 percent on the first $200 of eligible donations and 17.4 percent on amounts over $200.
- The dividend tax credit is 5.0 percent of the grossed-up amount of Canadian dividends.

- Manitoba repealed the Learning Tax Credit, introduced a Mineral Exploration Tax Credit (a 10-percent non-refundable credit for investment in certain flow-through shares or qualifying mineral exploration companies), extended the Equity Tax Credit (now due to expire June 30, 2008), and enhanced its Political Contributions Tax Credit (which now parallels the federal credit).
- There is no longer a flat tax or surtax levied in Manitoba.

Ontario

Janet Ecker delivered Ontario's 2002 budget on June 17, 2002. The key changes to personal taxes involved changes in the timing of previously announced cuts.

Taxable income in Ontario mirrors federal taxable income for 2002, and the tax rates and credits that apply for 2002 are as follows:

Taxable Income	Tax Rates: 2002	Tax Rates: 2003[1]
$0 to $31,892	6.05%	6.05%
$31,893 to $63,786	9.15%	9.15%
$63,787 and over	11.16%	11.16%

[1] Tax rates for 2003 were announced in the 2001 budget but may be changed in a budget or other announcement made subsequent to the time of writing. Tax brackets listed are for 2002 and will be indexed for 2003.

- The basic personal tax credit amount for 2002 is $7,686, and the spousal credit amount is $6,527. Your tax credit is equal to 6.05 percent of these amounts.
- Other tax credits are calculated at 6.05 percent of the applicable amounts and include: Age amount, dependant amount, CPP contributions, EI contributions, pension income amount, disability amount, disability supplement, tuition and education amounts, medical expenses, caregiver amount, and interest on student loans.
- Tax credits for charitable donations are 6.05 percent on the first $200 of eligible donations and 11.16 percent on amounts over $200 for 2002.
- Personal tax brackets and credit amounts were indexed by 3.5 percent for 2002. Decreases in the bottom and middle tax rates were implemented on October 1, 2001, sooner than the previously announced date of January 1, 2002. Reductions previously scheduled for January 1, 2003, have been delayed by one year. For

You're going to pay taxes in the province in which you were resident on December 31. So, if you're thinking of a move to a province with a lower tax rate, make that move before the end of the year to take advantage of that province's lower tax rates a year sooner. By the way, if it's not precisely clear where you're resident on December 31, the tax collector will look to which province you ordinarily reside in a permanent home and with which you have closer social and economic ties.

2004, tax rates applicable to tax brackets will be as follows: 5.65, 8.85, and 11.16 percent.

- The dividend tax credit is 5.13 percent of the grossed-up amount of Canadian dividends.
- Ontario still levies surtaxes for 2002 (c'mon, enough already), at the following rates: 20 percent of gross taxes in excess of $3,685, plus 36 percent of gross taxes in excess of $4,648 (these dollar thresholds will be indexed for 2003). In 2004, the surtax will become a one-tier tax of 56 percent (combining the 20 and 36 percent rates), and only the top threshold of $4,648 (to be indexed) will survive.
- The Equity in Education Tax Credit is a credit on the first $7,000 of private school (elementary and secondary) tuition. The credit rate was to be phased in over five years. The timing of that phase-in has been delayed so that the credit will start at 10 percent for 2002, reaching 50 percent in 2006 (the actual timing of phase-in is uncertain).

New Brunswick

Finance Minister Peter Mesheau released New Brunswick's 2002 budget on March 26, 2002. There were no significant personal tax changes made. Taxable income in NB mirrors federal taxable income for 2002, and the tax rates and credits that apply for 2002 are as follows:

- The basic personal tax credit amount for 2002 is $7,634, and the spousal credit amount is $6,482. Your tax credit is equal to 9.68 percent of these amounts.
- Other tax credits are calculated at 9.68 percent of the applicable amounts and include: Age amount, dependant amount, CPP contributions, EI contributions, pension income amount, disability amount, disability supplement, tuition and education amounts, medical expenses, caregiver amount, and interest on student loans.

Taxable Income	Tax Rates: 2002	Tax Rates: 2003[1]
$0 to $31,677	9.68%	9.68%
$31,678 to $63,354	14.82%	14.82%
$63,355 to $103,000	16.52%	16.52%
$103,001 and over	17.84%	17.84%

[1] Tax rates for 2003 had not been announced at the time of writing and so the assumption is made that they may not change from 2002. These rates for 2003 may be changed in a budget or other announcement made subsequent to the time of writing. Tax brackets for 2003 may be indexed for inflation.

- Tax credits for charitable donations are 9.68 percent on the first $200 of eligible donations and 17.84 percent on amounts over $200 for 2002.
- The dividend tax credit is 7.6 percent of the grossed-up amount of Canadian dividends.

Nova Scotia

On April 4, 2002, Finance Minister Neil LeBlanc brought down Nova Scotia's first balanced budget in 40 years. There were no new personal tax changes to speak of. Taxable income in NS mirrors federal taxable income for 2002, and the tax rates and credits that apply for 2002 are as follows:

Taxable Income	Tax Rates: 2002	Tax Rates: 2003[1]
$0 to $29,590	9.77%	9.77%
$29,591 to $59,180	14.95%	14.95%
$59,180 and over	16.67%	16.67%

[1] Tax rates for 2003 had not been announced at the time of writing and so the assumption is made that they may not change from 2002. These rates for 2003 may be changed in a budget or other announcement made subsequent to the time of writing. Tax brackets for 2003 may be indexed for inflation.

- The basic personal tax credit amount for 2002 is $7,231, and the spousal credit amount is $6,140. Your tax credit is equal to 9.77 percent of these amounts.

- Other tax credits are calculated at 9.77 percent of the applicable amounts and include: Age amount, dependant amount, CPP contributions, EI contributions, pension income amount, disability amount, disability supplement, tuition and education amounts, medical expenses, caregiver amount, and interest on student loans.
- Tax credits for charitable donations are 9.77 percent on the first $200 of eligible donations and 16.67 percent on amounts over $200 for 2002.
- The dividend tax credit is 7.7 percent of the grossed-up amount of Canadian dividends.
- NS still maintains its surtax equal to 10 percent of basic NS tax in excess of $10,000.

Prince Edward Island

PEI Treasurer Patricia Mella presented the 2002 budget on March 26, 2002. There were no significant personal tax changes announced. Taxable income in PEI mirrors federal taxable income for 2002, and the tax rates and credits that apply for 2002 are as follows:

Taxable Income	Tax Rates: 2002	Tax Rates: 2003[1]
$0 to $30,754	9.8%	9.8%
$30,755 to $61,509	13.8%	13.8%
$61,510 and over	16.7%	16.7%

[1] Tax rates for 2003 had not been announced at the time of writing and so the assumption is made that they may not change from 2002. These rates for 2003 may be changed in a budget or other announcement made subsequent to the time of writing. These tax brackets for 2003 may be indexed for inflation.

- The basic personal tax credit amount for 2002 is $7,412, and the spousal credit amount is $6,294. Your tax credit is equal to 9.8 percent of these amounts.
- Other tax credits are calculated at 9.8 percent of the applicable amounts and include: Age amount, dependant amount, CPP contributions, EI contributions, pension income amount, disability amount, disability supplement, tuition and education amounts, medical expenses, caregiver amount, and interest on student loans.

- Tax credits for charitable donations are 9.8 percent on the first $200 of eligible donations and 16.7 percent on amounts over $200 for 2002.
- The dividend tax credit is 7.7 percent of the grossed-up amount of Canadian dividends.
- PEI still maintains its surtax equal to 10 percent of basic PEI tax in excess of $5,200.

Newfoundland

Joan Marie Aylward presented the 2002 budget of Newfoundland and Labrador on March 21, 2002. Nothing new was announced on the tax front to speak of. Taxable income in Newfoundland mirrors federal taxable income for 2002, and the tax rates and credits that apply for 2002 are as follows below.

- The basic personal tax credit amount for 2002 is $7,410, and the spousal credit amount is $6,055. Your tax credit is equal to 10.57 percent of these amounts.
- Other tax credits are calculated at 10.57 percent of the applicable amounts and include: Age amount, dependant amount, CPP contributions, EI contributions, pension income amount, disability amount, disability supplement, tuition and education amounts, medical expenses, caregiver amount, and interest on student loans.

> **Did You Know?**
>
> At the time of writing, Canada's national debt stands at $547.4 billion. Our population is currently 31 million. This means that our country is indebted to the tune of $17,658 for every man, woman, and child in the country. Ouch. What's worse, 25 cents of every tax dollar raised goes to pay interest costs on the debt. While this is better than it was in 1992 when 42 cents of every tax dollar went to interest costs, there is room for significant improvement. The more debt that is paid down, the more of each tax dollar that is freed up for uses other than paying interest charges on the debt.

Taxable Income	Tax Rates: 2002	Tax Rates: 2003[1]
$0 to $29,590	10.57%	10.57%
$29,591 to $59,180	16.16%	16.16%
$59,181 and over	18.02%	18.02%

[1] Tax rates for 2003 had not been announced at the time of writing and so the assumption is made that they may not change from 2002. These rates for 2003 may be changed in a budget or other announcement made subsequent to the time of writing. There does not appear to be a plan to index the tax brackets annually, but this could change.

- Tax credits for charitable donations are 10.57 percent on the first $200 of eligible donations and 18.02 percent on amounts over $200 for 2002.
- The dividend tax credit was reduced for dividends declared and paid before March 20, 2002. The rate is now 5.0 percent of the grossed-up amount of Canadian dividends.
- Newfoundland still maintains a surtax equal to 9 percent of basic Newfoundland tax in excess of $7,032 for 2002.

Northwest Territories

Finance Minister Joseph Handley presented the 2002 NWT budget on February 20, 2002. There were some changes of note in personal tax credits announced in this budget. Taxable income in the NWT mirrors federal taxable income for 2002, and the tax rates and credits that apply for 2002 are as follows:

Taxable Income	Tax Rates: 2002	Tax Rates: 2003[1]
$0 to $31,677	7.2%	7.2%
$31,678 to $63,354	9.9%	9.9%
$63,355 to $103,000	11.7%	11.7%
$103,001 and over	13.05%	13.05%

[1] Tax rates for 2003 had not been announced at the time of writing and so the assumption is made that they may not change from 2002. These rates for 2003 may be changed in a budget or other announcement made subsequent to the time of writing. Tax brackets may be indexed for inflation.

- The basic personal tax credit amount for 2002 is $9,342, and the spousal credit amount is $8,766. Your tax credit is equal to 7.2 percent of these amounts. These amounts reflect a blend of the old amounts and the new amounts announced in the 2002 budget, which will apply for 2003. The new amounts are: basic personal tax credit amount of $11,050 and the spousal credit amount of $11,050.
- Other tax credits are calculated at 7.2 percent of the applicable amounts and include: Age amount, dependant amount, CPP contributions, EI contributions, pension income amount, disability amount, disability supplement, tuition and education amounts, medical expenses, caregiver amount, and interest on student loans.

- Tax credits for charitable donations are 7.2 percent on the first $200 of eligible donations and 13.05 percent on amounts over $200 for 2002.
- The dividend tax credit is 6.0 percent of the grossed-up amount of Canadian dividends.
- There are no surtaxes levied in NWT.

Nunavut

On April 30, 2002, Finance Minister Kelvin Ng gave his budget address. This represents the first year Nunavut has developed its own tax rates and credits apart from the Northwest Territories. The 2002 budget reduced all personal tax rates and credits. Taxable income in Nunavut mirrors federal taxable income for 2002, and the tax rates and credits that apply for 2002 are as follows:

Taxable Income	Tax Rates: 2002	Tax Rates: 2003[1]
$0 to $31,700	4.0%	4.0%
$31,701 to $63,400	7.0%	7.0%
$63,401 to $103,000	9.0%	9.0%
$103,001 and over	11.5%	11.5%

[1] Tax rates for 2003 had not been announced at the time of writing and so the assumption is made that they may not change from 2002. These rates for 2003 may be changed in a budget or other announcement made subsequent to the time of writing. Tax brackets may be indexed for inflation.

- The basic personal tax credit amount for 2002 is $10,000, and the spousal credit amount is $10,000. Your tax credit is equal to 4.0 percent of these amounts.
- Other tax credits are calculated at 4.0 percent of the applicable amounts and include: Age amount, dependant amount, CPP contributions, EI contributions, pension income amount, disability amount, disability supplement, tuition and education amounts, medical expenses, caregiver amount, and interest on student loans.
- Tax credits for charitable donations are 4.0 percent on the first $200 of eligible donations and 11.5 percent on amounts over $200 for 2002.
- The dividend tax credit is 6.0 percent of the grossed-up amount of Canadian dividends.
- There are no surtaxes levied in Nunavut.

Yukon

Pat Duncan presented the 2002 Yukon budget on April 4, 2002. Tax cuts were announced in the budget. Taxable income in the Yukon mirrors federal taxable income for 2002, and the tax rates and credits that apply for 2002 are as follows:

Taxable Income	Tax Rates: 2002	Tax Rates: 2003[1]
$0 to $31,677	7.04%	7.04%
$31,678 to $63,354	9.68%	9.68%
$63,355 to $103,000	11.44%	11.44%
$103,001 and over	12.76%	12.76%

[1] Tax rates for 2003 had not been announced at the time of writing and so the assumption is made that they may not change from 2002. These rates for 2003 may be changed in a budget or other announcement made subsequent to the time of writing. Tax brackets may be indexed for inflation.

- The basic personal tax credit amount for 2002 is $7,634, and the spousal credit amount is $6,482. Your tax credit is equal to 7.04 percent of these amounts.
- Other tax credits are calculated at 7.04 percent of the applicable amounts and include: Age amount, dependant amount, CPP contributions, EI contributions, pension income amount, disability amount, disability supplement, tuition and education amounts, medical expenses, caregiver amount, and interest on student loans.
- Tax credits for charitable donations are 7.04 percent on the first $200 of eligible donations and 12.76 percent on amounts over $200 for 2002.
- The dividend tax credit is 5.87 percent of the grossed-up amount of Canadian dividends.
- Yukon levies a surtax of 5 percent of Yukon tax in excess of $6,000.

Understanding the Quebec Difference

We should look at issues affecting taxpayers in Quebec in more depth. The reason? The differences between the federal and Quebec's system are more pronounced than in other provinces. We'll also look at some tax strategies to make you a winner if you live in Quebec.

Tim's Tip 91: **Understand the basics of the Quebec tax system.**

There are two key differences between the federal and Quebec tax systems to talk about: Quebec tax rates and Quebec's simplified tax filing system. Quebec's 2002 budget brought some minor changes, and we'll consider these too.

Quebec Tax Rates

In 1998, Quebec moved to a new three-bracket tax rate system, replacing the old five-rate system from 1997 and earlier years, and the 2002 Quebec budget introduced changes to these brackets and tax credits as the result of indexation for inflation at 2.7 percent for 2002. Here are the tax brackets and rates for Quebec for 2002:

Taxable Income	Tax Rates: 2002	Tax Rates: 2003[1]
$0 to $26,700	16.0%	16.0%
$26,701 to $53,405	20.0%	20.0%
$53,406 and over	24.0%	24.0%
Rate for non-refundable credits	20.0%	20.0%

[1] Tax rates for 2003 had not been announced at the time of writing and so the assumption is made that they may not change from 2002. These rates for 2003 may be changed in a budget or other announcement made subsequent to the time of writing. Tax brackets may be indexed for inflation.

The Simplified System

In 1998, the Quebec government introduced the simplified alternative tax system. I think we'd all agree that a simpler system is better. This simplified system is an optional way to file your tax return. It replaces more than 50 individual deductions with a single lump-sum tax deduction of $2,780 per person. This $2,780 amount may be adjusted annually based on a complex formula and is converted to a credit at the 20 percent rate to ultimately produce a $556 reduction in taxes. If you choose the simplified system, you'll be entitled to this credit, but you'll lose the ability to claim a number of expenses, including moving expenses, medical expenses, support payments, employment expenses, union or professional dues, investment expenses,

Revenue Quebec is trying to make it easy for you to choose between the general or simplified tax systems by providing a work chart to help you determine which system is best, and by telling you which system is better for you based on your previous year's tax return. If you're still not sure whether to file your tax return under the general or simplified system, just use the general system. Revenue Quebec will assess you under the simplified system if it is to your advantage.

the dividend tax credit, labour-sponsored fund credits, tuition fees, and others.

I should mention that, on June 30, 1999, the Quebec government amended the rules for the simplified system to allow for certain deductions and credits that were previously not permitted under this system. Check this list of these expenses in Information Bulletin 99-1, at the Web site **www.finances. gouv.qc.ca,** or call your local Revenue Quebec office. For the most part, these deductions are for the repayment of government benefits, tax-free rollovers to an RRSP, RRIF, or annuity, and certain payments made by disabled individuals.

But there's more. If you and your spouse both opt for the simplified system, the two of you can choose to file a joint Quebec tax return. This could mean half the paperwork. Finally, the simplified system will also allow one spouse to transfer the lump-sum credit to the other in order to minimize the family's overall tax burden.

Claude has been worrying about his 2002 Quebec tax return. He's not sure whether he should file under the general tax filing system or use the simplified filing system. In a nutshell, he'll be better off under the simplified system if his lump-sum credit is greater than the total of the replaced deductions. But he shouldn't worry about trying to decide whether to choose the general filing system or the new simplified system. If he chooses the general system and the simplified system would have been better for him, the government will assess his tax return under the simplified system to give him a bigger tax break. Claude can choose, if he wishes, not to have the government assess his return under the simplified system by sending notice to that effect on a prescribed form.

TO MAKE A LONG STORY SHORT:

- Quebec has had its own tax-on-income system for many years.

- In 1998 the Quebec government made it possible to file a tax return under the "simpli-fied system" that will replace a number of deductions with a single lump-sum tax credit.

Tim's Tip 92: **Understand the differences between federal and Quebec taxes, and plan accordingly.**

Let's take a look at the more significant differences between the federal and Quebec tax systems. If you don't understand these differences, your tax planning might work in one jurisdiction and not the other. Keep in mind that I'm not able to cover all the differences here, so you'd be wise to visit a tax professional before putting into place any fun and fancy tax strategies.

Personal and Family Tax Credits

Quebec offers a number of tax credits that are similar to the federal basic and related tax credits. Let me talk about four credits in particular. In each case, the base amount I refer to is multiplied by 20 percent (in 2002) to arrive at the tax credit amount: (1) the basic amount is a credit based on $6,060 in 2002 and is available to all taxpayers and coincides with the federal basic personal amount of $7,634 in 2002; (2) the amount with respect to age is a credit based on $2,200 for each spouse aged 65 or over; (3) the amount for a person living alone is a credit based on $1,080 for those living alone or with one or more dependent children; (4) the amount for retirement income is based on a maximum $1,000 and is available when you or your spouse report retirement income on your Quebec tax return. For credits 2 through 4 above, the actual amount claimed will be reduced by 15 percent for every dollar of family income over $26,700.

Refundable Childcare Tax Credit

Instead of a deduction for childcare expenses, Quebec offers a refundable tax credit. The credit is reduced as your income rises. The credit equals a certain percentage of your childcare expenses. For people in the lowest income bracket, a 75-percent credit is available, but this credit is reduced to 26 percent as income rises. Childcare expenses eligible for the credit are $7,000 for children under seven years of age at the end of the year, and $4,000 for other eligible children. While the lower-income spouse must claim childcare expenses for federal purposes, either spouse can claim them in Quebec.

Charitable Giving

The ceiling for charitable donations claimed in a given year is 75 percent of net income. This limit is increased to 100 percent in the year of death and the year before death. The limit for donations to the crown has been reduced from 100 percent of net income to 75 percent.

When total donations exceed $2,000 annually, the excess will provide greater tax relief in the form of a credit calculated at 24.0 percent (the rate of the highest tax bracket) of the excess amount (total donations of $2,000 or under attract a credit at 20 percent for 2002—the rate applicable to most non-refundable credits, generally). Donations in excess of the maximum that you can claim in a given year can be carried forward and used over the subsequent five years, or carried back to the previous year where the donor dies in the year of the contribution.

In order to encourage gifts of works of art to Quebec museums, the amount used to calculate the tax credit or the deduction for these gifts will now be equal to the fair market value of the work of art, plus 25 percent of that amount.

You should also be aware that Quebec has harmonized with the feds its rules regarding the donation of publicly traded shares, mutual funds, and segregated funds (so that just 25 percent of the gain realized when donating these securities is taxable. Consistent with the federal changes, this measure was extended so that it applies indefinitely.).

Tuition Fees

In Quebec, tuition fees will generate a 20-percent non-refundable tax credit. Unlike the federal law, any excess or undeducted tuition fees cannot be transferred to a spouse or parent but will be pooled and carried forward to offset future taxes. To compensate those who support students, the province introduced an enhanced non-refundable credit for dependants. This credit is equal to $339 per semester if the dependant is a full-time student at a post-secondary institution.

Academic Scholarships

In the 2000 budget, the Quebec government announced that the first $3,000 of scholarships, fellowships, bursaries, and prizes received by students would be tax-free. The 2001 budget took this a step further and announced that bursaries and prizes received other than by way of a registered education savings plan, through the carrying on of a business or by virtue of an office or employment, would be completely tax free, effective 2001.

Moving Allowances

If your employer requires you to move and gives you a moving allowance, you can exclude from income the portion of this allowance that equals two weeks of your salary at the new location. Quebec has also adopted the federal rules introduced in the 1998 federal budget regarding reimbursements for losses on the sale of a home, fair market value guarantees, and interest subsidies. See Chapter 3, Tip 24.

> **Action Step**
>
> Be sure to claim a non-refundable tax credit for interest paid on student loans. Quebec has adopted the federal rules that provide tax relief for these loans. In Quebec, the credit is equal to 20 percent of the loan interest paid. And if you choose not to claim a credit in a particular year for such interest paid, you'll be able to claim that credit in any future year. You'll have to file a general tax return, rather than a simplified return, to claim this credit.

Health Services Fund Contribution

This contribution (call it a tax if you want) is payable on all income other than employment income, Old Age Security, alimony and the 25-percent gross-up amount added to any Canadian dividends you receive. The income that is specifically included is generally business income, investment income, pension income, and capital gains. The contribution is calculated as 1 percent of such income that exceeds $5,000 in 2002 to a maximum of $150, plus an additional 1 percent of income over $40,000 to a maximum of $850. Once paid, it is eligible for a 20-percent non-refundable tax credit.

Union, Professional, and Association Dues

Union and professional dues are not allowed as a deduction for Quebec tax purposes (this changed in 1997). You'll now be eligible for a 20-percent tax credit on these fees instead.

Medical Expenses

You won't be entitled to claim any medical expenses unless they exceed 3 percent of your *family* income. As a result, many Quebec residents won't be able to claim the expenses. For those who can claim medical expenses, costs for training courses related to the care of disabled dependants may be claimed, thanks to the 1998 Quebec budget.

Disabled Persons' Credit

If you're disabled, the province will give you a credit worth up to $440 in tax savings in 2002. The credit is calculated as 20 percent of a base amount of up to $2,200 and can be transferred from a dependent child to a parent. The Quebec legislation leans heavily on federal law to define who is disabled, although the 2001 budget announced that a person will be entitled to the credit if he must undergo certain physician-prescribed therapy essential to the maintenance of a vital function.

Legal Fees and Marriage Breakdown

In Quebec, you can deduct legal fees paid in a court application to increase or decrease your alimony or maintenance. The federal rules allow a deduction only for legal fees to enforce a court-ordered payment of maintenance or alimony. The Quebec and federal governments agree on one thing here: Neither will allow a deduction for the legal fees to establish a right to receive payments.

Safety Deposit Box Fees

Not that this deduction was going to make you rich anyway, but you should realize that fees for safety deposit boxes are not deductible in Quebec, and haven't been since 1998.

Home Office

I touched on this issue in Chapter 4, Tip 39. The unfortunate fact is that Quebec has decided to limit home office expenses to just 50 percent of eligible expenses that are otherwise deductible. I'm talking about mortgage interest, property taxes, utilities, insurance, and similar expenses.

Refundable Infertility Credit

The costs associated with artificial insemination and *in vitro* fertilization that would normally be claimed as part of the medical expense credit will no longer qualify for that credit. But, to the extent they were not and cannot be reimbursed, they will instead be eligible for a refundable tax credit for the treatment of infertility. The credit will equal 30 percent of all the eligible expenses that were incurred during the year by the individual, or by the spouse, in order to enable the individual to become a parent. There is a $20,000 cap on the expenses that will qualify for this credit.

Adoption Expenses

If you adopt a child, either locally or from overseas, you may be entitled to claim a refundable tax credit for the costs incurred in the adoption process. The credit is 30 percent for up to $20,000 worth of expenses in 2002, to a maximum credit of $6,000 per child. The eligible costs include legal fees, travel costs, agency fees, and other costs.

> **Did You Know?**
>
> If you're a foreign researcher who works in Quebec on an eligible project and meet certain other conditions, you may be able to claim a deduction for 100 percent of your income for Quebec tax purposes. Likewise, foreign trainers employed by corporations carrying on business in Information Technology Development Centres may be eligible for similar tax relief. To top it off, certain specialists in international financial transactions and some Quebec sailors will also be provided a tax holiday!

Other Differences

You should be aware that there are differences between federal and Quebec tax rules in the following areas as well: family allowances for children; political contributions; the overseas employment tax deduction; artists' deductions; a refundable credit for athletes; the deductibility of private health services plan contributions for the self-employed; the Quebec sales tax credit; real estate tax refunds; alternative minimum tax; documentation for rental expenses; and income tax installments.

TO MAKE A LONG STORY SHORT:

• The federal and Quebec tax systems are different in many areas.

• Be sure to understand these differences so that your income tax planning works both federally and in Quebec.

Getting into the Game

Turn now to the Tax Planning Tip Sheet at the front of the book and review the strategies you've read about in Chapter 8. For each one, ask yourself, "Can this apply to me?" Armed with the *Yes* and *Not Sure* answers, visit a tax professional for more information on each strategy, or for help implementing the ideas. *Bonne chance.*

BOTTOM OF THE NINTH: PLANNING FOR YOUR ESTATE

Live your life, play the game, then tip your hat to the crowd.

9

Brace yourself: This chapter is about both death *and* taxes. You might be feeling tempted to pass by these next few pages. In fact, when I first wrote this chapter, I handed it to my neighbour George for his opinion. He claimed that he didn't have time to read it—he was going to the dentist. "George, what about next week? Can you read it by then?" I asked. "Uh, I don't see how, Tim. I'm hoping for a root canal," he said.

Hmm. I guess a root canal is decidedly more appealing than thinking about death any day of the week.

The only problem, of course, is that neglecting that day when you won't be here anymore is tantamount to handing a blank cheque to the tax collector. And make no mistake, estate planning is not simply for those who are in a later stage of life. Let's face it, even the best pitchers can be taken out of the game early. Whether you're 30 years old or 80 years young, you need to plan for your tax bill upon death.

I should mention that this chapter is meant to provide a general overview of estate planning strategies that will help you save tax. I cover in more detail all of this material and much more, including wills and powers of attorney, insurance, trusts, probate fees, business succession, planned giving, funeral planning, U.S. tax issues, and more, in my book *Winning the Estate Planning Game*.

Knowing What to Expect

Tim's Tip 93: **Understand the deemed disposition of your assets upon death.**

It's no secret that when you die, the tax collector usually follows the undertaker to your door. In fact, did you know that, upon your death, you are deemed to have sold everything you own at fair market value? It's true. And if you own any assets that have appreciated in value, you could face a tax bill on death that might just be large enough to wipe out the entire national debt, give or take. And while it would certainly be generous of you to think of your nation that way, my guess is that if you've got to choose between the tax collector and your loved ones, you'd rather leave your remaining assets to family, friends, or charity.

What this means, of course, is that you're going to have to plan for your taxes upon death—today! Once you're gone, so are the opportunities to minimize the tax collector's share of your estate. The lesson is simple: Calculate what you expect your tax bill to look like upon death, then use the strategies in this chapter to bring that tax liability down. If you're not sure how to crunch the numbers, visit a tax professional who can help you with the calculations.

TO MAKE A LONG STORY SHORT:

- Upon death you're deemed to have sold everything you own, which could result in a whopping tax bill.

- Once you're gone, so are the opportunities to minimize this tax hit.

- Calculate your tax bill expected upon death, and then use the ideas in this chapter to reduce the tax bite. Visit a tax pro to help with the calculations, if necessary.

Giving It Away Today

Tim's Tip 94: **Give assets away during your lifetime for tax and probate savings upon your death.**

One surefire way to avoid income tax and probate fees when you die is to die broke! Don't get me wrong, I'm not suggesting that you should spend the last few years of your life living on the streets and sleeping on a park bench just to beat the tax collector. You might, however, consider giving away some of your assets during your lifetime. A side benefit to this idea is that you'll be able to see your children or other heirs enjoy that inheritance while you're still around.

If you're going to take me up on this idea, just be aware that our tax law could create a tax bill for you in the year you give an asset away. You see, when you give something away, you're deemed to have sold it at its fair market value at the time you make the gift. If the asset has gone up in value, you might just trigger a taxable capital gain when giving it away.

> **Caution!**
>
> While it's true that your death will cause a deemed disposition, or sale, of all that you own, there are other common situations that can give rise to this same deemed disposition at fair market value. Here are the two most common: (1) where you give an asset away to someone other than your spouse and (2) where you give up Canadian residency. The problem with a deemed disposition is that since you're not actually selling anything, there are no sale proceeds with which to pay the tax bill. Proper planning can help to minimize the tax burden on a deemed disposition.

Make sure you don't cause a deemed disposition of your assets without realizing it. Canadians are notorious for doing this. For example, you may change your mutual fund account from "Jane Doe" to "Jane Doe and Sally Doe, joint with right of survivorship." Sure, this is going to avoid probate fees on your death—which is why people do this. The problem? Jane has just given away one-half of her investments to Sally. This generally results in a deemed disposition of one-half of those investments, and a potential tax bill. Count the cost of this tax hit before taking steps to avoid probate fees.

Caution!

There are a couple of ways to minimize any tax bill that might arise. First, give away assets that won't create a significant taxable gain. I'm referring primarily to cash, your principal residence, or assets that have not appreciated in value much, if at all. However, if you're going to give away the home, be sure to get legal advice first—there are some potentially harmful side effects since you may lose control over the property and expose it to the creditors or a disgruntled spouse of a family member. Second, if you're giving away assets that will lead to a tax bill, consider giving those assets away slowly, over a number of years, so that you don't trigger a huge tax bill in a single year. Otherwise, you could be pushed into a higher marginal tax bracket.

TO MAKE A LONG STORY SHORT:

- The tax collector can't tax you on assets you don't own at the time of your death.

- Consider giving assets away today to minimize taxes and probate fees upon death, but beware of the *deemed disposition* at fair market value that could lead to a tax bill when you make the gift.

Tim's Tip 95: Consider an estate freeze to minimize your tax bill on death.

Maybe you've heard of this thing called an estate freeze. It's a common technique used to freeze the value of certain assets today and to pass any future growth in value to your kids or other heirs. By the way, I deal with this issue more thoroughly in my book *Winning the Estate Planning Game*.

The Benefits

Here are some of the key benefits of an estate freeze:

- By freezing the value of certain assets today, you'll be able to establish, fairly accurately, what your tax liability is going to be upon death. This will allow you to plan for payment of those taxes.

- By passing the future growth in the asset's value to the next generation, you'll manage to defer income tax on that growth until a much later time. In fact, taxes may not be due until your heirs die, or until they sell the assets, whichever comes first.

- A freeze might allow you to take advantage of the *enhanced capital gains exemption* if you own shares of a qualified small business corporation or qualified farm property. This exemption is available to all Canadian residents and can shelter up to $500,000 of capital gains from tax—see Chapter 5, Tip 55, for more.

- There's no need to give up control over the frozen assets during your lifetime.

The Methods

How do you complete an estate freeze? I'd put you to sleep for sure if I tried to detail the many steps to completing a freeze. Let me just say that there are two very common methods of freezing an estate. The first is through use of a corporation. By transferring your growing assets to a company and taking back, in return, special shares in that company that are frozen in value, you'll manage a successful estate freeze. Common shares in the company, which may appreciate in value over time, can be issued to your children or anyone else. The second method is through use of a trust—called an *inter vivos* trust. The idea is that you'd transfer certain assets to a trust today for the benefit of your children or anyone you'd like.

In either case, you can bet you'll need the help of a tax pro to look after the nitty gritty details, because you may trigger a taxable event when placing your assets in the corporation or trust, although there are generally ways to avoid this in the case of the corporation.

TO MAKE A LONG STORY SHORT:

- By completing an estate freeze, you'll manage to pass the future growth of the frozen assets to your heirs or others of your choice.

- This will, among other things, freeze your tax bill upon death, enabling you to estimate and plan for those taxes ahead of time.

- A corporation or trust is most commonly used to freeze an estate.

- I've dealt with this issue in much more depth in my book *Winning the Estate Planning Game*.

Giving It Away at Death

Tim's Tip 96: **Leave it to your spouse to defer the tax hit longer.**

Remember, when you die you will be deemed to have sold your assets at fair market value. This could give rise to a tax bill. The common exception to this rule is when you leave assets to your spouse. You see, when you leave something to your spouse, the ugly *deemed disposition* that takes place will no longer take place at fair market value. Rather, you will be deemed to have sold those assets at your cost base. The result? No tax to pay! In this case, you'll manage to defer the tax bill until the death of the surviving spouse, or until he or she sells the assets.

*B*ill *passed away last year. His assets consisted of a home, Registered Retirement Savings Plans (RRSPs) of $400,000, non-registered investments worth $100,000 for which he had paid $60,000, and cash of $100,000. Bill left everything to Lois, his wife, with the exception of the cash of $100,000 and some life insurance proceeds of $100,000. How much tax do you suppose was triggered by Bill's death? The answer is zero. Nil. He managed to escape* *tax on any assets that had appreciated in value by leaving those assets to Lois. Since he wanted to leave something to his kids, he left them those assets that weren't subject to income tax at the time of his death.*

Do you follow what happened in Bill's situation? Bill left his wife any assets that might have given rise to a tax hit upon his death. This included his RRSPs and non-registered investments. He also left the home to Lois, not because it would have otherwise been subject to tax (since his principal residence exemption can work, even on death, to shelter any gains from tax), but because Lois still needed the home to live in.

Here's a final point worth noting. If you wish, you can transfer your assets to a spousal trust upon your death. This will have the same tax-free effect as if you had left the assets directly to your spouse. With a spousal trust, all the income earned on the assets placed in the trust will accrue to your spouse while he or she is still alive. And no one other than your surviving spouse can access the assets (the capital of the trust) while that spouse is still alive. There may be many reasons to set up a spousal trust rather than leaving the assets directly to your spouse. I'll talk about one of the key reasons in Tip 99.

> Leaving assets to your spouse on your death will defer a tax hit. Leaving assets to your kids or other heirs will generally give rise to tax if the assets have appreciated in value since you bought them, or on your RRSP or Registered Retirement Income Fund (RRIF). So, if you're going to leave anything to your kids or other heirs, leave them the assets that won't be subject to much tax, if any. There are four assets in this category: cash, life insurance benefits, a principal residence, and investments that have not appreciated in value very much.
>
> **Caution!**

TO MAKE A LONG STORY SHORT:

- Leaving assets to your spouse or a spousal trust upon death will allow you to avoid the effect of a deemed "sale" at fair market value of those assets when you die.

- If you're going to leave assets to the kids upon your death, leave them with those assets that will be subject to little tax, if any: cash, life insurance benefits, a principal residence, or assets that have not appreciated much in value.

Tim's Tip 97: Minimize the tax on your RRSP or RRIF assets upon death by naming the right beneficiaries.

A common question pondered by many Canadians is this: "How can I avoid tax on my RRSP or RRIF assets when I die?" The answer isn't always easy. Your first line of defence is always to name your spouse as the beneficiary of your plan. Beyond this, the opportunities to avoid tax become slim, but if you have certain dependants, there may be other opportunities.

Your Spouse as Beneficiary

If you name your spouse as the beneficiary of your RRSP or RRIF, then your plan assets will transfer directly to your spouse's plan upon your death on a tax-free basis. If your surviving spouse is aged 69 or younger in the year of your death, those assets can be transferred to his or her RRSP, otherwise they'll be transferred to your spouse's RRIF. Your spouse generally has 60 days following the year of your death to make the deposit to his or her own plan.

Your Dependants as Beneficiaries

Rather than leaving your RRSP or RRIF assets to a spouse, maybe you've decided that you're going to leave the assets to your kids or grandchildren. In the vast majority of cases, this is going to mean a tax bill. Typically, you'll face tax on these plan assets on your final tax return; then the balance is distributed to the children or grandchildren. But like many rules in tax, there are exceptions. In this case, there are two:

- **Infirm Dependants.** You'll manage to avoid the tax collector if you leave your RRSP or RRIF assets to a child or grandchild, of any age, who was financially dependent on you at the time of your death due to a physical or mental infirmity. Your dependant will be eligible to transfer your plan assets tax-free to his or her own RRSP, RRIF, or annuity.
- **Minor Dependants.** If a minor child was financially dependent on you at the time of your death, the child will be eligible to buy an annuity to age 18 using your RRSP or RRIF assets. This won't defer tax for very long in most cases, but it beats paying tax on the plan assets in one year. If the minor is infirm, then the rules for infirm dependants apply.

It's always best to name the appropriate person as beneficiary of your RRSP or RRIF on the plan application form itself. However, naming the appropriate person in your will accomplishes the same thing.

I should mention that, prior to the 1999 federal budget, you could take advantage of this tax-free rollover to your dependants only when you did not have a surviving spouse. Today, you can transfer your RRSP or RRIF assets to those dependants under these rules even if you have a surviving spouse (generally, however, your simplest bet will be to leave the assets to your spouse first). This change is effective for 1999 and later years, although the measure will be available for deaths after 1995 and before 1999 if the recipient of the RRSP or RRIF assets and the deceased's estate make a joint election for the new rules to apply.

Charity as Beneficiary

The 2000 federal budget changed the rules so that it is now possible to designate a registered charity directly as the beneficiary of your RRSP or RRIF. In this case, you'll receive a donation credit in the year of your death that could offset all the tax owing as a result of your RRSP or RRIF.

Action Step

I've met many Canadians who have been divorced and are remarried, and who have decided to leave their RRSP or RRIF to the kids rather than the new spouse. If you plan to leave your new spouse anything on your death, leave all or a portion of those RRSP or RRIF assets—it's generally the only way to avoid tax on those assets. Leave the kids with other assets—perhaps even a principal residence (with instructions that the house is to be occupied by your new spouse until his or her death). Leaving the kids with the full RRSP or RRIF will create a tax bill that could wipe out half of those assets—a high price to pay.

TO MAKE A LONG STORY SHORT:

- You'll always manage to avoid tax on your RRSP or RRIF assets upon death by naming your spouse as the beneficiary of your plan.

- You may also manage to defer tax on your plan assets by transferring your RRSP or RRIF to a person who is financially dependent on you at the time of your death.

- Designating a charity as beneficiary could eliminate all tax owing on your RRSP or RRIF upon your death.

Tim's Tip 98: Instruct your executor to make a final contribution to your RRSP after your death.

Believe it or not, the tax collector won't mind one bit if the executor of your estate makes RRSP contributions on your behalf once you're gone. But keep some things in mind here:

- After your death, no contributions can be made to your own RRSP. Rather, contributions will have to be made to a spousal RRSP on your behalf. You'll receive the deduction, but your surviving spouse will pay the tax on any withdrawals.
- Your spouse must be under age 69 on December 31 of the year you die in order for a contribution to be made to a spousal RRSP—otherwise no contribution can be made.
- You must have RRSP contribution room available at the time of your death to enable your executor to make a spousal RRSP contribution on your behalf.
- Any contribution to a spousal RRSP after your death will provide a deduction on your final tax return. This can help to minimize the taxes that would otherwise arise on your death.

The tax savings that will be passed to your heirs from an RRSP contribution after your death will range from about 25 percent to 46 percent of the contribution, depending on your province and the level of income reported on your final tax return.

TO MAKE A LONG STORY SHORT:

- The executor of your estate may be able to make final RRSP contributions on your behalf after you're gone.

- The contributions must be made to a spousal RRSP, within your contribution limits.

- A deduction may be claimed on your final tax return for these contributions.

Tim's Tip 99: Save your heirs tax by setting up a testamentary trust in your will.

A testamentary trust is a terrific tool for splitting income. It works this way: A trust would be created upon your death through instructions in your will. All or a portion of your assets would be transferred to the trust upon your death, and your intended heirs would be the beneficiaries of the trust.

Any investment income earned on the inheritance each year may now be taxed in the trust, rather than in the hands of your beneficiaries. You see, the trust is considered to be a separate person for tax purposes and will be taxed at the same graduated tax rates as any individual. Rather than adding any investment income directly to the beneficiary's income where it will be taxed at his or her marginal tax rate— very likely between 35 and 46 percent—simply split income with the trust by having the trust pay tax on the income instead, at graduated rates.

*R*ic died last year and left assets directly to his wife Shirley, now living in Kelowna, BC. Ric's assets generate $60,000 annually in investment income for Shirley. Since Shirley already has income of $60,000 annually from other sources, she now has $120,000 of income to report on her tax return each year. The tax bill to Shirley is going to total $38,350 in 2002. Ric could have done things differently. He could have set up a testamentary trust for Shirley through his will upon his death, and Shirley would be enjoying the benefits of splitting income with the trust. In this case, the trust would now be

paying tax on the $60,000 earned on the inheritance each year, while Shirley
would continue to pay tax on her other income. But the combined total tax
bill between Shirley and the trust would be just $29,933—a full $8,417 less
than without the trust! By the way, that's $8,417 in tax savings each year.
Now that's something worth writing home about!

Action Step

When setting up a testamentary trust, the option exists to have the income of the trust taxed in the hands of the beneficiary in any given year. This is done by *paying* the income to the beneficiary or by making it *payable* to the beneficiary. And this may be a good idea if, for example, the beneficiary has little or no other income and will enjoy the first $7,634 (in 2002) of income tax-free due to the basic personal amount.

The reason for the tax savings with the testamentary trust is simple: Both Shirley and the trust are entitled to low marginal tax rates on the first $31,677 of income. By having both Shirley and the trust paying tax, the number of dollars taxed in the lowest tax bracket is multiplied. Your tax savings may not be as high as in the example I've given here, but savings of up to about $12,960 (a Canada-wide average) each year are possible. The actual amount will depend on your income and province of residence.

Here are some last thoughts: You may want to set up a separate trust for each beneficiary, to maximize the number of dollars that can be taxed in the lowest bracket. The trusts would provide that income may accumulate in the trusts, and that tax-free capital distributions could be made to beneficiaries.

TO MAKE A LONG STORY SHORT:

- A testamentary trust provides an opportunity for your heirs to split income with the trust, maximizing the number of dollars that will be taxed in the lowest tax bracket.

- Setting up a testamentary trust must be done in your will.

- The tax savings can be up to about $12,960 (a Canada-wide average) annually, depending on your income level and your province of residence.

Tim's Tip 100: Consider an alter ego trust for probate savings and other benefits.

I've often wondered what life would be like if I could clone myself. I could do all those things I'm not crazy about doing—like mowing the lawn, painting the fence, and massaging my wife's feet—while simultaneously spending the day on the golf course. The "other me"—my alter ego—could do the dirty work (not that Carolyn's feet are offensive) while I continue a schedule of rest and relaxation.

Now, what may take hundreds of years to accomplish genetically, our Department of Finance has accomplished with one stroke of the pen from a tax perspective. That's right—it's now possible to "clone" yourself under our tax law. I'm referring to an "alter ego trust," and with it, there are some definite estate planning benefits to be had.

Legislation containing this gem known as an alter ego trust received royal assent in June 2001. It's a trust that can be set up by an individual after 1999 provided he or she has reached age 65. The terms of the trust have got to provide that the individual establishing the trust (the settlor) is alone entitled to all of the income of the trust earned before his or her death. And there's more. The trust must also provide that no one other than the individual is entitled to receive any of the capital of the trust before the individual's death. When the trust agreement is prepared, the contingent beneficiaries to receive the income and/or the capital of the trust after the settlor dies, are named.

Generally, when you transfer legal and beneficial ownership of assets to a trust (or to anyone other than a spouse, for that matter), you're deemed to have sold those assets at fair market value. This can give rise to a taxable capital gain, and a tax hit, where the assets have appreciated in value. In the case of an alter ego trust, transferring property to the trust won't give rise to a taxable disposition thanks to the new rules (unless you elect that the disposition should take place at fair market value). In addition, the clock for the 21-year rule (which deems the property of a trust to have been disposed of on the trust's twenty-first anniversary) won't start ticking until your death in the case of an alter ego trust.

At the time of your death, there will also be a deemed disposition at fair market value of the property of the trust—just as there would have been if you had continued to own the property directly.

There are at least four potential estate planning benefits to an alter ego trust:

- **Probate fee savings.** Transferring assets to an alter ego trust results in a change in legal and beneficial ownership of those assets. The bottom line? The assets fall outside of your estate and you'll avoid probate fees on those assets upon your death.

- **Compulsory succession avoided.** It may be possible for your will to be contested after your death if you leave behind an unhappy family member or two. An alter ego trust can avoid this problem by passing assets outside of your will. The trust cannot be challenged nearly as easily.

- **Power of attorney replacement.** An alter ego trust can name a successor trustee and/or provide other direction in the event of your mental incapacity. In this way, your property in the trust will be looked after if you can't handle it.

- **Privacy preserved.** When your will is probated, it becomes a public document, along with the value of your estate. The alter ego trust offers privacy both before and after your death.

By the way, it's also possible to set up the same type of trust for you and your spouse or common-law partner jointly. The same rules apply, except that both of you will be named beneficiaries of the trust and the deemed disposition at death will not take place until the second of you dies. This type of trust is referred to as a *joint partner trust* rather than an alter ego trust—but they're basically the same thing.

TO MAKE A LONG STORY SHORT:

- An alter ego or joint partner trust can be created after 1999 by those 65 or older.

- There is no taxable disposition when transferring assets to the trust.

- These trusts have four key benefits: minimizing probate fees; avoiding compulsory succession; replacing a power of attorney; and protecting privacy.

Tim's Tip 101: **Give to charity and save a bundle. But do it properly!**

Let's face it, one of the joys of giving to charity is seeing your donations put to good use, so you may want to consider giving to charity during your lifetime. And if you want to avoid probate fees, giving to charity today is going to help, since you'll no longer own those assets on the date of your death. Having said this, making a donation upon your death could go a long way toward reducing any tax bill you might face at that time. Regardless of whether you plan to make your donations during your lifetime, after your death, or a bit of both, why not give in a manner that's going to save the most tax? There are three out-of-the-ordinary methods of giving to charity that I want to talk about.

Donating Securities

The tax collector changed the rules around charitable giving in the 1997 federal budget to make things easier for charities, and the new rules could help you save more tax than ever on certain donations. The rules say that you'll be entitled to claim donations totalling up to 75 percent of your net income annually. This increases to 100 percent in the year of your death. And if your donations exceed this amount in the year of death, the excess can be carried back and claimed in the year before your death—up to 100 percent of your income in that year as well.

The new rules also favour donating mutual funds, stocks, bonds, and other securities, rather than cash.

*B*ernadette *owned shares in XYZ Corporation on the date of her death. XYZ is traded on the Toronto Stock Exchange, and the shares were worth $25,000 on the date she died, but she had paid just $10,000 for the shares a few years earlier. These shares were deemed to have been disposed of upon Bernadette's death, which would have triggered a $15,000 capital gain and a* *tax bill of about $3,450 if she had not left the shares to charity. Bernadette, however, left instructions in her will for her executor to donate these shares to her favourite charity after her death. The result is that the $15,000 gain is only 25-percent taxable! That's right, just $3,750 ($15,000 × 25 percent) of the gain is subject to tax. Normally, one-half of the gain would have been taxable under the usual capital gains rules. The result? The tax owing on this $15,000 gain will now be just $1,725—half of what it would have been. To top it off, a donation credit will be provided based on the $25,000 fair market value of the shares. This credit will be claimed on Bernadette's final tax return and will amount to about $10,000 in tax savings (varying slightly by province and income level).*

> **Caution!**
>
> There are two things to remember if you're going to set up a charitable remainder trust. First, the trust will be irrevocable—once it's set up, there's no turning back. Second, transferring investments to a charitable remainder trust could trigger a taxable capital gain if those investments have appreciated in value. The donation credit received from the gift, however, will soften the blow of any taxable gain.

You'll notice that Bernadette paid $1,725 in taxes on her capital gain, but received a donation credit of $10,000 to more than offset these taxes. The net benefit to Bernadette's estate is $8,275 ($10,000 minus $1,725).

So here's the game plan: Instead of cash, consider leaving securities that have appreciated in value to your favourite charity. This can be done by leaving instructions in your will for your executor to donate specific securities to a charity of your choice. Your heirs will thank you, since the tax savings could be significant.

By the way, the preferential 25-percent taxable rate for donated securities was to apply until the end of the year 2001, but the Department of Finance announced in the fall of 2001 that this measure would be extended indefinitely.

Establishing a Charitable Remainder Trust

With a charitable remainder trust (CRT), you can donate certain investments to a trust during your lifetime. Your favourite charity is named as the capital beneficiary of the trust so that, upon your death, or upon the death of a surviving spouse, the investments pass to the charity. During your lifetime, you're entitled to all income generated by the investments in the trust. You get tax relief right away for the investments you have transferred to the trust. The value of the donation credit is determined by an actuarial calculation based on your age and interest rates. The older you are, the greater the tax credit when setting up a CRT.

Giving Life Insurance

There are generally three ways to help your favourite charity with life insurance: (1) make the charity the beneficiary of your policy; (2) transfer ownership of a policy to the charity and make the charity the beneficiary; or (3) make your estate the beneficiary and leave instructions in your will for a donation to be made to charity.

In the first scenario, you'll be entitled to claim a donation credit on your final tax return as a result of designating the charity as beneficiary of the policy you own. This was not the case prior to the 2000 federal budget, but this change has made things better for all deaths after 1998. This credit could go a long way to reducing your tax bill in the year of your death. I like this option most of the three listed here.

In scenario two, transferring ownership of a policy will provide you with a donation credit for any cash value that exists at the time of transfer, plus a credit for any premiums paid by you after that date. Sorry, you won't receive a credit for the death benefit when it's paid to the charity upon your death. There may be a tax hit on any cash surrender value that exceeds the cost base of the policy in this scenario, but the donation credit should outweigh this.

Scenario three used to be my favourite because it provided the most tax relief—but not anymore. The drawbacks of naming your estate as beneficiary and then leaving instructions in your will to donate the cash to charity are these: (1) probate fees will be due on the amount of the life insurance, and (2) if your will is contested, the charity may never get the money you intend it to receive. Now that a credit is provided for directly designating a charity as the beneficiary of a life insurance policy you own (the first scenario), it makes much more sense simply to make this designation in the policy.

TO MAKE A LONG STORY SHORT:

- Giving to charity during your lifetime or upon death can provide significant tax savings. Making donations during your lifetime will also save probate fees.

- Consider donating securities instead of cash.

- Consider a charitable remainder trust or life insurance as tax-efficient ways to help your favourite charity.

Providing Tax-Free Death Benefits

Tim's Tip 102: Use life insurance to soften the blow of a tax bill at the time of your death.

Sometimes, avoiding a tax hit on death is impossible. In this event, life insurance may be your answer if you're hoping to leave a little more behind.

The Role of Life Insurance

The deemed disposition that I talked about in Tip 93 can leave your estate with a large enough tax bill to wipe out half the assets you were hoping to leave to your heirs. Consider also the result when the second spouse in a family dies and leaves any remaining RRSP or RRIF assets to the kids: Virtually half the assets of the plan will disappear when the tax collector comes knocking.

Further, some assets can create a hefty tax bill upon your death without providing the cash for those taxes to be paid. For example, private company shares that have appreciated in value, or a vacation or rental property, can give rise to taxes, and yet it can be difficult to sell these assets in order to provide the necessary cash to pay the taxes owing.

This is where life insurance can be your friend. If you're able to estimate today your taxes upon death, you may be able to buy enough life insurance to cover the taxes owing. Remember our talk on estate freezes (Tip 95)? A freeze can help you to establish your tax bill ahead of time, which is going to make it easier for you to buy the appropriate amount of insurance.

Paying for the Insurance

Obviously your age and health will be important considerations in deciding whether this idea is for you. Life insurance may not be an option if you're in poor health or you're elderly (generally, over age 80). But even where the premiums are high, these may still cost you less than the tax bill at the time of your death. Hey, why not approach your kids or other heirs to see if they are able and willing to help cover the cost of these premiums? After all, they're the ones who stand to benefit from a reduced tax burden when you die.

People usually get a good laugh out of my suggesting that the kids pay for the life insurance. But let me tell you how to sell it to them. Your kids should think of these premiums as an investment that will lead to tax-free investment returns down the road. Suppose, for example, it's going to cost $8,000 each year in premiums for $400,000 of insurance on your life. If you've got four kids, that's $2,000 each per year. If you live for another 20 years, that's a total investment by each child of $40,000 ($2,000 times 20 years) at which time each child would receive $100,000 tax-free ($400,000 for four children). That works out to an annual return of 8.8 percent for each child—tax-free! Of course, the sooner you die, the higher the return for your beneficiaries. Not to scare you, but you might want to watch the brakes on your car on a regular basis! (Yes, I'm kidding.)

When buying life insurance to cover your taxes owing on death, consider joint, second-to-die insurance. This is a policy that will pay out benefits upon the death of the second spouse. This insurance is easier to get since only one spouse needs to be insurable, and the premiums are generally cheaper since two events have to take place before the insurance proceeds are paid: both you and your spouse must die. This type of policy makes sense because you won't generally need the insurance until the second spouse has died. After all, there will be little tax to pay on the death of the first spouse if most assets are left to the surviving spouse.

Here's one last point: There are actually many reasons to buy life insurance and covering a tax bill on death is just one of them. I devote a whole chapter to life insurance in my book *Winning the Estate Planning Game*.

TO MAKE A LONG STORY SHORT:

- Sometimes it's impossible to avoid a tax bill on death. If you want to minimize the impact of this, life insurance may be your best bet.

- Life insurance will be particularly important when you expect a tax bill on death with little cash available to pay those taxes.

- Consider asking your heirs to pick up the tab for the insurance; after all, they're the ones who will ultimately benefit.

- There are many reasons to buy life insurance and covering a tax bill on death is just one of them. My book *Winning the Estate Planning Game* devotes a whole chapter to the use of life insurance.

Planning for U.S. Estate Taxes

Tim's Tip 103: Forecast your U.S. estate tax and apply nine strategies to minimize the tax bill.

Prior to changes introduced in 1995 to the Canada–U.S. tax treaty, Canadians who owned U.S. assets were subject to U.S. estate taxes on the value of those assets as figured on the date of death. A meagre $60,000 deduction from the value of those assets was provided when making the estate tax calculation. The U.S. estate tax was levied in addition to the taxes paid in Canada, if any, upon death. The result? Double taxation.

The Rules Today

Today, you could still face a tax bill, but you'll now find greater relief. Which assets are subject to U.S. estate tax? Anything considered a *U.S. situs* property, including:

- real estate (a vacation property, rental property, private home, or business property)
- shares of a U.S. corporation (public and private companies)
- debt obligations issued by U.S. residents (individuals or government)
- personal property located in the U.S. (cars, boats, jewellery, furnishings, club memberships, and more)

The tax is levied on the fair market value of these assets on the date of your death, and the tax rate for U.S. estate taxes ranges from 18 to 55 percent of your U.S. assets, with most people facing a tax bill between 25 and 35 percent.

Now for the tax breaks offered: Canadian citizens residing outside of the U.S. who have worldwide estates of $1.2 million (U.S.) or less will only be subject to U.S. estate taxes on certain U.S. property. For the most part, this property will include real estate, business assets when a permanent establishment is maintained in the U.S., and resource properties. But that's not all. Canadians will be entitled to a unified credit of up to $345,800 in 2002. This credit can be used to offset, dollar for dollar, the U.S. estate tax bill otherwise owing and effectively shelter from estate tax the first $1 million of U.S. assets in 2002. In actual fact, Canadians won't generally receive the full credit of $345,800 since it's prorated based on the percentage of total assets located in the United States.

Lynda owned a condominium in Colorado worth $300,000 (U.S.) on the date of her death. Her total assets upon death were valued at $1,500,000 (U.S.). Lynda's U.S. estate taxes were calculated to be $87,800 (U.S.) before the unified credit. The unified credit that she was able to

Action Step

Okay, here's some advice for those of you who have a sense of humour and are likely to pay U.S. estate taxes in the year of your death. Given that the current law in the U.S. has scrapped the U.S. estate tax for the year 2010 only, you could save yourself a bundle by dying in that year! Apart from this strategy, the next best way to completely avoid U.S. estate taxes is by never dying at all!

claim was $69,160, calculated as follows: $345,800 × $300,000/1,500,000.
Lynda's total estate tax bill was $18,640 (U.S.) ($87,800 minus $69,160).

The unified credit is reduced when only some of your assets are located in the
U.S., and this will be the case for most Canadians. You'll be glad to know that an
additional marital property credit of up to $345,800 is available in 2002 if you
leave your U.S. assets to your spouse upon your death. Further, you generally won't
have to worry about the double-taxation problem anymore since any U.S. estate
taxes paid will typically be eligible for a foreign tax credit in Canada (that is, the
U.S. estate taxes paid can be used to reduce your Canadian tax bill in the year of
death). You should note that the rules for a U.S. citizen who happens to be living in
Canada are slightly different, but if you're in this boat you'll be eligible for similar
tax relief.

Minimizing U.S. Estate Taxes

Try these nine ideas on for size to minimize the impact of U.S. estate taxes:

- Keep your U.S. assets below $1.2 million to avoid estate tax on all but your U.S.
  real estate and a couple of other uncommon U.S. assets.
- Consider holding your U.S. assets inside a Canadian corporation.
- Give property to your spouse and children over time, since each person is entitled
  to his or her own unified credit.
- Share ownership of U.S. assets with someone else.
- Buy life insurance to cover any U.S. estate tax liability.
- Restructure your debt so that non-recourse loans are secured by your U.S. assets,
  since this debt will reduce the value of your taxable estate.
- Move your U.S. assets back to Canada.
- Leave your U.S. property to a qualified domestic trust (QDOT). This type of trust
  does not eliminate U.S. estate tax but can defer it until the death of the second
  spouse.
- Rent instead of owning. You're not going to pay estate tax on assets you don't
  own, so consider renting a place in your favourite location down south rather
  than buying.

U.S. Estate Tax Repeal

You might have heard that estate taxes in the U.S. have now been scrapped. While it's true that on June 7, 2001, President George W. Bush did sign the *Economic Growth and Tax Relief Reconciliation Act of 2001*, this won't mean much estate tax relief for most. You see, the estate tax will be reduced slightly between now and the year 2010. In 2010, the tax will be scrapped altogether—but only for that one year. The legislation that scraps the estate tax is itself repealed in 2011, so that the estate tax will apply again in 2011 and later years. In order for the estate tax to be repealed permanently after 2010, new legislation will have to be enacted by the government of that day.

TO MAKE A LONG STORY SHORT:

- U.S. estate taxes will apply to any *U.S. situs* property you own on the date of your death.

- Recent changes in the Canada–U.S. tax treaty make this estate tax blow easier to take, but you still need to plan.

- Apply one or more of the nine most common strategies to minimize U.S. estate tax.

- New legislation has scrapped the U.S. estate tax—but only for the year 2010 at this point. Plan your affairs as though the estate tax may still apply.

Getting into the Game

Maybe you can't take it with you, but you can certainly have a say in where it goes after you're gone. Start now by turning to the Tax Planning Tip Sheet at the front of the book and reviewing the tips for Chapter 9. Ask yourself, "Can this tip apply to me?" Your *Yes* and *Not Sure* answers could lead to big tax savings for your estate—and that's good news for you, your heirs, and your favourite charitable causes.

Glossary of Abbreviations

ABIL	allowable business investment loss	**HBP**	Home Buyer's Plan
ACB	adjusted cost base	**HST**	Harmonized Sales Tax
CCA	capital cost allowance	**IPP**	Individual Pension Plan
CCPC	Canadian-controlled private corporation	**IRA**	Individual Retirement Account
CCRA	Canada Customs and Revenue Agency	**LSVCC**	Labour-sponsored venture capital corporation
CESG	Canada Education Savings Grant	**OAS**	Old Age Security
CGRM	Capital gains refund mechanism	**PA**	Pension adjustment
CICA	The Canadian Institute of Chartered Accountants	**QDOT**	Qualified domestic trust
		QPP	Quebec Pension Plan
CNIL	cumulative net investment loss	**QSBC**	Qualified small business corporation
CPP	Canada Pension Plan	**QST**	Quebec Sales Tax
DPSP	Deferred Profit Sharing Plan	**RESP**	Registered Education Savings Plan
EI	Employment Insurance	**RPP**	Registered Pension Plan
GAAR	general anti-avoidance rule	**RRIF**	Registered Retirement Income Fund
GIC	Guaranteed Investment Certificate	**RRSP**	Registered Retirement Savings Plan
GST	Goods and Services Tax	**SAR**	Stock appreciation right
		SIN	Social Insurance Number
		TONI	Tax-on-income system

Marginal Tax Rates for 2002

These tables will help you determine your 2002 marginal tax rate and the amount of tax you will owe for 2002.

Your Marginal Tax Rate

When it comes to tax planning, this is probably the most important number for you to understand. It will help you to calculate both your tax savings from a deduction and your after-tax investment returns. It will also tell you how much tax you will pay on your last dollar of income. For example, if you live in Alberta and your taxable income is between $31,677 and $63,354, you'll pay tax of 32 percent on your next dollar of regular or interest income, 16 percent on your next dollar of capital gains, and 15.33 percent on your next dollar of Canadian dividends. Foreign dividends are taxed at the same rate as regular income.

Your Tax Balance Owing

These tables will also help you to calculate how much tax you'll have to pay in 2002. All you have to do find the table for your province, then look in the left column of the table and find the figure that comes closest to your taxable income without going over your actual taxable income. This is your tax bracket. Now it's easy to calculate your actual tax bill. Consider Glenda's example.

*G*lenda lives in British Columbia and had taxable income of $45,000 in *2002. How much tax will Glenda have to pay for 2002? First, she will find the tax table for B.C. Next, she'll find her tax bracket by looking at the column on the left for the figure that comes closest to her taxable income without going over her income. Her tax bracket starts at $31,677 in B.C. in 2002. Her marginal tax rate on regular income is 31.15 percent (second column in the table). Glenda will pay taxes of $5,286 on her first $31,677 (the column on the far right). On her next $13,323 ($45,000 minus $31,677), she will pay taxes of $4,150 ($13,323 times 31.15 percent). Glenda's total tax bill for 2002 will be $9,436 ($5,286 plus $4,150). This tax balance takes into account the basic personal credit and all provincial surtaxes and tax reductions, but no other credits.*

Marginal Tax Rates for 2002

BRITISH COLUMBIA 2002

Taxable Income Bracket[1]	Marginal Tax Rates (%)			Tax Owing Up to Bracket[5]
	Interest and Regular Income[2]	Captial Gains[3]	Canadian Dividends[4]	
$ —	—	—	—	—
7,634	16.00	8.00	3.33	—
8,168	22.05	11.03	4.51	85
31,124	25.15	12.58	8.39	5,147
31,677	31.15	15.58	15.90	5,286
62,249	33.70	16.85	19.08	14,809
63,354	37.70	18.85	24.08	15,182
71,470	39.70	19.85	26.58	18,242
86,785	40.70	20.35	27.83	24,322
103,000	43.70	21.85	31.58	30,921

ALBERTA 2002

Taxable Income Bracket[1]	Marginal Tax Rates (%)			Tax Owing Up to Bracket[5]
	Interest and Regular Income[2]	Captial Gains[3]	Canadian Dividends[4]	
$ —	—	—	—	—
7,634	16.00	8.00	3.33	—
13,339	26.00	13.00	7.83	913
31,677	32.00	16.00	15.33	5,681
63,354	36.00	18.00	20.33	15,817
103,000	39.00	19.50	24.08	30,090

SASKATCHEWAN 2002

Taxable Income Bracket[1]	Marginal Tax Rates (%)			Tax Owing Up to Bracket[5]
	Interest and Regular Income[2]	Captial Gains[3]	Canadian Dividends[4]	
$ —	—	—	—	—
7,634	16.00	8.00	3.33	—
8,000	27.25	13.63	7.39	59
30,000	29.25	14.63	9.89	6,054
31,677	35.25	17.63	17.39	6,544
60,000	37.50	18.75	20.21	16,528
63,354	41.50	20.75	25.21	17,786
103,000	44.50	22.25	28.96	34,239

MANITOBA 2002

| Taxable Income Bracket[1] | Marginal Tax Rates (%) | | | Tax Owing Up To Bracket[5] |
	Interest and Regular Income[2]	Captial Gains[3]	Canadian Dividends[4]	
$ —	—	—	—	—
7,634	16.00	8.00	3.33	—
8,884	27.90	13.95	11.96	200
22,500	26.90	13.45	10.71	3,999
30,544	31.40	15.70	16.33	6,163
31,677	37.40	18.70	23.83	6,519
63,354	41.40	20.70	28.83	18,366
65,000	43.40	21.70	31.33	19,047
103,000	46.40	23.20	35.08	35,539

ONTARIO 2002

| Taxable Income Bracket[1] | Marginal Tax Rates (%) | | | Tax Owing Up to Bracket[5] |
	Interest and Regular Income[2]	Captial Gains[3]	Canadian Dividends[4]	
$ —	—	—	—	—
7,634	16.00	8.00	3.33	—
10,347	28.10	14.05	5.61	434
13,008	22.05	11.03	4.47	1,182
31,677	28.05	14.03	11.97	5,298
31,892	31.15	15.58	15.85	5,359
56,160	32.98	16.49	16.85	12,918
63,354	36.98	18.49	21.85	15,291
63,786	39.39	19.70	24.87	15,450
66,163	43.41	21.70	27.58	16,387
103,000	46.41	23.20	31.33	32,378

QUEBEC 2002

| Taxable Income Bracket[1] | Marginal Tax Rates (%) | | | Tax Owing Up to Bracket[5] |
	Interest and Regular Income[2]	Captial Gains[3]	Canadian Dividends[4]	
$ —	—	—	—	—
7,575	16.00	8.00	6.46	—
7,634	29.36	14.68	9.24	9
26,700	33.36	16.68	14.24	5,607
31,677	38.37	19.18	20.50	7,268
53,405	42.37	21.18	25.50	15,605
63,354	45.71	22.85	29.68	19,820
103,000	48.22	24.11	32.81	37,942

NEW BRUNSWICK 2002

Marginal Tax Rates (%)

Taxable Income Bracket[1]	Interest and Regular Income[2]	Captial Gains[3]	Canadian Dividends[4]	Tax Owing Up to Bracket[5]
$ —	—	—	—	—
7,634	16.00	8.00	3.33	—
11,000	30.68	15.34	12.18	539
17,520	25.68	12.84	5.93	2,539
31,677	36.82	18.41	19.86	6,174
63,354	42.52	21.26	26.98	17,838
103,000	46.84	23.42	32.38	34,695

NOVA SCOTIA 2002

Marginal Tax Rates (%)

Taxable Income Bracket[1]	Interest and Regular Income[2]	Captial Gains[3]	Canadian Dividends[4]	Tax Owing Up to Bracket[5]
$ —	—	—	—	—
7,634	16.00	8.00	3.33	—
10,302	25.77	12.89	5.92	427
15,000	30.77	15.39	12.17	1,638
21,000	25.77	12.89	5.92	3,484
29,590	30.95	15.48	12.40	5,697
31,677	36.95	18.48	19.90	6,343
59,180	38.67	19.34	22.05	16,506
63,354	42.67	21.34	27.05	18,120
79,527	44.34	22.17	28.17	25,021
103,000	47.34	23.67	31.92	35,428

PRINCE EDWARD ISLAND 2002

Marginal Tax Rates (%)

Taxable Income Bracket[1]	Interest and Regular Income[2]	Captial Gains[3]	Canadian Dividends[4]	Tax Owing Up to Bracket[5]
$ —	—	—	—	—
7,634	16.00	8.00	3.33	—
9,963	25.80	12.90	5.96	373
15,000	30.80	15.40	12.21	1,672
20,000	25.80	12.90	5.95	3,212
30,754	29.80	14.90	10.95	5,987
31,677	35.80	17.90	18.45	6,262
51,859	37.18	18.59	19.22	13,487
61,509	40.37	20.19	23.21	17,075
63,354	44.37	22.19	28.21	17,820
103,000	47.37	23.69	31.96	35,411

NEWFOUNDLAND 2002

Marginal Tax Rates (%)

Taxable Income Bracket[1]	Interest and Regular Income[2]	Captial Gains[3]	Canadian Dividends[4]	Tax Owing Up to Bracket[5]
$ —	—	—	—	—
7,410	10.57	5.29	6.96	—
7,634	26.57	13.28	10.29	24
29,590	32.16	16.08	17.28	5,857
31,677	38.16	19.08	24.78	6,529
58,598	39.61	19.81	26.04	16,802
59,180	41.64	20.82	28.58	17,032
63,354	45.64	22.82	33.58	18,770
103,000	48.64	24.32	37.33	36,865

NORTHWEST TERRITORIES 2002

Marginal Tax Rates (%)

Taxable Income Bracket[1]	Interest and Regular Income[2]	Captial Gains[3]	Canadian Dividends[4]	Tax Owing Up to Bracket[5]
$ —	—	—	—	—
7,634	16.00	8.00	3.33	—
9,342	23.20	11.60	4.83	273
31,677	31.90	15.95	15.71	5,455
63,354	37.70	18.85	22.96	15,560
103,000	42.05	21.03	28.39	30,507

NUNAVUT 2002

Marginal Tax Rates (%)

Taxable Income Bracket[1]	Interest and Regular Income[2]	Captial Gains[3]	Canadian Dividends[4]	Tax Owing Up to Bracket[5]
$ —	—	—	—	—
7,634	16.00	8.00	3.33	—
10,000	20.00	10.00	0.83	379
31,677	26.00	13.00	8.33	4,714
31,700	29.00	14.50	12.08	4,720
63,354	33.00	16.50	17.08	13,900
63,400	35.00	17.50	19.58	13,915
103,000	40.50	20.25	26.46	27,776

YUKON 2002				
Taxable Income Bracket[1]	Interest and Regular Income[2]	Captial Gains[3]	Canadian Dividends[4]	Tax Owing Up to Bracket[5]
$ —	—	—	—	—
7,634	23.04	11.52	4.80	—
31,677	31.68	15.84	15.60	5,540
63,354	37.44	18.72	22.80	15,575
74,203	38.01	19.01	23.14	19,637
103,000	42.40	21.20	28.63	30,583

Notes:

1. This column indicates the amount of taxable income at which particular tax rates apply.

2. This column shows the marginal tax rates that apply to interest and regular income (which includes most other types of income such as net rental, net business, pension income, and more).

3. This column shows the marginal tax rate on capital gains, and already takes into account the 50-percent inclusion rate for capital gains.

4. This column shows the marginal tax rate on actual dividends from taxable Canadian corporations. Dividends from foreign corporations are taxed at regular income rates.

5. This column shows the amount of tax owing for interest and regular income up to the beginning of the tax bracket indicated. The calculation takes into account the basic personal credit and all provincial surtaxes and tax reductions, but no other credits.

Federal Personal Tax Rates for 2002

Your total tax bill is made up of both federal and provincial taxes. The following table shows the federal component only. For the provincial personal tax rates, see the next section. Your federal tax rate is applied to the taxable income figure on line 260 of your tax return.

FEDERAL PERSONAL TAX RATES FOR 2002			
Taxable Income			**Tax Payable**
$ —	to	$31,677	16% of income
$31,678	to	$63,354	$5,068 plus 22% on income over $31,677
$63,355	to	$103,000	$12,037 plus 26% on income over $63,354
$103,001	and	over	$22,345 plus 29% on income over $103,000

Notes:

1. The former federal surtax of 5 percent of basic federal tax was eliminated effective January 1, 2001.

2. The tax amounts shown are before any credits, which will reduces taxes owing. In particular, the basic personal credit will eliminate taxes on the first $7,634 of income and will reduce taxes owing by $1,221 ($1,020 in Quebec). For other tax credits, see "Personal Tax Credits for 2002" below.

Provincial Personal Tax Rates for 2002

By the year 2001, all provinces and territories had moved to the new tax-on-income (TONI) system. Provinces and territories used to calculate tax based on a percentage of federal tax (a tax-on-tax system). Today, all jurisdictions calculate tax based on taxable income (tax-on-income, or TONI system).

I discussed in Chapter 8 the key tax changes introduced in each province and territory, and detailed the tax rates and credits that currently apply in each jurisdiction. Turn to that chapter for all the details.

Personal Tax Credits for 2002

Personal tax credits are applied to reduce your tax bill, dollar for dollar, each year. The credits listed here are non-refundable credits, meaning that they can be used to bring your tax bill to nil, but are not refundable for cash if they happen to exceed your tax liability.

I have shown the federal base amount and the actual taxes saved federally (which will equal 16 percent of the base amount for each credit). I have then shown the amount of tax that will be saved in each province for the same credit. These tax savings do not reflect any provincial surtax savings, which might increase the total savings slightly.

| PERSONAL TAX CREDITS FOR 2002 FEDERAL AND PROVINCIAL VALUES | | | | | |
Jurisdiction	Basic Personal Amount[1]	Married or Equivalent[1,2]	Age Amount for Over 65[3]	Disability Tax Credit[3,4]	Dependant Credits[1]
Federal base amount	7,634.00	6,482.00	3,728.00	6,180.00	3,605.00
Federal	1,221.00	1,037.00	596.00	989.00	577.00
British Columbia	494.00	423.00	222.00	371.00	216.00
Alberta	1,334.00	1,334.00	374.00	620.00	362.00
Saskatchewan	900.00	900.00	419.00	695.00	406.00
Manitoba	832.00	707.00	406.00	674.00	393.00
Ontario	465.00	395.00	227.00	376.00	219.00
New Brunswick	739.00	627.00	361.00	598.00	349.00
Nova Scotia	706.00	600.00	345.00	419.00	233.00
Prince Edward Island	726.00	617.00	355.00	431.00	240.00
Newfoundland	783.00	640.00	368.00	447.00	249.00
Northwest Territories	673.00	631.00	329.00	545.00	260.00
Nunavut	400.00	400.00	300.00	400.00	144.00
Yukon	537.00	456.00	262.00	435.00	254.00
Quebec[5]					

Notes:

1. This credit is reduced for a dependant's income over $649 for the married/equivalent-to-spouse credit, and over $5,115 for the dependant's credit.

2. To qualify for the equivalent-to-spouse credit, eligible dependants are those under age 18 living with and related to the taxpayer, or the taxpayer's parents/grandparents, or other persons who are related to the taxpayer and are infirm.

3. These credits may be transferred to a spouse. The credits available for transfer are reduced by the amount resulting from the application of the credit reduction rate to the transferor's net income in excess of $7,634. The age amount will be clawed back for seniors with incomes over $27,749.

4. These credits may be transferred to a supporting parent or grandparent. The credit is reduced when the transferor's income exceeds $7,634.

5. The following are the Quebec personal tax credits for the simplified Quebec provincial income tax system:

- Basic personal amount: base amount of $6,060 (credit of $1,212 at 20 percent).

- Spousal amount: base amount of $6,060 (credit of $1,212 at 20 percent).

- Person living alone or with dependant: base amount of $1,080 (credit of $216 at 20 percent). The base amounts for a person living alone, aged 65 and over, and pension income credits are added together and reduced by 15 percent of family income in excess of $26,700.

- Single parent: there is no equivalent-to-married credit in Quebec, but a single parent is entitled to a base amount of $1,335 (credit of $267 at 20 percent). The base amounts for the single parent, dependent children, and dependent student credits are added together and reduced by the dependant's net income.

- Dependent children: base amounts of $2,670 first child, and $2,465 for each subsequent child (credits of $534 and $493 respectively at 20 percent). See "Single parent" above for reductions.

- Other dependants: base amount of $2,465 for each dependant (credit of $493 at 20 percent). The base amount for infirm dependants is $6,060 (credit of $1,212). The base amounts are reduced by the dependant's net income.

- Age 65 and older: base amount of $2,200 (credit of $440 at 20 percent). The credit is transferable to a spouse, but the amount transferable is reduced by any income tax payable by the spouse. See "Person living alone" above for more reductions.

- Disability amount: base amount of $2,200 (credit of $440 at 20 percent). The credit is transferable to a spouse, but the amount transferable is reduced by any income tax payable by the spouse.

- Pension income amount: base amount is the lesser of $1,000 and the actual pension income received (maximum credit of $200 at 20 percent). See "Person living alone" above for reductions.

- Other credits available include: dependent student ($339), QPP ($335 for employed, $335 for self-employed, plus a deduction of $1,673), EI ($172), Health Services Fund ($200).

- Many other credits and a number of deductions are replaced under the simplified income tax system with a lump-sum base amount of $2,780 (credit of $556 at 20 percent).

Minimum Annual RRIF Withdrawals

Minimum annual withdrawals from a registered retirement income fund (RRIF) are based on the value of the assets inside the RRIF on January 1 each year. Simply find the appropriate percentage in the table below and multiply it by the value in the RRIF on January 1. RRIFs established before 1993 are generally *qualifying RRIFs* and annuitants should use the right-hand column, below.

The appropriate age for this calculation is your age at the start of January 1 each year. If you are under age 65, the formula to calculate your minimum withdrawal percentage is 1 *divided by* (90 *minus* your age).

MINIMUM ANNUAL RRIF WITHDRAWALS (%)					
Age	General	Pre-1993 Qualifying RRIFs	Age	General	Pre-1993 Qualifying RRIFs
65	4.00	4.00	81	8.99	8.99
66	4.17	4.17	82	9.27	9.27
67	4.35	4.35	83	9.58	9.58
68	4.55	4.55	84	9.93	9.93
69	4.76	4.76	85	10.33	10.33
70	5.00	5.00	86	10.79	10.79
71	7.38	5.26	87	11.33	11.33
72	7.48	5.56	88	11.96	11.96
73	7.59	5.88	89	12.71	12.71
74	7.71	6.25	90	13.62	13.62
75	7.85	6.67	91	14.73	14.73
76	7.99	7.14	92	16.12	16.12
77	8.15	7.69	93	17.92	17.92
78	8.33	8.33	94 or		
79	8.53	8.53	older	20.00	20.00
80	8.75	8.75			

Index

A

abbreviations, glossary of, 285
active businesses, 110–11, 157–60
adjusted cost base (ACB), 27, 143, 150,
    158–59, 232–33
adjustment request, 3
adult children
    adventure in the nature of trade, 138–39
    advertising in foreign media, 123
    after-tax investing, importance of, 132
    age credit, 28
    aircraft expenses, 87
Alan Wayne Scott v. The Queen (1998), 88
Alberta, 242–43, 286, 287
allowable business investment losses (ABILs),
    159, 160
allowances, 68
alter ego trusts, 273–74
alternative minimum tax (AMT), 197
annuity, purchase of, 216, 217
artist's expenses, 89
assessment, disputing your, 12–14
assets
    classes of, for CCA purposes, 119–20
    deemed disposition on death, 262– 63, 266,
        273
    deemed sale on contributions to RRSP, 190
    deemed sale on transfer, 7, 23, 33, 263,
        267
    home business and CCA, 115
    non-qualifying, 189
    non-registered, 131–32, 150
    personal value, 70, 77
    sale of, and tax on capital gains, 139–40,
        151
    swapping, 22
    transfer before leaving country, 25, 263
    transfer of, to corporation, 156–57
    transfer of, from friend, 19
    transfer of, to others, on your death,
        266–67, 268–69
    U.S., on your death, 238
assistant's salary, 87
attendant care and costs, 57–58, 88
attribution rules, 19–20, 21, 22, 35, 203–4
    sidestepping, 20–32, 37–38
    See also income splitting
automobile
    allowances, 93–97, 123

business use, 117–18
    disadvantages of company car, 92–94
    employer's, 91–97
    expenses, 87, 95–97
    loan from employer, 79–80
    maximize employment use of car, 97
    operating cost benefit, 93
    reimbursements, 94–97
    standby charge, 70, 92–94
avoidance of taxes, 2–3

B

back-to-back prescribed annuity, 164–67
bare trusts, 43
big events, and taxes, 11–12
bonuses, 100–1, 151, 191, 192
borrowing to invest, 13, 167–75, 183, 190–91
Brian J. Stewart v. The Queen (2002), 126
British Columbia, 241–42, 286, 287
business deductions
    advertising in foreign media, 123
    automobile allowances, 123
    automobile deductions, 117–18
    automobile expenses, 93–94, 97
    capital cost allowance (CCA), 89
    CCA, eligibility, 119–20
    club dues, 123
    conventions, 123
    entertainment expenses, 118–19
    golf dues, 123
    home office expenses, 88, 115–17
    life insurance premiums, 124
    living expenses, 122
    meal expenses, 88, 118–19
    office rent, 88
    personal expenses, 122
    personal services business expenses, 122
    prepaid expenses, 122
    private health services plan (PHSP), 123
    recreational facilities, 123
    salaries to family members, 30–31, 121–22
business losses, 124–25, 137–39
Business and Professional Income Tax Guide
    (CCRA), 120
business structures
    corporations, 110–12
    partnership, 31, 109–10
    proprietorship, 108–9

C

Canada Child Tax Benefits, 29, 61–62
Canada Customs and Revenue Agency
(CCRA)
interest costs deduction, 80, 172–73
prescribed interest rate calculations, 119
prescribed loan interest rate, 20–21, 79
Canada Education Savings Grants, 40–43
Canada Pension Plan (CPP)/Quebec Pension
Plan (QPP)
and disability, 56
and employer-direct RRSP contributions,
191
employment deduction for assistant's salary,
87
income splitting of benefits, 30
and self-employment, 107, 127–28
Canada Savings Bonds, 33, 133, 184
Canada–U.S. tax treaty, 228, 232–34, 235,
237, 280
Canada's national debt, 249
Canadian-controlled private corporation
(CCPC), 81
Canadian development expenses (CDEs),
149–50
Canadian exploration expenses (CEEs), 149
Canadian Institute of Chartered Accountants'
In-depth Tax Course, 12
capital cost allowance (CCA)
automobile expenses, 97
eligibility, 89, 119–20
half-year rule, 120
home office expenses, 116–17
and non-capital losses, 124–25
undepreciated capital cost (UCC), 120
capital gains
and contributions to RRSP, 190
and donations to charities, 276–77
election to treat all gains and losses as, 138
enhanced exemption, 158, 265
and family trusts, 35
and flow-through share investing, 151
investment profits, 133, 137–39
marginal tax rate, 4, 135–36
mutual fund distributions, 153
portfolio turnover, 135–36, 183
reserve, 139–40
rollover, 158–59
and transfer of property, 33, 43–44, 48–50
and upvesting, 172
U.S., 228, 231–33
capital gains refund mechanism (CGRM),
143–44

capital losses
vs. business losses, 137–39
and flow-through share investing, 150
and small corporations, 159
transfer to spouse, 26–28
capital-protected closed-end funds, 154–55
cascading life insurance, 162–64
cash flow, need for, 135
charitable gifts
charitable remainder trust (CRT), 276–77
charity as RRSP beneficiary, 269
and estate planning, 275–78
life insurance, 277–78
Quebec, 256
securities, 275–76
charitable remainder trust (CRT), 276–77
childcare expenses
babysitting costs, 24–25
and business expenses, 53–54
daycare as taxable benefit and deduction,
71
earned income, 53–54
increased base for claim, 55
maximum claims, 54–55
Quebec, 255–56
restrictions on deductions, 53–54
single-parent and two-parent families, 53
children
adult. *See* adult children
allowances, 24
Canada Child Tax Benefits, 29
capital gains in hands of, 22–23, 199–200
and corporate dividends, 31
custody, 59–60
and disability credits, 56–57
and employment, 24–25, 121
in-trust accounts, 43–47
life insurance policy transfer to, 162–64
RESPs, 29–30, 39–43, 45–47
as RRSP/RRIF beneficiaries, 41, 132,
268–69
Social Insurance Number, 29
tax returns for, 29, 199–200
clergy deduction, 90
club dues, 123
commissioned employee expenses, 86, 88
commissions on sales for personal use, 72
common-law partner, 20
commuted value of pension, 197, 223–24
company pension plans. *See* RPPs
contributions in kind, 189–90
control test, 107
conventions, 123
corporate mutual funds, 142–45

corporations
    active business income, 110
    drawbacks, 111
    ownership with family members, 31, 127
    as separate persons, 110
    tax deferral, 110–12
    trapped losses, 111, 113
    use of two, to transfer money, 32
couriers, 88
Court of Quebec, 13
credits
    age, 28
    attendant care, 57–58
    vs. deductions, 4–6
    disability, 28, 56–57
    dividend tax, 32, 36, 37, 141
    dollar-for-dollar tax savings, 4–6
    donation to charity, 269, 276
    education, 28
    equivalent-to-married, 59–60
    medical expense, 6, 58
    non-refundable, 6
    pension, 28
    personal tax, for 2002, 292–94
    and provincial surtaxes, 6, 28
    for Quebec residents. *See* Quebec
    refundable, 6
    and spouses, 6, 59, 141
    transfer of, 28
    tuition, 28, 256
Current Year Method, 10
custody, 59–60

D

daycare services, 71
death benefits, 72
debt swap, 173
deductions
    attendant care, 53–54, 57–58
    automobile, 95–97
    babysitting costs, 24–25
    for beneficiaries, of your final RRSP
        contribution, 270
    capital gains reserve, 139–40
    childcare expenses. *See* childcare expenses
    corporate loans to students, 24
    vs. credits, 4–6
    defined, 4
    employment. *See* employment deductions
    and flow-through shares in RRSP, 150
    interest on debt swap, 173
    interest on loan from employer, 79–80
    moving expenses, 51–52

    RRSP contributions and clawback of OAS
        benefits, 201
    self-employment. *See* business deductions
    spousal RRSPs, 29, 203–5, 270
    tax savings at marginal tax rate, 5–6,
        18–19
    and upvesting, 168, 172–74
deemed sale on transfer, 7–8, 33, 49–50
deferral of taxes, and true cost in future, 8
deferred compensation
    bonuses, 100–1, 191, 192
    Deferred Profit Sharing Plan (DPSP),
        98–100
    leave of absence, 102
    RPPs, 98–99
    RRSPs, 99
    sabbatical plan, 102
Deferred Profit Sharing Plan (DPSP), 99–100,
    197
defined benefit plan, 221–22
defined contribution plan, 221
dependants. *See* children
depreciation, 93–94, 97, 119
disability
    credits, 28, 56–58
    deduction for attendant costs, 88
    insurance plan, 71
    top-ups, 72
discounts on merchandise, 73
diversification, 50, 84, 149–52, 171, 185–86
dividend receivable, 157
dividend sprinkling, 36
dividend tax credit, 32, 36, 37, 141
dividends
    marginal tax rate, 4
    spouse's, 31, 141
    taxation of, 134–37
    transfer of, and clawback of OAS benefits,
        31, 155–56
    U.S., 229
divorce. *See* separation and divorce
Don't Just Invest, Upvest (Cestnick), 170
draw, 109

E

earned income
    attendant care costs, 57–58
    for childcare purposes, 53–54
    children's, 24–25, 199–200
    RRSPs, 24, 25, 156, 187, 199–200
economic reality test, 107
education
    Canada Child Tax Benefits invested for, 29

costs, employee payment of, 74
credits, 28
Lifelong Learning Plan (LLP), 210–13
parents in full-time attendance, 53–54
Quebec, 256, 257
withdrawing from RRSP for adult, 211
See also Registered Education Savings Plans
(RESPs)
employee compensation
deferred, 98–102
non-taxable benefits as. *See* non-taxable
employment benefits
stock option plans. *See* stock option plans
employer-direct contributions, 191–92
Employer Health Tax (EHT), 128
employer home-purchase, 68, 69
employment benefits
assets of personal value, 70, 77
automobile loan from employer, 79–80
family benefits, 70–72
home benefits, 68–70
home loan from employer, 79
individual benefits, 72–75
interest subsidies, 68
investment loan from employer, 79–80
loan from employer, 13, 78–80
non-taxable. *See* non-taxable employment
benefits
stock options, 80–86
taxable benefits, where advantageous,
76–78
tips, waiters/waitresses, 73
workplace benefits, 75–76
employment deductions, 86–91
aircraft expenses, 87
artist's expenses, 89
assistant's salary, 87–88, 89
attendant costs, 88
automobile expenses, 87
clergy deduction, 90
commissioned employee expenses, 86
couriers, 88
home office expenses, 88
legal fees, 89
meals and lodging, 86–87
musician's instruments, 89
office rent, 88
professional dues, 88
requirement to pay costs, 87
supplies, costs of, 87
travel expenses, 86–87
union dues, 88–89
Employment Insurance (EI), 107, 127–28, 191
entertainment expenses, 118–19
equity investments, 133–34, 161–62

mutual fund, 153, 171, 172–73, 179, 182
equivalent-to-married tax credit, 59–60
estate freeze, 264–66, 279
estate planning
alter ego trusts, 273–74
charitable gifts, 275–77
deemed disposition of assets on death,
262–63, 266–67
estate freeze, 264–66, 279
final RRSP contribution after death, 270
final tax return, 157, 270
giving away assets during lifetime, 263–64
life insurance, 72, 267, 278–80
minimizing taxes and probate fees on your
death, 34, 156–57, 163–64, 263–64,
266–83
RRSPs/RRIFs, beneficiaries of, 198, 268–70
spouse, assets left to, 266–67
tax-free death benefits, 278–79
testamentary trusts, 34, 271–72
U.S. estate taxes. *See* U.S. estate taxes
evasion, 2–3, 227
exercise price, 80, 81

F
fair market value guarantee, 75
fairness rules, 14–15
Family Allowance. *See* Canada Child Tax
Benefits
family employment benefits, 70–72
family tax planning
attendant care, 57–58
attribution rules, 19–20, 21, 22, 35, 203–4
disability credits, 28, 56–57
divorce. *See* separation and divorce
family care costs, 53–55
family trusts, 31, 32–39, 271–74
income splitting. *See* income splitting
moving expenses, 51–52
principal residence exemption, 48–50, 115
principal residence left to heirs to minimize
tax, 267
salaries to family members and EI, 127
second property, ownership of, 48–50
separation. *See* separation and divorce
tax exemption rule on assets transferred
between spouses, 7, 20
family trusts
advantages, 23, 31, 32, 34–39
dividend sprinkling, 36
income in, 35–36
for income splitting, 19–21, 22–23, 25–26,
31–36
kiddie tax, 36–37

portfolio investments, 34–35
private corporation shares, 35–37
property, transfer of, 33, 50
taxation of, 31, 33–37, 271–74
trust, defined, 33
21-year rule, 273
Federal Court of Appeal, 14
federal personal tax rates, for 2002, 291–92
fitness facilities, 75
fitness professionals, 75
fixed income investments, 133–34
flow-through shares, 149–52
foreign content rules for RRSPs, 143, 146, 185–86
formal or general procedure, for appeal, 13–14

G

gambling losses, 234–35
general employment-related training, 74
gifts from employer, 73
glossary of abbreviations, 285
golf course meals, 118
golf dues, 123
Goods and Services Tax (GST)
    rebate, 91, 97
    self-employment, 128
    on taxable benefits, 93
Granovsky v. The Queen (1998), 157
group plan premiums, 71
Guaranteed Investment Certificates (GICs), 33, 133, 165, 184, 189

H

half-year rule, 120
Harmonized Sales Tax (HST), 128
holding companies, 155–57
Home Buyers' Plan, 207, 208–10
home employment benefits, 68–70
home loan from employer, 79
home office expenses, 88, 115–17, 259
    See also business deductions, self-employment
host/hostess trip, 74–75
household expenses, and income splitting, 28

I

in-trust accounts, 43–47
income splitting
    allowance to working child, 24
    asset swapping, 22
    babysitting payments, 24–25
    Canada Pension Plan benefits, 30

capital gains in children's hands, 22–23
capital losses, transfer to spouse, 26
Child Tax Benefits, investing in child's name, 29
    and child's education, 40, 121
corporate loan to related student, 24
family trusts, 32–39
household expenses paid by higher-income spouse, 28
inheritances, investment in right name, 28
loan between family members, 18–21, 22
loans for more than five years, 21
ownership with family members corporation, 31
partnership with family members, 31, 37, 110
pay adult child to help move, 25
personal tax credits, transfer of, 28
RESPs, 29–30, 40–43, 47
room and board charges, 23
RRSPs, 203–5
salary to family members, 30, 89, 121–22, 127
spousal RRSPs, 29, 60, 203–5
spouse's dividends on your tax return, 30, 141
transfer assets before leaving country, 25
transfer investment income to adult children, 23
transfer money for business purposes, 21
transfer money for interest expenses, 22
two corporations to transfer money, 32
Income War Tax Act (1917), 11
incorporation, 113, 114
individual employment benefits, 72–75
Individual Pension Plan (IPP), 223–24
Individual Retirement Account (IRA) (U.S.), 199
informal trusts, 43
inheritances, investment of, 28
installments, 9–10
integration test, 107
inter vivos trust, 33–34
interest costs, deduction of, 171–75
interest income, 132–42, 153–54
    marginal tax rate, 3–4, 133–34
    U.S. income, 227–28
international organization, employment by, 90
investment holding corporation, 155–57
investment loan from employer, 78–80
investment strategies
    active businesses, 157–60
    after-tax investing, importance of, 132
    back-to-back prescribed annuity, 164–67

borrowing to invest, 167–75
business losses, 124–25, 137–39
Canadian development expenses, 149–50
Canadian exploration expenses (CEE), 149
capital gains, 137–39, 276
capital gains refund mechanism (CGRM),
    143–45, 171
capital gains reserve, 139–40
capital-protected closed-end funds, 154–55
cash flow, need for, 135
corporate mutual funds as tax deferral,
    142–45
debt swap, 173
dividends, 133, 135
flow-through shares, 149–52
holding companies, investment in, 155–57
interest costs, deduction of, 171–75
labour-sponsored funds (LSVCCs), 145–49
life insurance, 72, 161–67, 267, 277–80
money market corporate funds, 153–54
non-registered portfolios, tax impact on,
    131–37, 150, 183
portfolio make-up, 84, 132–34, 183, 185
portfolio turnover, 135–37, 183
private companies, 155–60
spouse's dividends, 141–42
"upvesting," 167–75

J
joint partner trust, 274

K
kiddie tax, 36–37

L
labour-sponsored funds, 145–49
labour-sponsored venture capital corporations,
    145–49
leave of absence, 102
legal fees
    as employment deduction, 89
    for family trusts, 32
    on marriage breakdown, 63, 258
    for support collection, 63
"leveraged investing," 167
liability, 109–11, 112
life insurance
    back-to-back prescribed annuity, 164–67
    cascading, 162–64
    to charities, 277
    and commissions on sales to self, 72
    and estate planning, 267, 278–80

exempt policy, 161–62
    joint, second-to-die, 279
    leveraged, 161
    premiums, 124
    and RRSPs, 189
Lifelong Learning Plan (LLP), 210–13
living expenses, 122
loan from employer, 13, 78–80
loans to family members
    for business purposes, 21
    corporate loan, to related student, 24
    corporate loans between spouses, 32
    for five or more years, 21
    guarantee, 22
    interest and repayment, 21, 22
    proper documentation of, 21
loss-on-home reimbursement, 69
losses
    capital, 26–28
    deducting interest costs of, 175
    See also non-capital losses
lottery winnings, 234–35
Ludco Enterprises Inc. v. The Queen (2001),
    172–73

M
Manitoba, 244–45, 288
marginal tax rates
    Alberta, 286, 287
    British Columbia, 286, 287
    capital gains, 4, 133–35
    defined, 3–4
    dividends, 4, 133–34
    inter vivos trust, 33–34
    interest income, 4, 133
    knowing your, 3–4
    Manitoba, 288
    New Brunswick, 289
    Newfoundland, 290
    and non-residency, 25–26, 213–15
    Northwest Territories, 290
    Nova Scotia, 289
    Nunavut, 290
    Ontario, 288
    Prince Edward Island, 289
    Quebec, 288
    Saskatchewan, 287
    for 2002, 287–92
    Yukon, 291
marriage breakdown. *See* separation and
    divorce
meal expenses, 88, 118–19
meal subsidies, 75

medical expense credits, 6, 58, 258
membership fees, 73
Min Shan Shih v. The Queen (2000), 26
Mintz Report (1998), 168
money market corporate funds, 153–54
money market investments, 133–34
money purchase plan, 221
mortgage payments, vs. RRSP contributions, 202
mortgage subsidies, 68, 79
moving expenses, 51–52, 257
musician's instruments, 89
mutual funds, 152–55
    capital gains distributions, 153
    capital-protected closed-end funds, 154–55
    corporate, 142–45
    as corporations vs. trusts, 142–45, 153–55
    money market corporate funds, 153–54
    and portfolio, 132–37, 166
    and RRSPs, 189
    switching, and taxable events, 7–8, 142–43, 264

N

National Child Benefit Supplement, 61
net rental income method, 230–31
New Brunswick, 246–47, 289
Newfoundland, 132–34, 249–50, 290
non-capital losses, 111
    application of, 124–25
    expiry of, 124
    investment losses as, 137–39
    reasonable expectation of profit (REOP), 138–39
non-refundable credits, 6
non-registered assets, 131–32, 150, 187, 193
non-taxable employment benefits
    assets of personal value, 70, 77
    commissions on sales for personal use, 72
    daycare services, 67, 71
    death benefits, 72
    disability top-ups, 72
    discounts on merchandise, 73
    education costs, 74
    employer home-purchase, 69
    fair market value guarantee, 69, 257
    family benefits, 70–72
    fitness facilities, 75
    fitness professionals, 75
    gifts and awards, 73
    group plan premiums, 71
    home benefits, 50, 68–70
    host/hostess trip, 74–75
    individual benefits, 72–75
    loss-on-home reimbursement, 69
    meal subsidies, 75
    membership fees, 73
    mortgage subsidies, 68
    out-of-town trips, 74
    personal counselling, 70–71
    private health services plans (PHSPs), 72
    recreational facilities, 75
    relocation costs, 68, 79
    remote location benefits, 70
    special clothing and uniforms, 75
    transportation passes, 71
    transportation to work, 76
    travel expenses, 86–87
    vacation property use, 74
    vehicle purchase from employer, 70
    workplace benefits, 75–76
Northwest Territories, 250–51, 290
Notice of Appeal, 89
Notice of Objection, 12–13, 57, 89
Nova Scotia, 247–48, 289
Nunavut, 251, 290

O

office rent, 88
Old Age Security
    clawback of benefits, 31, 150, 155–56, 201
    and residency status, 229
Ontario, 245–46, 288
open money, 131, 178, 184
operating cost benefit, 93
organization test, 107
out-of-town trips, 74
over-contributions to RRSPs, 193–95

P

partnership
    with family members, 31
    and self-employment, 109–10
    written partnership agreement, 110
payroll taxes, 128
penalties
    on RRSP over-contributions, 193
    tax evasion, 2–3
    waiver of, under fairness rules, 14–15
pension adjustment (PA), 98–99, 221–22
pension credits, 28
personal counselling, 70–71
personal expenses, 122
personal interest training, 74
personal services business expenses, 122
personal tax credits, for 2002, 292–94

phantom stock plans, 85
portfolio investments, 34–35
portfolio make-up, 132–34
portfolio turnover, 135–37
prepaid expenses, 122
prescribed annuity, 166
prescribed area, 70
Prince Edward Island, 248–49, 289
principal residence exemption
avoiding taxes on, on your death, 267
deemed sale on transfer, 49–50
home office and CCA, 115
multiplying, 49–50
pre-1982 gains, 48–49
U.S. real estate, 233
Prior Year Method, 10
private corporation
active businesses, 157–58
allowable business investment losses, 159
capital gain rollover, 158–59
enhanced capital gains exemption, 158–60, 265
holding companies, 155–57
investment in, 155–60
qualified farm property, 160
qualified small business corporation (QSBC), 158–60
and RRSPs, 189
shares, 35–36, 155–60
private health services plans (PHSPs), 72, 123
professional dues, 88
promissory notes, 21
property. See real estate
proprietorship, 108–9
provincial personal tax rates, for 2002, 292
provincial tax issues
Alberta, 146, 242–43, 286, 287
British Columbia, 241–42, 286, 287
corporate mutual funds, 144
disability tax credit for children, 56–57
interprovincial moves, 52, 245
labour-sponsored venture capital corporations, 146
Manitoba, 244–45
New Brunswick, 146, 246–47
Newfoundland, 146, 249–50
Northwest Territories, 250–51
Nova Scotia, 247–48
Nunavut, 251
Ontario, 245–46
payroll taxes (provincial), 128
Prince Edward Island, 248–49
provincial surtaxes, and credits, 6, 59
Quebec. See Quebec

residency, 245
Saskatchewan, 243
Tax Collection Agreements, 241
Yukon, 252

Q

qualified domestic trust (QDOT), 282
qualified farm property, 160
qualified small business corporation (QSBC), 146, 158–60
Quebec
academic scholarships, 257
adoption expenses, 259
charitable donations, 275–78
Court of Quebec, 13
disabled persons' credit, 258
exemptions from taxation, 259
family tax credits, 255
federal taxes, differences from, 9, 241, 253–60
foreign researchers, 259
health services fund contribution, 257, 260
home office expenses, 116, 259
installment payments, 9–10
interest on student loans, 257
legal fees on marriage breakdown, 63, 258
marginal tax rate, 288
medical expenses, 258
moving expenses, 51–52, 257
personal tax credits, 255, 292, 293–94
prescribed interest rate, 119
refundable childcare tax credit, 255–56
refundable infertility credit, 259
safety deposit box fees, 258
simplified system vs. general system, 253–55
student loans, interest on, 257
tax rates, 253
tax system in, 9, 252–55
tuition fees, 256
union, professional, and association dues, 258
withholding tax on RRSP withdrawals, 207
work chart, 254
The Queen v. Jack Walls et al. (2002), 126
The Queen v. Singleton (2001), 173

R

real estate
as capital asset, 138–40
deducting interests costs when borrowing money to invest in, 172–75
division on marriage breakdown, 62–63

employer's vacation property, use of, 74
Home Buyers' Plan, 207, 208–10
principal residence exemption, 48–50
and RRSPs, 189
second property, ownership of, 48–50
U.S. *See* U.S. real estate
reasonable expectation of profit (REOP), 126
recreational facilities, 75, 123
refundable credits, 6
Registered Education Savings Plans
and Canada Education Savings Grants
(CESGs), 40–43, 46
choosing, 40
and income splitting, 29–30, 40, 46
vs. in-trust accounts, 43–47
rules, 41
using, 39–43
Registered Pension Plans (RPPs). *See* RRPs
Registered Retirement Income Fund. *See*
RRIFs
Registered Retirement Savings Plans. *See*
RRSPs
reimbursements, 95
relief, request for, 14–15
relocation costs, 68, 79
remote location benefits, 70
residency
Certificate of Foreign Status (U.S.), 227
Closer Connection Statement (Form 8840)
(U.S.), 236–37
date of giving up, 25–26
deemed disposition of assets on giving up,
25–26, 263
exempt person, 237
Form NR73, 26
Form 1040NR (U.S.), 232, 234–35
giving up properly, 26, 215
and RRSPs, 213–16
and spouses, 26
and stub period, 114
substantial presence test, 236
tie-breaker rules, 237
U.S. citizen in Canada, 228, 282
resource companies, 149–52
retirement strategies. *See* investment strategies;
RRSPs
retiring allowance rollover, 103–4, 196–97
rights or things return, 157
RPPs (Registered Pension Plans)
deferred compensation, 98
defined benefit plan, 221
defined contribution plan, 221
Individual Pension Plan (IPP), 223–24
money purchase plan, 221

opting out when possible, 221–22
pension adjustment, 98–99, 222
retiring allowance, rollover from, 103–4,
196–97, 211
rollover of assets to RRSP, 197–98
separation and divorce, 60–61, 198, 269
RRIFs (Registered Retirement Income Funds)
beneficiaries, 60, 268–70
charity as beneficiary, 269
delayed first withdrawal, 220
drawback, 218
and flow-through share investing, 150
labour-sponsored funds, and foreign
content, 146
minimum amount of withdrawals, 220,
295
mutual fund corporation shares, and
foreign content, 143
rollover from RRSPs, 217–18
vs. an RRSP, 217–18
tax deferral, 7
transfer of assets to investment holding
company not permitted, 157
transfer of RRSP to, 217–18
withdrawals, 60–61, 150, 218–20
withholding taxes, 220
wrap fees, 187
younger spouse, 219–20
"RRSP freeze," 180–84, 196, 206
"RRSP meltdown," 182–84, 196
RRSP withdrawals
annuity purchase, 166, 216–17
contribution room, 203, 207
cost of, 181, 206
divorce or separation, 60–61
education costs, 210–13
and flow-through tax deductions, 150
Home Buyers' Plan (HBP), 208–10
leaving the country, 213–16
Lifelong Learning Plan (LLP), 210–13
lump-sum, 196, 198, 216–17
no or low-income periods, 188, 206–7
and over-contributions, 193
periodic, 214, 228
to purchase home, 208–10
repayment of, 212
residency in U.S., 213–15
rollover into RRIFs, 217–19
and RRSP freeze, 180–84, 206
and spousal RRSPs, 203–5
transfers between, 196
from U.S. IRA, 199
RRSPs (Registered Retirement Savings Plans)
administration fees, 184–85, 186

beneficiaries, 132, 268–70
borrowing to make contributions, 190–91
charity as beneficiary, 269
and children's earned income, 24, 199–200
and children's education, 41
contribution with deceased's assets, 205
contribution limit, 187–88, 203, 204
contribution room, 24, 156–57, 187–88,
    199–200, 204
contributions in kind, 189–90, 191
contributions vs. mortgage payments, 202
deductions in right year, 200–1
deferred compensation, 98
deregistration, 189
earned income, 156–57, 187, 194–95
eligible investments, 185, 189
employer-direct contributions, 191–92
excess, investment outside plan, 193–94
fees, payment from outside plan, 186
final contribution after death, 205, 270–71
and flow-through share investing, 150
vs. labour-sponsored funds, 146–48
loans from, 191
locked-in, 197–98, 223–24
mutual fund corporation shares, and
    foreign content, 143
non-qualifying assets, 187, 189
Notice of Assessment, 188
over-contributions, 193–95
retiring allowance rollover, 103–4, 196–97
vs. a RRIF, 217–18
"RRSP freeze," 182–84, 196
 "RRSP meltdown," 182–84, 196
self-directed, 184–86, 190, 196
senior's over-contribution to RRSP, 194–95
separation and divorce, 60–61, 198, 269
spousal, 29, 203–5, 270
stepping up book value, 195, 214–15
tax deferral, 7, 132, 177–78, 267
tax-free growth, 178–80
tax-free rollovers, 195–98, 224
too much in, 180–84
transfer of assets to investment holding
    company not permitted, 157
transfer to spouse after death, tax-deferred,
    198, 268
withdrawals. *See* RRSP withdrawals
and withholding tax, 191–92, 207
wrap fees, 187

S

sabbatical plan, 102
salary to family members, 30, 89, 121–22, 127

same-sex couples, tax status of, 18
Saskatchewan, 243–44, 287
Second Prior Year Method, 10
second property, ownership of, 48–50
self-directed RRSPs, 184–86
self-employment
    business structures, 108–12
    Canada/Quebec Pension Plan (CPP/QPP),
        107, 127–28
    control test, 107
    corporations, 110–13
    deductions. *See* business deductions
    draw, 109
    economic reality test, 107
    EI premiums, 107, 127
    vs. employment, 106–8
    employment of family members and
        Employment Insurance, 127
    Goods and Services Tax, 128
    installments, 9
    insurance, 109
    integration test, 107
    non-capital losses, 124–26
    organization test, 107
    partnership, 31, 109–10
    proprietorship, 108–9
    provincial payroll taxes, 128
    reasonable expectation of profit, 126
    specific results test, 107
    stub period, 114
    true substance of business relationship,
        106–8
    various "taxes," 127–29
    Workers' Compensation, 128
    written contract, 107
    year-end, choice of, 113–15
senior's over-contribution to RRSP, 194–95
separation and divorce
    Canada Child Tax Benefits, maximization
        of, 61–62
    custody, 59–60
    equivalent-to-married tax credit, 59–60
    legal costs of collecting support payments,
        63
    one-income status, application for, 61–62
    real estate, division of, 62–63
    RPPs, 60–61, 198, 269
    RRIFs, 60–61
    RRSP/RRIF beneficiaries, 60
    RRSPs, 60–61
    statistics, 58–59
    support agreements, pre–May 1997, 64–65
    tax-free rollovers, 198
short-selling, 139

social security, 228–29
source withholdings, 8–9
special clothing and uniforms, 75
specific employment-related training, 74
specific results test, 107
"split income," 37
spousal RRSPs, 29, 203–5
spouses
    assets left to, on death, 266–70
    capital losses, transfer of, 26–28
    dividends of, 30, 141–42
    household expenses, payment of, 28
    multiple, 59
    personal tax credits, transfer of, 28
    as RRSP/RRIF beneficiaries, 60, 198,
        268–69
    tax credits, 6, 30, 58
    See also family tax planning
standby charge, 70, 92–93
Statistics Canada, 58–59
Stewart A. Bell v. The Queen (2001), 55
stock appreciation rights (SARs), 85
stock option plans
    Canadian-controlled private corporation, 82
    conditions to meet for 50-percent
        deduction, 81
    deferral, effect of, 83–84
    deferral, eligibility for, 82–83
    defined, 80–82
    eligible options, 82
    exercise price, 80, 81
    $100,000 limit, 82–83
    "in the money," 80, 81, 84
    new rules for options, 82–84
    phantom stock plans, 85
    pros and cons, 81, 84–85
    reporting requirements, 83
    risk of acquiring shares, 84
    stock appreciation rights (SARs), 85
stub period, 114
substantial presence test, 236, 238
superficial loss rules, 27–28
supplies, costs of, 87
support agreements, pre–May 1997, 64–65
support payments, collection of, 63
Supreme Court of Canada, 14, 126, 172, 173
Symes v. Canada (1993), 54

T

tax avoidance, 2–3
tax basics
    assessment, disputing your, 12–14
    big events, and taxes, 11–12
    credits, 4–6
    deductions, 4–6
    fairness rules, 14–15
    marginal tax rates, 3–4, 286
    tax evasion, 2–3, 227
    taxable events, 7–8, 11–12
    timely payment, 8–10
Tax Collection Agreements (1962, 1997), 241
Tax Court of Canada, 13, 57
tax evasion, 2–3, 73, 227
tax-free rollovers
    inherited RRSP assets, 198
    lump-sum transfers, 196
    retiring allowance rollover, 103–4, 196–97
    RPP assets to RRSP, 197–98
    RRSPs to RRIFs, 217–19, 268–69
    transfers on marriage breakdown, 198
    transfers from one RRSP to another,
        195–96
    U.S. IRA to RRSP, 199
tax-on-income system (TONI), 6, 255, 292
    See also provincial tax issues
tax professionals, 12
tax refunds
    as interest-free loan, 9
    problem with, 9
tax software packages, 58, 141
taxable events, 7–8, 135
termination of employment, 103–4
testamentary trusts, 34, 271–72
Thomas Vanka v. The Queen, 115
timely payment, 8–10
tips, 73
traders, 138
transportation passes, 71
transportation to work, 76
travel expenses, 86–87
trusts
    administration costs, 32
    alter ego, 39, 273–74
    bare or informal, 43
    charitable remainder (CRT), 276–77
    deemed sale, 33
    defined, 33
    and income paid out to beneficiaries,
        33–35, 36
    inter vivos, 33–34, 265
    qualified domestic (QDOT), 282
    spousal, on your death, 267–68
    testamentary, 34, 271–72
    transfer of assets to, 23, 43–45
    See also family trusts
TSX Venture Exchange stocks, 159–60
tuition credits, 28, 256

tuition fees, 210–11, 256

U

undepreciated capital cost (UCC), 120
unified credit, 281–82
union dues, 88–89
United Nations, employment by, 90
"upvesting"
   interest cost deductions, 168–70, 172–75
   rewards of, 167–69
   risks, 169–70
   rules of prudent, 171
U.S. estate taxes
   domicile in U.S., 238
   forecasting, 238, 280–83
   minimizing, 281, 282
   new rules, 281–82
   repeal, 283
   substantial presence test, 236, 238
U.S. income
   alimony, 229
   capital gains, 228
   death taxes, 238
   dividends, 228
   employment income, 229
   foreign tax credit, 37, 227–29, 233, 282
   interest income, 227–28
   lottery winnings, 235
   maintenance, 229
   pension payments, 228
   residency, 237
   social security, 228–29
   U.S. situs property, 281
   withholding taxes, 227–29, 232, 234–35
U.S. IRA, transfers from, 199
U.S. real estate
   capital gains, 228
   net rental income method, 230–31
   principal residence sales, 232, 233
   property owned pre–September 27, 1980,
     232
   situs property, 281
   social security, 228–29
   taxable gains, minimization of, 232–34
   unified credit, 181–82
   withholding certificate, 232
   withholding tax, minimization of, 230–32

U.S. residency status, implications of, 236–37,
   282

V

vacation property use, 74
vehicle purchase from employer, 70
voluntary disclosure, 2, 3

W

waiters/waitresses, 73
Winning the Education Savings Game
   (Cestnick), 39–40, 41
Winning the Estate Planning Game (Cestnick),
   264, 280
Workers' Compensation, 128
workplace benefits, 75–76
wrap fees, 187
written partnership agreement, 31, 110

Y

Yukon, 252, 291